T0373392

THE BOOK OF YERBA MATE

The Book of Yerba Mate

A STIMULATING HISTORY

CHRISTINE FOLCH

PRINCETON UNIVERSITY PRESS

PRINCETON & OXFORD

Published by Princeton University Press
41 William Street, Princeton, New Jersey 08540
99 Banbury Road, Oxford OX2 6JX

press.princeton.edu

All Rights Reserved

ISBN 978-0-691-24639-0
ISBN (e-book) 978-0-691-24643-7

British Library Cataloging-in-Publication Data is available

Editorial: Fred Appel and James Collier
Production Editorial: Jill Harris
Jacket Design: Chris Ferrante
Production: Erin Suydam
Publicity: Kate Hensley and Kathryn Stevens

Jacket images: George Dolgikh / Sklyarov / Adobe Stock

This book has been composed in Arno

Printed in the United States of America

10 9 8 7 6 5 4 3 2 1

To my grandmothers, Ondina and Germania, whose culinary virtuosity inspired a lifelong love of cuisine. And to my grandfather Antonio, who shared Materva with us when we were kids.

CONTENTS

ILLUSTRATIONS

PREFACE AND ACKNOWLEDGMENTS

THIS IS A BOOK about food. Because eating and drinking are a common human experience, food gives us a way to connect with others, to learn about and experience different cultures, and to express our own creativity, to make art in everyday moments. When my roommate brought yerba mate back to Boston from a trip to Chile in 2001, it wasn't so easy to find in the United States as it is now. Instantly intrigued by the dark brown gourd and the metal straw with the capped end, I opened the tightly packed bag to find crushed grayish-green leaves with a smoky, herbal fragrance that filled the room. But I didn't know how all the pieces came together until I was in New York and drank it regularly with Argentine friends who insisted that I learn the right way to drink mate ("Don't move the bombilla!" they told me when I began to adjust the drinking straw). When I ran into a mate café in the mountains of Lebanon, selling cups made out of local hardwood and bombillas next to rent-your-own narghiles, a bit of an obsession began.

Once I started looking, I noticed yerba mate everywhere. The great writers and artists of the "Southern Cone" region of South America render yerba in their works. Jorge Luis Borges opens a poem about an evening walk with a line that describes the night as "fragrant as a cured mate." "Yerba" [**YER** bah] refers to the leaves; "mate" [**MAA** teh] generally refers to the gourd drinking vessel and sometimes to the beverage itself. Two decades ago it was customary to see the name written as "yerba maté" in English, with the acute accent on the "e" as a pronunciation guide to let readers know that mate rhymes with café. But the recent yerba mate boom in North America has had an orthographical effect and even Microsoft spellcheck knows to autocorrect the accent mark, which is fortunate because "maté" (emphasis on the second syllable) sounds like a homicide confession in Spanish. It means "I killed."

An unexpected outcome of my vocal fascination with mate was that friends became informal research assistants—they started sending me images whenever mate crossed their paths: in beauty products, on a store shelf in France, graffitied on the side of a building in Lebanon. They made writing this book much easier. Deep gratitude goes to my students at Duke and Wheaton who've tried ice-cold *tereré* and hot mate with me and who've even gone on foraging adventures in Durham to pluck, roast, and then steep our local caffeinated *Ilex* phenomenon yaupon. Above all, I am grateful to our cultural anthropology Ph.D. student Samar Zora who, week after week, came to my office with her discoveries on the connections between mate use and the Middle East during her first semester as my research assistant. Samar's eyes lit up with excitement as she showed me pages of mate advertising in Arabic, maps of trade routes, the debate over mate's acceptability that led to a fatwa, and even the stills from an online Syrian finger-puppet show where all sorts of characters drank mate. We lost Samar in the tragic February 2023 earthquake in Turkey and Syria; her curiosity and love of learning infuse the pages of chapter 6.

I thank the hundreds of mate drinkers, vendors, producers, and harvesters in Argentina, Brazil, Chile, Paraguay, Uruguay, Lebanon, Syria, Jordan, France, Canada, and the United States who shared their recipes, knowledge, and love of yerba mate with me. I am particularly grateful to the staff at the Archivo Nacional in Asunción, Paraguay, for helping me navigate fragile early colonial manuscripts, Milda Rivarola and her unparalleled visual archive Imagoteca Paraguaya, and Paraguayan anthropologists and historians Marilín Rehnfeldt, Ana Barreto Valinotti, Herib Caballero, Anahi Soto Vera, and Claudio Armadans and the Comité Paraguayo de Ciencias Históricas. The Museo Antropológico Andrés Barbero, helmed by Adelina Pusineri, Universidad Comunera, led by Antonieta Rojas and Carla Fernández, and CPES/FLACSO with Magda Rivarola and Rudi Elias have been intellectual homes in Asunción. The paraguayólog@ community across the hemispheres is a source of inspiration, including Caroline Schuster, Kregg Hetherington, Joel Correia, Gustavo Setrini, Bridget Chesterton, Amber Wutich, John Tofik Karam, and Paola Canova.

I thank Marcus Folch for his felicitous encouragement to check out *I. paraguariensis*'s North American cousin yaupon, which just so happened to be growing outside our living room window— providing my first taste of North America's stimulant *Ilex*. Support for research on yerba mate, yaupon, and guayusa was provided by a Fulbright Scholar award, by the Duke Arts & Sciences Council Committee on Faculty Research, the Franklin Humanities Institute, and by the New York Public library Wertheim Study Writer-in-Residence program. At Duke, my work has benefited from a wide range of collegial engagement, including the Latinx Faculty Writing Group, the CLACS community, my colleagues in the Department of Cultural Anthropology, and many others.

I thank Fred Appel, James Collier, Jill Harris, and the editorial board at Princeton University Press for their vision for the book on yerba mate, Jennifer Backer for her careful copyediting eye, and the book's anonymous readers for the rigorous review and generative engagement with the text. Portions of the historical work on yerba mate and yaupon found in chapter 1 and 2 are drawn from two articles published by *Comparative Studies of Society and History* as "Stimulating Consumption: Yerba Mate Myths, Markets, and Meanings" (2010) and "Ceremony, Medicine, Caffeinated Tea: Unearthing the Forgotten Faces of Yaupon (*Ilex vomitoria*)" (2021); editor David Akin was one of the earliest believers in this project. The germ of the ideas in this book started in a graduate school class taught by my thesis advisor Marc Edelman. I thank Juan Carlos Cristaldo, Silvia Arévalos, and Lorena Silvero at the Facultad de Arquitectura, Diseño y Arte (FADA/UNA) for their work in making the maps and tables come to life to tell the story of mate. Images for this book project came from the Diran Sirinian Collection and the lenses of Diego Kartaszewicz and Henry Maillet.

The recipe for any good book starts with a creative community and I'm blessed to be surrounded by many writers who inspire, including Larycia Hawkins, Julie Rodgers, and Carey Wallace; college friends/long-standing conversation partners Lydia Johnson, Katy Goldsborough, Elliot DeHaan, Nathanial Barksdale, Jane Rubio, Liza Cagua, Abena Osseo Asare, Agbenyo Aheto, Julie Thwing, Yang-Sze Choo, Olamide Jarrett, Robyn and Jonathan Liu, Naunihal Singh, and the entire Class of 1998; and Kwame Akowuah, Li Lian Tan, Rebecca and Patrick Ray, Adrienne Lotson, Brian Howell, Christa Tooley, Amy Hsiao, Eduardo Espina, Alessandro Angelini, Cam McDonald, Melissa Zavala, Julie Skurski, Bryan Lowder, Nicole Labruto, Michael Gately and Laura Kent, Johanna and John Villalobos, and so many more. Most of all, I thank my family: Juan Carlos, Daniel, Juani, Liliana, Juan and Julie, Marcus, Celeste, Elias, Mattin, Emmeline, Candace, Jakob, Andromeda, Freja, Saga, Astrid, Diana, Victor, Soledad and Emilita, Victor and Mercedes. I dedicate this book to my Cuban and Dominican grandparents, who taught me the love of cooking and how cuisine builds community, and even gave me my first sip of mate in Materva.

THE BOOK OF YERBA MATE

FIGURE I.I. Mate gourd and bombilla. Image credit: Henry Maillet.

Introduction

TO PREPARE MATE, take the cured gourd or the cattle horn *guampa* or whatever else you wish to use as a cup and fill it two-thirds with dried yerba leaves. Cover the opening tightly with your hand, turn the receptacle upside down, and shake it gently to break up any clumps in the powder and to make sure that the leaves and small twigs are evenly distributed. Then take the long drinking straw bombilla and jam its filtered end all the way to the bottom of the yerba, keeping it closer to one side of the cup. This will give you a lot of surface area on the loose-leaf mate over which to pour the water. If you're drinking mate that is hot, pour heated but not boiling water onto the yerba in the gourd, filling it up so that the liquid lifts the leaves ever so gently and air bubbles start to form on the surface. If you're using a cow horn to drink ice-cold *tereré*, the water you'll use is chilled and may already be infused with fresh *yuyos*, herbs for traditional remedies.

Wait a few seconds until the loose-leaf yerba has absorbed the water and then pour a bit more water into the cup. Sip the bombilla to drain the infused water from the gourd or the guampa until you can hear that you are sucking air. That sound is where the word "tereré" comes from—an onomatopoetic rendition in Guaraní for the sounds of sucking up the drink in a bombilla. It's customary for the *cebador*, the person preparing mate for a group, to take the first sip to remove the initial bitterness from the drink before pouring water into the cup again and passing it to someone else. Everyone in a round of mate or tereré takes a turn fully emptying the cup with the same bombilla, passing it back to the cebador, who refills it and gives it to the next person.

Yerba mate is the world's third-most popular naturally caffeinated drink, behind tea and coffee. It inspired the world's first written tango lyrics. It was an economic engine for early Jesuit and German nationalist utopias, albeit separated by centuries. The secret of its cultivation was found, hopelessly lost, and then rediscovered. Jealousy over its wealth lay at the heart of one of modern history's most devastating wars and fueled great Catholic conspiracies. On its more global circuit, mate is currently starring in puppet shows put on by Syrian dissidents. And the Argentine national team proudly hoisted their mates for all to see en route to their 2022 FIFA World Cup victory.

Made from the dried leaves and tender shoots of *Ilex paraguariensis*, mate comes from an evergreen holly tree that grows in the subtropical Atlantic Forest in the heart of South America. In Argentina, southern Brazil, Paraguay, and Uruguay, mate is the stimulating brew of choice, giving its drinkers the jolt of liquid effervescence others might get from Colombian coffee or English breakfast tea. Consumed from precolonial times in South America by Indigenous communities, under Spanish colonial rule mate expanded far beyond its natural growing range to become the leading beverage, after wine and water, in the Viceroyalty of Peru as it was wildly popular in Argentina, Bolivia, Chile, Ecuador, Paraguay, Peru, and Uruguay.[1] Today, mate culture has traveled far enough to make its mark in the Levant—bombilla included—as Lebanon and Syria have become the world's leading importers of mate outside South America. And the drink has been given new life in the North Atlantic world as a blended energy drink and prepackaged in single-serving tea bags. No bombilla required.

But if mate is so delightful, as its popularity attests, why don't North Americans generally drink the world's major stimulant beverage commodity that comes from the Americas? For that matter, why do we drink coffee in North America, especially since the

United States has a famous tea moment in its national founding? The answer isn't who got there first. All three exotic beverages came into European orbit at about the same time and it took centuries for North Atlantic caffeine preferences to solidify. The Spanish were introduced to mate and chocolate in the 1500s, a hundred years before coffee or tea became known in western Europe. So, technically, mate got there first. Coffee moved westward from the Ottoman Empire in the 1600s via the institution of the coffeehouse, then (as now) a space for public sociality, debating new ideas, and even transacting business.[2] Fittingly, England's first coffeehouse was opened in Oxford in the early 1650s, setting a precedent for university town cafés the world over. Black tea arrived shortly thereafter as a novelty item in a London coffeehouse; it made such an impression on English writer Samuel Pepys that he recorded the first time he drank it in his diary on September 25, 1660.[3]

Consumables like yerba mate are popular subjects of books because of what they teach us about ourselves and the world we live in. Over the last few years salt, cod, sugar, and the hamburger have all received celebrity treatment.[4] Red wine, coffee, tea, and (especially) chocolate are perennial favorites. It's high time for yerba mate to take center stage. What can we learn from a biography of the South American stimulant? The first thing to know is that mate has multiple personas: commodity, recipe, drink, highly stylized ritual, and plant. These different facets help us learn about the economics of drugs (legal and otherwise), the botany of psychoactive subjects, the symbolic meanings of consumption, the political histories of South America, and more.

Mate draws people together across time and space, from the chilly mornings on the Argentine countryside and the torrid afternoons in the Paraguayan Chaco to the souk of Damascus, the nightclubs of Berlin, the cafés of Kraków, and the rugged Pacific Northwest coastline. Cuisine is fun to talk about because it opens up to us both the symbolic and the material dimensions of human life; the food (and drink) we consume has an inordinate ability to

FIGURE I.2. Customs of Uruguay: mate. A. Marchetti, 1900. Image credit: Biblioteca Nacional, Uruguay.

embody paradox. At one moment food is mundane, the daily bread we eat to live; at the next, it is extraordinary, a religiously inflected feast or a great wedding banquet. A single meal can juxtapose the large, impersonal economic forces that produce and move what ends up on our dinner plates and the intimate personal experience of taste and the evocative memory of grandma's cooking.[5] At the very same moment, the act of eating and drinking unites people and distinguishes them as separate from others. Food is simultaneously, indivisibly, both symbolic and pragmatically material.[6]

This book follows the cultures of yerba mate, from its Indigenous and colonial beginnings to its current incarnation as a global caffeinated commodity, tracing the varied political-economic structures that brought the drink to market as well as mate's changing symbolic significance—its meanings. Social meanings, rather than just some unmoored rational calculus, shape consumer choices within markets. But consumables also show us how larger structures (corporations, colonialism, and capitalism, to name a few) affect the conduct of our daily lives. This is one of the main tenets of economic anthropology and why ethnographic methodologies of observing how people do their daily shopping or click through websites have so much to teach us. One of the lessons from coffee, tea, and mate is that the uptake of stimulating beverages has to do with both market structures and social meanings.

To uncover who drinks mate and why, it's helpful to think in terms of "commodity chains," the differing dynamics of production and consumption, and the commerce that links the two.[7] When we attend to the production side of the commodity chain, we ask questions about laborers and labor processes, materials, and the environment, as well as the costs of production. Consumption invites us to think about who uses the product and to what end, the rituals and moral economy built around the experience. To wit, the political-economic history of coffee and tea in the West features (1) exotic ceremony (orientalized tea) or convivial sociality (coffeehouses): consumption; (2) the creation of imperial or private transnational corporations for trade: commerce; and (3) the structuring of landscapes for extractive monocrops (coffee enclaves and tea plantations) that move from periphery to core: production. Scholars like to study the commodity chains of major consumables because they reveal the emergence of nothing less than global capitalism.

But mate is not just any product. It has powerful psychoactive properties that affect the mind and the body. Not only does it possess the alkaloid caffeine, it also contains significant amounts of theophylline (found in tea) and theobromine (found in chocolate). The interplay between these compounds gives mate a kick distinct from that of coffee or tea, each of which possesses a tad more caffeine per average cup, earning mate a reputation as a less jittery stimulant. But, of course, the potency of these drinks is affected by how you prepare them. Dried tea has more caffeine per gram than ground coffee, which is why we use more coffee to make a single cup. Not to be outshone because of mate's lower caffeine content, mate drinkers in South America will fill a gourd with a good half cup of dried yerba leaves multiple times a day. The similarity of effects between plant products hailing from different corners of the globe long puzzled observers; it was through the study of psychoactive plants that disciplines like biomedicine, botany, and lab chemistry got their start.[8]

Mate was commodified as it was drawn into European-administered circuits of trade, a process that changed both how it was produced and how its users consumed it. The historical transformations by which goods become exchanged commodities uproot objects from their embedded meanings. A tomato becomes something that we get through money that we acquired by selling our labor, instead of something we struggled to grow and which we triumphantly now pick after waiting for months as the seedling bursts through soil we tended, weeded, and watered. Ready-made mac and cheese is mass produced and frozen, rather than laboriously cooked from a family recipe handed down over generations. Economic philosophers have noted that an economy based on monetary exchange hides the social relations underlying commodities because we can't see the labor and conditions of production that went into the product or service we're purchasing.[9] This gives us the illusion that what we do when we buy things is exchange money for a commodity when what we're doing is interchanging the labor that we exerted to earn the money for the labor that went into producing the good.

Marx called this phenomenon the "commodity fetish" because the inert commodity takes on almost agentive power, as if it could move on its own, when the real creative force behind it is human ingenuity. To teach college students about the commodity fetish, a well-respected colleague used to ask his (simultaneously horrified and enthralled) students what, if anything, they knew about the toilet paper they used, where or how it was made. Because the production and consumption of commodities are separated, it's practically impossible to know what's involved in how goods are

FIGURE I.3. Embossed cattle horn *guampas* for cold *tereré*. With permission from Centro Cultural Citibank/Museo del Barro, Asunción, Paraguay. Image credit: author.

made unless we actually go to the site of production. And that's why this book attempts to get beyond the commodity fetish by telling stories of mate production *and* of mate consumption.

At the same time, plants have power over people. In his classic work of Cuban anthropology, *Cuban Counterpoint: Tobacco and Sugar*, Fernando Ortiz explored the relationship between the two dominant plants of the largest island in the Antilles: one native to the New World, the other brought from the Old; one artisanally crafted, the other mass produced. The counterpoint treats sugar and tobacco as historical actors, as agents in their own right with the power to shape human society. This "counterfetishism" reveals the interwoven nature of commodities as their material qualities are inextricably linked to economic structures and symbolic interpretations.[10] New scholarship on plants, from biology to philosophy, also challenges common understandings of plants as inert backdrops to animalistic action. Darwin noted that the radicle (the root tip) of plants acts like a "primitive" animal brain, touching, sensing, and making decisions about where to turn.[11]

We know now that plants communicate with each other by smell.[12] They release chemicals when injured or eaten so that other plants nearby learn that one of their species is in distress. In short, plants solve problems. The strategies they use to do so—to reproduce, to avoid predators, to find water—may be thought of as "vegetal" or "plant-thinking."[13] Similarly, people look to plants to solve ostensibly human problems. While lab chemistry may tell us why coffee makes us alert or cannabis relaxes, the desirability of those chemical reactions resides in a wider milieu, which is why some are deemed morally licit and why that licitness changes over time.

Speaking of chemical reactions, the popularity of certain drugs over others comes from not only the sensations they cause but also the social contexts around those effects. It's no coincidence that drugs accompanied European colonial expansion or that Adderall makes the rounds on college campuses for off-script use during final exams. In fact, there's a direct connection between what drugs do and the kind of economy in which they circulate.[14] And, to be clear, legal substances like caffeine still count as drugs.[15] In the early stages of European colonialism, the chemical and biological properties of psychoactive plants made them instrumental in trade and in securing labor.

Drugs were used to force people into relations of dependency with European trading partners. Pem Davidson Buck's historical work on race, class, and power in Kentucky shows that Native Americans who refused to sell land to British settlers in North America in the seventeenth century were gifted alcohol to induce addiction.[16] But when they attempted to acquire more liquor to quench their thirst, they were met with a new demand. British traders would only accept money for payment rather than bartered goods and the only way to get that money was to sell something that the merchants would buy: in the case of Kentucky, deerskins or land. A hundred years later, the British East India Company ran a similar scheme. They smuggled opium into China in the eighteenth century knowing that it would create addiction. Once that goal was achieved, they demanded that China open their desirable market to British goods in exchange for the drug. The two Opium Wars (1839–42, 1856–60) fought between China and European powers resulted from various Chinese attempts to suppress the opium trade. Both times, Western military forces triumphed and the trade continued.

Stimulants took center stage when colonial priorities changed under a new phase of imperialism and drugs focused on intensifying the amount of labor extracted from workers. As the kind of labor changed from agriculture and mining to industry, there was a move from numbing drugs (alcohol, marijuana, opium) used to deaden the boredom and physical discomfort associated with hard labor to stimulants like coffee and tea, which had the opposite effect of heightening alertness and sobriety.[17] The coffee pot became ubiquitous in offices and factories as companies realized providing it for free boosted worker productivity. Yerba mate, the "green gold" (*oro verde*) of South America, both follows and complicates this schematization because then as now it was primarily consumed where it was produced. The psychoactive substance's importance changed in its native environs over the course of Iberian imperialism and into the early years of the newly independent nations as the dominant economic logic was shifting from mercantile to free-market capitalism. And now that mate use has finally transcended a South American circuit as a drink associated with the Levant in the Middle East and as a youthful energy drink in the North Atlantic, mate trains our eye to see new connections between markets and the meanings of psychoactive experiences.

But if psychoactive plants like mate were able to mobilize empires, it's because they were able to capture the imaginations and aspirations of millions. The symbolically laden consumption rituals, the intricate accoutrements to serve the drinks, and even the specific recipes for how to prepare them the "right" way show that caffeinated beverages have strong cultural resonances. George Orwell himself penned a widely circulated essay titled "A Nice Cup of Tea" (1946) that still inspires debate today. More recently, Bosnian women migrants living in Chicago in the aftermath of the Balkan conflict follow precise steps to roast, grind, and then brew coffee to create "multisensory encounters" that nostalgically link them to their old, lost homes as they establish new homes half a world away.[18] Mate, too, is a multisensory encounter. From the predawn hours on the streets of Asunción, the sound of herbs being pounded in a wooden mortar can be heard as *yuyeros* (traditional herbalists) meticulously prepare roots, leaves, and stems to be mixed with ice-cold water and yerba mate to make the refreshing tereré Paraguayans prefer.

And, surely some of my mate-drinking readers have taken issue with the instructions at the opening of this book, while others agree that it is indeed the right way to *cebar* mate. But the reality for mate, as with all caffeinated beverages, is that the experience of consuming it is highly diverse. Yerba mate is as much a recipe as it is a plant and there are slight, but important, differences in how the leaves are prepared for consumers in the four chief South

American markets for the drink. Mate for the Spanish-speaking markets of Argentina, Paraguay, and Uruguay is usually slowly dried via roasting, a process that imparts a smoky flavor to the drinks. Skilled mate processors will carefully choose specific local woods whose essence complements mate to make the firepit. Brazilian-style mate consumed in Rio Grande do Sul has the bright bold flavor of fresh *I. paraguariensis*, but yerba for River Plate palates is aged (*estacionado*) and mellowed in storehouses: two years for tereré in Paraguay; three years for a more tempered flavor (*suave*) for mate in Argentina.

The flavor we think is right, it turns out, is not simply due to personal preference. Pierre Bourdieu's study of French citizens' taste (in food, music, literature, and visual art) demonstrated that something that seems so personal—individual taste—correlates tightly with socioeconomic class status as denoted by the father's occupation and with personal educational attainment.[19] Bourdieu also found that part of the performance of elite identity was to look down on the consumption practices of those from less privileged backgrounds. Elites marked a distinction by preferring abstract art, daring literature, and pure music rather than the "simple" or "obvious" cultural production preferred by the French working classes.

We don't just consume what we like. We learn to like what we consume. This is especially true of bitter drinks like coffee, tea, mate, beer, and wine, which are often described as "acquired" tastes. And so, it's not just the conspicuous consumption of status symbols (a sports car, an immaculate green lawn, a large diamond ring) that has a public dimension. All consumption has social implications and therefore all consumption is semiotic—it communicates meaning through objects, words, and images. We demonstrate belonging and identity through what we wear, what music we listen to, and what food we eat; consequently, fashion, musical styles, and cuisine can be "read" to learn about the raced/gendered/classed communities that use them. If so, negative (or positive) conversations about a certain kind of music or a particular way to

FIGURE 1.4. Organic yerba mate, ready to be harvested. Itapúa, Paraguay, 2019. Image credit: author.

wear an article of clothing map onto social hierarchies. Common sayings like "look the part" and "dress for the job you want" indicate that consumption itself may even be aspirational, a way to perform a desired identity. Recipes similarly communicate important social values by making claims about what is authentic and who has authority—think of how sommeliers and gourmands determine what kind of wine or dish is "good." Through a specifically Uruguayan way of preparing mate, Uruguayans emphasize that they are distinct from Argentines. By drinking mate that has been processed locally, gaúchos from the southern Brazilian state of Rio Grande do Sul show that they are a community different from the rest of coffee-drinking Brazil.

Yet, the social resonance of cultural goods like cuisine and musical compositions can change over time. Like the exotic spices that once traveled on the Silk Road, coffee, tea, and sugar entered Europe first as rarities from the Orient. Although they are common today, these substances imported from afar were luxury items, indexing elite status because of their expense. In *Sweetness and Power*, Sidney Mintz tracks how cane sugar became the world's top agricultural commodity, a position it comfortably held for centuries. To produce sugar for North Atlantic consumption, European empires seized land and labor in the tropics, unleashing demographic and political dilemmas that reverberate into the present. As mass production drove down the cost and sugar became accessible to the growing industrial working classes, the sweetener no longer signaled a high social rank. Coffee and tea have similar histories where European and North American powers sought control of colonies with the right climate to produce "drug foods" (Mintz's term) at industrial scales and thus what was once exceptional became ubiquitous in North Atlantic cupboards.

Yerba mate and its cultural meanings migrate alongside people as they, too, move. In mate's journeys with and between communities, it has animated multiple processes of cultural transition and transformation from the colonial expansion of Spain in the New

World to the plant's globalization as an iconic Levantine beverage in the Middle East and as a healthy lifestyle product in the North Atlantic. Even if the ingredients are basically identical, mate isn't the same thing if it's an energy drink gulped on a quick break while scaling the sheer side of a cliff versus a gourd passed around a circle in the early morning hours before work. The chapters here catalogue those disadjustments and readjustments, the losses and acquisitions, the new cultural creations that have something of the past lives of mate but are nevertheless different. Cuban anthropologist Ortiz prefers to use his term "transculturation" rather than "acculturation" to describe these experiences of cultural change because communities do not merely enter or adopt an already existing, complete culture. Rather, something new is forged in the simultaneous loss and gain.[20] New mate cultures have new recipes and rituals or new meanings for old recipes and rituals.

As we follow the stimulant drink from South America on its odysseys around the globe, we encounter worlds built by mate. The drama unfolds in three acts. Part 1 explores the deep origins of yerba mate and its burst onto the Spanish colonial stage by beginning with mate's caffeinated *Ilex* kin in the Americas. In part 2, yerba mate, already entrenched in South American markets for centuries, plays a key role in the political, economic, cultural, and scientific development of newly independent nations as they struggle to find their footing. Finally, part 3 traces yerba mate's recent journeys to the Middle East and to the North Atlantic, experiences that shed light on mate culture transformations in the past and illuminate the globalized present.

Because production and consumption change over time and place, we can use yerba mate to explore the processes of commodification and their countervailing forces to see how accidents of botany intersect with political economic systems and personal taste. The economic imperial logics of the Spanish Empire under mercantile capitalism and the material difficulty in transplanting *I. paraguariensis* have as much to do with the geographical limits of yerba mate as do the strategic marketing plans of coffee and tea merchants who saw in mate a troubling rival. So, too, did the consumption rituals affect how exotic tropical products got adopted—tea got a boost from orientalist admiration of the ceremony and delicate porcelain accoutrements. There's even a whole field of study about the "Art of Tea" to describe the aesthetic pleasure of these rituals. But because yerba mate is often taken using the shared bombilla drinking pipe and a rustic communal vessel, a cured gourd or cow horn or even a carved hoof, it violated European notions of hygiene and respectability. Yet there's a comparable "Art of Mate" of structured ritual with highly intricate designs for the bombilla and exquisite precious-metal plating of mate gourds or tereré horns that incorporate the mining riches of the New World.

Just as some of the best mate grows *bajo sombra* (in the shade of other trees), other psychoactive plants near and far help tell the story of South America's supreme stimulating infusion, which means we'll also learn more about the histories of coca, khat, yaupon, coffee, kola nut, black tea, caapi, and more. The wide range of data used here—colonial archival documents, ethnographic observation of organic yerba mate harvesting, nineteenth-century scientific reports, twenty-first-century Arabic social media, interviews with mate producers and consumers in South America, North America, the Middle East, and more—attests to how a simple beverage unlocks the complicated interplay between economic forces and the tastes and choices of individuals. But each chapter has repeated themes: commodification and resistance, mate and migrations, consumption rituals, and the tension between pharmacological effects and social priorities. One common thread binds all the stories in this book: the way mate has served, throughout its history, as a force that brings people together.

PART I

Origin Stories

1

Ilex in the Americas and Indigenous Beginnings

WHILE YERBA MATE is the best known, the Americas have an *Ilex* fix. There's a good chance that anyone reading this book in the Western Hemisphere lives not too far from a naturally occurring stimulant *Ilex*. In 1528, Spanish explorer Álvar Núñez Cabeza de Vaca shipwrecked off the coast of Texas. He survived, taking an eight-year meandering trek through the mainland and eventually into central Mexico—a journey he recorded in his memoirs of the people and customs he encountered in North America—and mentioning the yaupon holly (*Ilex vomitoria*) and the Black Drink ceremony in print for the very first time:

> They drink there another thing that they make from the leaves of trees like that of the holly oak and toast them in pots on the fire and after they are toasted, they fill the pots with water and have them there over the fire. And when they have boiled twice, they toss it into another vessel and cool it with half a gourd. And when it has a lot of foam, they drink it as hot as they can handle. And from the moment they take it from the pot until they drink it, they cry out, saying "who wants to drink?" . . . And that which they have drunk, they throw up, which they do very easily and without any shame.[1]

In 1542, less than twenty years after the shipwreck, Cabeza de Vaca was appointed governor of the Rio de la Plata Province, with its seat in Asunción, Paraguay, where he again encountered Indigenous nations that prepared and drank yet another stimulating *Ilex*. In fact, Cabeza de Vaca's entire sojourn in the Americas from Florida to Texas to Paraguay was among *Ilex*-consuming groups, though he only wrote about it once.

Yerba mate is part of a larger continuity of *Ilex* usage for caffeine and spiritual potency in the Western Hemisphere. Of the more than four hundred species of hollies distributed across the world, three found in the Americas are known to possess a combination of psychoactive substances—caffeine, theophylline, and theobromine—that set them apart. Mate (*I. paraguariensis*) and guayusa (*I. guayusa*) in South America and yaupon (the unfortunately named *I. vomitoria*) in North America have been continually used from pre-Contact to the present.[2] Though hollies throughout the Old World have served as medicinal plants, only in China does it seem that there may be an *Ilex* that also yields a caffeinated drink, the large-leafed kudingcha from *I. kudingcha*. Scientists speculate that New World hollies radiated out of the Northern Hemisphere, possibly East Asia, beginning some twenty-eight million years ago.[3] Kudingcha has lower levels of caffeine than its American cousins and, more importantly, than *Camellia sinensis* (Chinese tea), which perhaps explains why it is not as prominent a drink in Asia.

Stretching from the southeastern coast of North America through central Mexico, across the headwaters of the Amazon River, and tracing the curves of the Paraná River in the heart of South America, vastly different species of *Ilex* were used by Indigenous groups since time immemorial to make stimulating drinks (figure 1.1). Early Spanish explorers, on a quest for New World riches and wonders, were taken by the rituals around *Ilex*, and first-contact writings about the drinks date as early as the mid-sixteenth century. In spite of the great distances and the vast differences between the three, there are striking similarities in how they were prepared and consumed according to the earliest reports: all three were first dried before being prepared as a drink (yaupon and mate were roasted); guayusa and yaupon featured in core rituals accompanied by other potent plants (the Ayahuasca ceremony for the former; the Black Drink ceremony for the latter); all three were associated with ritualized, convivial emesis; and all three were consumed out of gourds.

But whereas mate is a globalized beverage, having expanded throughout the southern part of the Spanish Empire and then beyond, guayusa and yaupon are relatively obscure today. The Spanish quickly noted the similarities between the three *Ilex* stimulants. In spite of yaupon's first-mover advantage, mate took the lead. Colonial and early national writers often compared yaupon and guayusa to yerba mate, admiring the latter's economic success. What is it that makes mate so different from its cousins? Why are guayusa and yaupon so unknown, even (in the case of the latter) where they are grown as common yard decor? The answer partly lies in how people have related to these plants in the past. The three *Ilex* beverages have iterated between ceremony, medicine, and caffeinated tea as inhabitants of the Americas—Indigenous, Black, settler colonial, immigrant—have wielded the leaves' properties to different, culturally situated aims. These three identities for the drinks (ceremony, medicine, caffeinated tea) offer a way to think about plant-human relationships.

Readers in the United States are probably wondering why we lost general knowledge of yaupon's stimulant qualities. Much of the research on the history of medicine traces how plant knowledges move from the colonial periphery to the North Atlantic core; important and contestatory work, however, has focused not just on how knowledge is built but on ignorance. Londa Schiebinger writes of the "nontransfer of important bodies of knowledge from the New World into Europe" as she traces why abortifacient properties of West Indian plants did not make it to Europe even as the plants themselves did, which she explores as "agnotology"—"the study of culturally-induced ignorances."[4] The

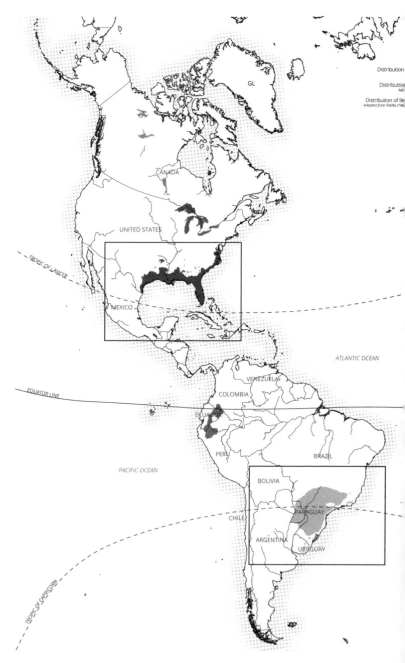

FIGURE 1.1. The Americas' *Ilex* fix: Western Hemisphere map with growing ranges of *Ilex vomitoria*, *Ilex guayusa*, and *Ilex paraguariensis*. Image credit: Juan Cristaldo and Silvia Arevalos, Exponencial S.A.

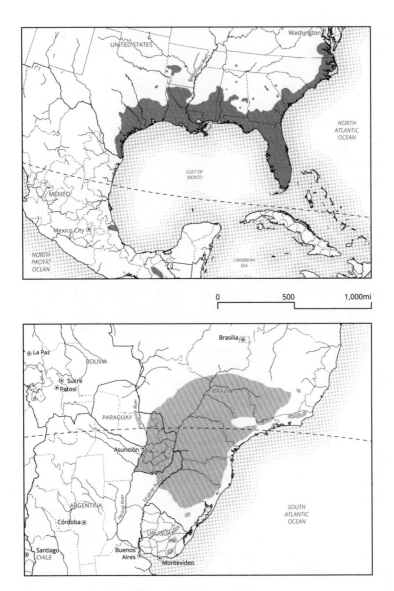

| 0 | 500 | 1,000mi |

phrase "culturally-induced ignorance" attributes the loss of knowledge to cultural priorities; a key priority at play with surprising and perhaps even counterintuitive outcomes for the *Ilex* beverages of the Americas was economic incentive.

When Cabeza de Vaca firmly brought *Ilex* stimulants into Western thought through writing, he inaugurated a debate over the proper role of stimulant *Ilex* in society. The competition to define *Ilex* stimulants' rightful place in society is an epistemological contest over what kinds of knowledge are properly authoritative and, especially, *whose* knowledge. Simply put, epistemology has to do with how we know things, the kinds of data we gather, how knowledge is constructed and transmitted, and the kinds of logics that are authoritative. Putting mate in a community of plant practices in the New World helps us think through plant epistemologies. We like to say that knowledge is power, but deciding what counts as legitimate knowledge is a power play and so talking about plants is also a coded way for talking about people. That is why we will see that the story of mate's *Ilex* cousins yaupon and guayusa is more than just about how people relate to plants but how they relate to other people.

Yaupon

Desperate for a cup of coffee or tea, both of which were inaccessible as a result of the Union blockade during the U.S. Civil War (1861–65), Walter Lenoir wrote to his mother about the solution he and his company had found at Camp Lee, South Carolina: "We have been out of coffee for some time, but are doing very well without it, & have all become so fond of Yeopon tea that we will continue to use it."[5] European expansion into the Western Hemisphere famously began as a pursuit of exotic consumables, many with desirable psychoactive properties.[6] Lenoir's happy experience with the yaupon holly was just one of many colonial and settler encounters with the evergreen shrub that grows along the southeastern coast of North America. Separated by hundreds of years and hundreds of miles, both Cabeza de Vaca and Lenoir stumbled upon the sole caffeinated beverage native to North America: yaupon, sometimes called "cassina." Yaupon gained traction beyond the Indigenous nations in North America that enjoyed the drink. It was once so popular in Europe that it was traded and consumed in Paris and London throughout the eighteenth century. And it was so common in Europe during that time that when American hosts served it to French visitors in Mississippi, they recognized the drink as something they had already tasted. The puzzling question is, then, why is yaupon not the caffeinated drink of choice in the United States?

The name "yaupon" comes from the Catawba for "small tree"; "cassina" comes from "assi," Creek/Muskogee for "leaf"; and both have meanings similar to the original Guaraní "ca'a miri" (small plant) for yerba mate. In spite of how it's written, locals pronounce yaupon as "**YOH** pon" (rhymes with "mow" not "wow"). A large evergreen shrub capable of growing into a small tree, yaupon is naturally found in the sandy soils of the North American coast from Virginia Beach to Texas. A discontiguous population exists in Chiapas, Mexico, where the plant is known as "tza'los te'" and "sakil winik te'" in Tzeltal (a Maya language), perhaps harkening to a wider pre- or early colonial consumption.[7] Like yerba mate, in addition to caffeine, yaupon possesses the stimulant alkaloids theobromine and theophylline.[8] These and other properties made yaupon desirable.

Brewed yaupon can taste bright and floral or honeyed with a hint of malt depending on how long it is roasted. It lacks the tannins that make tea and wine bitter, so it can be steeped longer to draw out its complicated flavors. The average cup of yaupon has a little less caffeine than a cup of coffee or tea, but it still gives a good rush while the other alkaloids it contains extend the stimulant powers of the drink. In my experience of hosting yaupon tastings, North Americans start out intrigued by the idea of a caffeinated plant hidden right in plain sight, but the reaction turns to surprise because the drink is delightful, and then confusion as to why it's not better known in the United States. Part of the answer is that

personal consumption is a way to demonstrate community belonging. Though the plant yields a pleasant beverage, social forces
around the identities of its consumers (Indigenous, Southern,
Black) branded it as an inferior buzz in the past. Yaupon is currently
experiencing a surge in popularity because those earlier associations
no longer have the same valence.

Yaupon propagates easily from seed and transplants successfully, as attested to by the holly's current distribution to the hilly
inland of the Carolinas, Georgia, and Texas and which eighteenth-
century writer James Adair noted in saying that "the Indians transplant [it] and are extremely fond of it."[9] By measuring the residue
presence of all three alkaloids in drinking vessels, archaeologists
have recently determined that yaupon, and possibly Black Drink
ceremonialism, was present at Cahokia, the pre-Columbian city
(c. 1040–1350) located in what is now southwest Illinois, hundreds
of miles outside of yaupon's growing range, indicating a lively
trade in the leaf.[10] John Brickell, an Irish physician who composed
The Natural History of North Carolina (1737), wrote that Indigenous inhabitants of the coast "frequently carry it [yaupon] to the
Westward Indians, who give Deer Skins, and other Necessaries
they want for it."[11] In 1763, British botanist Mark Catesby also
wrote of trade in yaupon throughout the Southeast, including an
important comparison to yerba mate: "The Indians on the sea-
coast supply those of the mountains therewith and carry on a considerable trade with it in Florida; just as the Spaniards do with
their South-Sea tea from Paraguay to Buenos Aires."[12]

Anthropologist Jessica Cattelino has argued that money and
individual private property, or the lack thereof, were crucial ideological justifications for dispossession of North American Native
nations.[13] John Locke, for example, claimed that America was "va-
cant" (his word) and free for the taking not because it was unin-
habited but because Indigenous nations did not farm the land or
produce industry the same way the British would.[14] Although the
claim that Native nations had no "real" economy was a mobilized
stereotype, the repeated mentions of yaupon trade—corroborated

by archaeological evidence—demonstrated a kind of value that would have been recognizable as such by European settlers. And so, anglophone settlers were faced with a dilemma. A key legitimation for the British right to land occupied by Native nations was challenged by Indigenous trade in yaupon. Instead, the attention shifted to how to disqualify yaupon's ceremonial use.

The Black Drink ceremony (so named in English because of the color of the liquid) immediately caught the attention of explorers, missionaries, and military alike, who described the cultural context for the drink.[15] Black Drink was taken during council meetings and before important events, notably during the annual Green Corn harvest celebration—the busk—which featured heavily in American literature, including, for example, Thoreau's *Walden*. Women first heated water in which to boil the leaves. By pouring the drink from one container to another, preparers frothed the liquid. The (male) leader of the ceremony (a position of high prestige and honor) would then sing a series of notes before partaking of the drink and then passing it around. Frothing and foaming seem to have been an important part of preparing sacred beverages; chocolate, for example, was frothed in Mesoamerica.[16] According to early writers, women prepared yaupon as a decoction, boiling the leaves in water for a set length of time rather than steeping or percolation, which are common for tea and coffee. Cabeza de Vaca's male hosts used gourds; French colonist Jacques Le Moyne depicted Timucua men using conch shells to consume the drink in sixteenth-century Florida (figure 1.2). The colonial- and early national-era writers analyzed here were all men, and they describe Black Drink ceremonialism as a gendered event with women as only preparers and men as singers and consumers. They give no indication as to whether there might have been a context for female consumption. However, Florida historian John Hann, based on his reading of Spanish Florida mission records, maintains that women of a chiefly class were permitted to drink yaupon.[17]

But it was not the preparation or consumption that caught the attention of colonial writers in English. Instead, the focus was on

FIGURE 1.2. Jacques Le Moyne (published in 1591 by Theodore de Bry) depicts the Timucua tribe in Florida in their Black Drink ceremony, using a nautilus shell for the beverage, c. 1564. French observers are in the lower left. Plate XXIX. Image credit: P. K. Yonge Library of Florida History, Special and Area Studies Collections, George A. Smathers Libraries, University of Florida, Gainesville.

what happened after imbibing: ceremony participants easily and regularly regurgitated the Black Drink (also seen in the Le Moyne drawing). For comparison, though the association with ritualized vomiting captured the imagination of anglophone writers, French explorers did not bother to mention it aside from Le Moyne.[18] By the early eighteenth century, yaupon was known as "apalachine" in French literature because it "derived its name from the Apalache, an Indian nation which makes great use of it" and was associated as a drink of war.[19] Spanish writers also tended to downplay the emesis and instead connected yaupon to a traditional ball game played by North Florida's Indigenous inhabitants (different from the well-known ball game of the Aztecs).[20] Still, the influence of the anglophone fixation on regurgitation left so strong a rhetorical link between yaupon and vomiting that the U.S. Department of Agriculture Fire Service listed *Ilex vomitoria* as an emetic well into the twentieth century.[21]

In spite of its unfortunate name, yaupon is no more emetic than coffee or tea. Scientific studies testing its chemical components have repeatedly found no known emetics and its many users report no urge to regurgitate.[22] Anthropologist Charles Hudson, in his extensive work on Black Drink ceremonialism, asserted that the vomiting associated with the beverage was learned behavior.[23] The contemporary example of ritualized regurgitation of guayusa in the *wayus* ceremony supports Hudson's hunch, but we also know that to induce regurgitation additional ingredients were mixed with yaupon at other times. Sixteenth-century Spanish writers explicitly noted that Indigenous groups in Florida mixed salt water with yaupon to encourage regurgitation and some Southeast Indigenous groups today mix other local plants with yaupon to make the Black Drink emetic.[24] Vomiting, like frothing, seems to have been understood as purifying.

Public ritualized regurgitation disrupted anglophone notions of gentility and was instrumentalized to depict Native Americans as culturally defective. Early nineteenth-century Methodist missionary William Capers writes of the Creek chiefs that "none drink without spitting or puking when they have done. . . . [T]hey drink and puke with equal readiness—perhaps with equal ease. . . . [T]hey seem to drink to puke; and puke to drink again."[25] This was either conscious hyperbole or a sign that Capers only witnessed yaupon consumption once, in a Black Drink ceremony performed by Creek chiefs. Regurgitation as cultural practice was configured as moral deficiency, just one example of a long-standing settler-colonial fascination with the imagined grotesque in Indigenous consumption.[26]

Food can be used to construct cultural hierarchies. Just like the supposed lack of a real economy legitimated European dispossession of Indigenous nations, the diet of Native groups was used to build arguments around cultural inferiority. European criticism of Native foodstuffs dates to the very beginning of Contact. For European colonists, Native communities "ate wrong" by consuming what historian Rebecca Earle calls "un-food"—frogs, spiders, and insects, which were seen as inadequate and unhealthy.[27] Corn and yuca were slated as inferior starches to wheat, though they were adopted. Chocolate, on the other hand, was one great exception and colonial writers raved about the drink. Because of yaupon's strong association with Indigenous spirituality and with a specific ceremony, its treatment differed from that of other culinary goods (corn, beans, squash, buffalo, and turkey—all of which were also spiritually inflected) that were inserted into European settler-colonial foodways in preexisting, familiar categories as grain, vegetable, meat, and so forth. Regurgitation, too, was disordered eating that let anglophones frame yaupon as a kind of un-food and thus situated Indigenous practitioners as having a disordered relationship with nature.

Yet, politicians and writers around the time of U.S. independence recognized and appreciated the importance of the Black Drink. In a 1775 speech to the "Beloved Men, Head Men and Warriors of the Cherokee Nation" on the eve of war, one of the "Beloved Men of South Carolina," Congressman Will H. Drayton, tried to convince the federation not to join the British side but instead ally with the revolutionaries by appealing to the Black Drink:

> And in particular they ordered, that if we drink Tea, we must pay so much money to the Great King.—I must tell you, this Tea is somewhat like your black drink—But as we know that this order is contrary to our agreement; and also, as we know the evil consequences of our paying this money, so your Brothers the white people in America have resolved that they will not pay it.[28]

Drayton's usage of the term "beloved" is notable and probably arises from Cherokee practices around the word. Nancy Ward (1738–1822), Cherokee political leader and heroine in later recounts of U.S. history because she advocated conviviality between the Cherokee and European settlers in the years before forced removal, takes her title "Beloved Woman" from her important role in preparing the beverage for the Black Drink ceremony.[29] Pennsylvania naturalist William Bartram, who visited the Cherokee Nation in 1776, wrote that the Cherokee called yaupon the "beloved tree."[30]

The beloved tree was given an inauspicious scientific name at the hands of botanists across the Atlantic. Because North America's southern coast lay for centuries divided between French, Spanish, and British rule, imperial divisions arose within the scientific treatment of yaupon and its biomedical study. Even the scientific naming of the plant involved competing European empires. Though the Spanish and French chroniclers first wrote about yaupon, William Aiton, head botanist at the Royal Botanic Gardens at Kew, recognized yaupon as a unique species, giving it its official scientific name *Ilex vomitoria* in 1789.[31] The choice of the term is curious, not only because the leaf had been marketed to a British public for decades under the moniker "Carolina Tea" but because yaupon had been cultivated in Britain since 1700, as Aiton himself noted, and *was actually cultivated at Kew Gardens* under Aiton's care at that very time.[32] Aiton's word choice might simply have come from the influence of British imperial writing that prioritized the ritualized regurgitation of the Black Drink ceremony. But University of Florida applied ecologist Francis Putz believes it was actually something more sinister: economic sabotage.

Putz claims that Aiton was secretly employed by Ceylon tea merchants who feared competition from Carolina Tea and deliberately gave a name designed to invoke disgust.[33] After all, yaupon was at the time consumed on both sides of the English Channel— Aiton could have, if he were curious, verified the emetic properties of the drink. Whether Aiton was covertly working for conflicting tea interests or not, his proximity to the Royal Society (Linnaeus's botanist "apostle" Daniel Solander, who worked with him on the cataloging project, was a fellow) meant that he had regular contact with the East India Company, which turned to the society for advice on the latest scientific developments. Despite Aiton's official description, many writers misapplied *Ilex cassine* to denote yaupon throughout the nineteenth century perhaps as an attempt to distinguish yaupon from its emetic reputation.[34] And well into the twentieth century, scientists have debated the correct scientific name for yaupon.[35]

Yaupon was consumed in the North American South long before Walter Lenoir wrote to his mother about the privations experienced during the Civil War. But it also circulated in the circum–North Atlantic. Multiple attempts at commercializing yaupon had to contend with caffeinated competition as well as with the intersection of identity and usage. In a 1722 letter, Pierre Francois Xavier de Charlevoix wrote of yaupon's presence in Paris:

> Cassine, otherwise called Apalachine, grows here [Biloxi] every where in abundance: it is a very small shrub, the leaves of which, infused like those of tea, are a good solvent and an excellent sudorific, but its main quality is in being diuretic. The Spaniards make great use of it over all Florida: it is even their ordinary drink. It began to be in some repute at Paris when I left it.[36]

Half a century later, Thomas Skinner announced his intention to auction a 1775 shipment of "the Leafe and Good-will of the CAROLINA TEA" at Deptford-Bridge in London.[37] And northern ports along the East Coast of North America, like New York and Halifax, regularly received bundles of yaupon from sailors hailing from or having stopped at port in North Carolina, both before and after U.S. independence.[38] Provenance was key to yaupon's branding—whether in the name "Carolina Tea" or "apalachine"—tightly identifying the plant with geography.

During the lead-up to the American Revolution, yaupon was marked as an "American" beverage consumed as a manner of protest against the British East India Company and against crown attempts to tax tea consumption. Later U.S. history books for schoolchildren recounted, "The Americans were not contending for a little money, but for a principle, and they refused to receive the tea. They began to drink tea made of sassafras-roots, sage, raspberry-leaves, yaupon, and other American plants."[39] But once the conflict died down, so too did the urgency to drink yaupon as a manner of defiance and a newly forged patriotism. And trade in yaupon appears to have subsided. Instead, the southern plant became a solidly southern drink. "Almost all the southern coasters who frequent the port of New-York, are in the constant use of Yapon-tea made from this vegetable," wrote the New York–based *Medical Repository* in 1806.[40] Through its geographical association with the U.S. South, yaupon moved from being a cultural stand-in for things (and people) Indigenous to things (and people) Southern.

The U.S. Civil War (1861–65) remapped race, region, and cuisine in important ways, which led to a significant reduction in the use and knowledge of yaupon in the present day. In the first half of the nineteenth century, U.S.-based writing on yaupon focused on it as ceremony through settler ethnographies (often from missionaries) of Indigenous communities or on the medical and scientific import of the plant. But in 1863, Francis Porcher's *Medical Botany of the Confederate States* catalogued plants that might be useful in the Confederacy, especially attentive to those that substituted for products previously accessed from the North or abroad. He writes of yaupon using the South Carolinian nomenclature: "The inhabitants of North Carolina purify brackish water by boiling in it Cassina leaves. In North and South Carolina much use is made of the leaves of cassina for making tea."[41] Rumors of yaupon usage during the Civil War made their way to the Union. An 1861 letter to the editor of *Scientific American* asserts: "Messrs. Editors: In consequence of the scarcity of tea at the South, the Southerners are said to be reviving the use of the Yopon or Yaupon (*Ilex Cassine*), of which the North Carolina Indians made their 'black drink,' and which has been more or less used ever since in that region, though mainly by the poorer classes."[42] In her manuscript memoirs, Texan Lillie Barr Munroe recalled the day-to-day hardships experienced during the war, writing that "one of the clearest memories I have of them is that mother had no tea, we gathered the leaves of Upon [yaupon] shrub . . . they made a substitute, but only a substitute."[43]

Yaupon became, for the North and the South, an emblem of wartime suffering in the U.S. South, which may help explain why it was treated as a second-rate substitute to be abandoned once opportunity arose. Northern cosmopolitan disdain toward white Southerners attached to yaupon drinking after the war. One writer in Pennsylvania recounted (invented?) an exchange between an unidentified Southern man and his wife over the size of the yaupon gourd in which she served the drink:

> "Is that the gourd you gave me my yaupon in to-night?" "Yes, honey." Up sprang the invalid and gave his wife striking proofs of his vitality. "It's a two quart gourd," he shouted, "and you skeered a fellow to death. One quart is my allowance, and you know it. I thought when I couldn't go my gourd of yaupon that I myself was a goner."[44]

The husband, having been served yaupon in a two-quart gourd (which apparently he could not distinguish in size from a one-quart gourd), thought his inability to finish the drink was a sign of illness; when the mistake was discovered, he beat his wife in anger. The account was part of a yaupon-skeptical article titled "Spurious Substitutes" and argued against yaupon presumably because of attempts to encourage consumption and commercialization of the Southern leaf. Notably, denigrating humor at domestic violence and white Southern ignorance form the backbone of this sketch, part of what historian James Cobb describes as "an already well-established tendency among northern whites to see the South as a primitive and exotic land distinctly apart from the rest of America."[45] And so, a link between yaupon and Southernness transferred the negative valences of the latter to the former.

Even within the South, yaupon suffered from strong geographical association. As early as the eighteenth century, yaupon consumption among white settlers was a marked characteristic of the Carolina sea coasts and continued for centuries.[46] North Carolina's Outer Banks are steeped in historical lore around their isolation from the mainland. Here, the Roanoke colony vanished and most likely relocated to the island of Hatteras and intermarried with the yaupon-consuming Indigenous community on the island.[47] Centuries of distance have resulted in linguistic and cultural distinctives (including the "hoi toider" dialect of American English). Post–Civil War estate sales of deceased Outer Banks residents show that one lot of yaupon fetched the price of $1 in 1869.[48] And a man named Quidley in Hatteras Township listed his occupation as "Yappan manuf[acturer]" in the census of 1860.[49] In the late nineteenth and early twentieth centuries, yaupon consumption was both a hallmark of the Outer Banks and part of derogatory, "hillbilly"-like stereotypes of island inhabitants.[50] The term "choppers"—from "yaupon-choppers," as part of processing the leaf—was an insult used against islanders by North Carolina mainlanders and phrases like "Kinnakeeter, yaupon eater" were used to taunt children in Avon, Hatteras Island.[51] Yaupon production and consumption have continued in the Outer Banks uninterrupted to this day.

But perhaps most importantly, for Northern and Southern whites, yaupon was racialized. In 1864, the New York–based Farmer's Club featured a small update on yaupon with these details:

> The leaves of these shrubs have been in use by the aborigines of that district from time immemorial, and the Ilex cassine or Yaupon, constitutes the tea in universal use there among the negroes, which has given currency to the common negro adage, "Fried hominy, possum fat, and Yaupon tea is too good."[52]

The association of "possum fat" with yaupon is illuminating. Historian Nicolas Proctor makes a case for "racially ordered preferences" when it came (and comes) to cuisine from the perspective of whites in the United States and the perceived inferiority of the consumption of racial minorities and particularly Black

communities. Opossum as Black game and a Black meal is a repeated trope that appears in both *Twelve Years a Slave* and Frederick Douglass's *Narrative*.[53] In his book on hunting in the U.S.
South, Proctor writes that in the mid-1840s, "English naturalist
Charles Lyell wrote that although he considered raccoon and
opossum meat 'too coarse and greasy for the palate of a white
man, . . . the negroes relish them much.' "[54] Moreover, opossum
and raccoon hunting were nocturnal activities and thus would not
interfere with daytime duties.[55] If opossum and yaupon were parallels, as the dubiously "common" negro adage implies, then the
very Black taste for yaupon meant that a white public might not
want to consume it.

During Reconstruction and Jim Crow, the strong association between race and yaupon continued. A Hatteras Democratic leader
wrote to a local Democratic congressman in 1898 complaining that
"the backbone of the Republican Party here are 'Yeopon-
choppers.' "[56] Perhaps "chopper" as an insult for Outer Banks residents carried racial undertones. Whatever the case, in 1905 North
Carolinian amateur historian H. H. Brimley visited Hatteras Island
to document the last remaining "Yaupon Factory," which was owned
and operated by "Old Man Scarborough," an elderly Black man who
gathered, chopped, processed, and dried yaupon along with his
family (figure 1.3).[57] And even in 1923, *Nature Magazine* featured an
article on yaupon processing and use among Black residents of
South Carolina's Sea Islands with photographs of young women
stripping leaves from twigs and adult men operating ovens and machinery to dry and chop the leaves.[58] Important details from both
pieces suggest a strong cultural continuity between island forms of
preparing yaupon and Indigenous techniques. An 1806 article about
the Creek and the 1905 account of Scarborough describe the same
process: after being chopped with a hatchet, the yaupon is placed
into a barrel and covered with hot stones to sweat the leaves before
finally being laid out to dry.[59]

Although Brimley wrote of yaupon's supposed emetic and purga-
tive qualities, Scarborough commended the drink to him for the

FIGURE 1.3. Scarborough stands next to a yaupon shrub and yaupon processing equipment, Hatteras, North Carolina, 1905. Photograph by H. H. Brimley. Image credit: Brimley Photograph Collection, North Carolina Digital Collections.

"smooth and easy way in which the drinking of his tea would remove fevers from the system with a guarantee of no bad after-effects."[60] But even the praise from Scarborough fit into a pre-structured dismissal of Black medical knowledge in the South, which historian Sharla Fett asserts was shaped by both "social relations of slavery and the cultural heritage of African herbal practitioners."[61] Black knowledge of plant medicine grew from day-to-day laboring practices under slavery and from contact with Indigenous groups.[62] Moreover, the caffeine-bearing kola nut had been widely used, cultivated, and traded across West Africa from at least the thirteenth century and, following local custom, was even used to refresh the stagnant drinking water on ships crossing the Middle Passage; many enslaved Africans arrived to the Americas with the knowledge of caffeine's powers.[63] Because the very structures of slavery and the

U.S. racial caste system meant that Black populations had to manage their own medical well-being, herbalism was a crucial part of everyday health for Black communities despite the disparagement by white advocates of biomedicine.[64] Well into the twentieth century, writers asserted that "Cassina or Black Drink is still prepared (1924) by the natives and negroes along the coast wherever the source-plant is abundant."[65]

Indeed, while familiarity with yaupon's pharmacological prowess has subsided in the mainstream, knowledge around use of the plant remains in Black coastal communities in the South.[66] By interviewing elderly community members, medical sociologist Roman Johnson has studied alternative medicine use by Gullah-Geechee residents in Georgia's coastal McIntosh county.[67] The Gullah-Geechee are descendants of enslaved Africans who live along the southern coast from North Carolina to Florida, with cultural and linguistic traditions preserved from Africa. Their distinct English-language creole possesses loanwords and structures from various West African languages.[68] Among the many plant remedies assembled by the Gullah-Geechee, yaupon was recorded by Johnson as an "herbal medicine [that] prevents the onset of colon cancer."[69] This traditional remedy resonates with some of the latest findings in cancer medicine: recent studies suggest that coffee drinkers have lower risk for death from colorectal cancer.[70]

Whatever the reasons for yaupon's post–Civil War ebb, the long twentieth century and the twenty-first have seen repeated attempts to popularize the beverage for consumption, with success only more recently.[71] Chicago physician Edwin Hale wrote an 1891 booklet on the history of yaupon for the U.S. Department of Agriculture with an aim to see its use resuscitated and "to inquire into its possible economic value."[72] The U.S. Bureau of Chemistry (part of the Department of Agriculture and a direct antecedent to the Food and Drug Administration) prepared a circular in 1922 to advocate for the production of beverages from yaupon and even tested soft drinks made from the plant at the Charleston

FIGURE 1.4. "Drinking Cassina, a South American drink, made in Department of Agriculture," July 1924. Yaupon tasting of "cassina mate," prepared by the U.S. Department of Agriculture. Photograph by Harris and Ewing. Image credit: Library of Congress Prints and Photographs Division, Washington, D.C., Reproduction Number LC-DIG-hec-32428. Note the erroneous attribution of cassina to South America.

County Fair (figure 1.4). The bureau's explicit mission was applied research—combining scientific inquiry with economic aims. The writers enthused:

> It was found during these experiments that these products can be produced very cheaply in comparison with commercial tea because of the fact (1) that unlike tea, all the leaves on the plant contain the active principle, caffeine, (2) that unlike tea, all the leaves can be removed from the pruned branches with live steam, (3) that the number of steps in the process of production

can be substantially reduced, and (4) that in the preparation of cassina a very small amount of hand labor is necessary.[73]

Yaupon might have distinct advantages to imported tea, but just at that time, Coca-Cola was on its ascent and the newly public company was capitalizing on Prohibition plus a sophisticated advertising scheme that extended to the shape of its bottle and even the modern image of Santa Claus.[74] And so, whatever cultural space there might have been for a new caffeinated beverage was filled by an ice-cold soft drink.

Although yaupon was treated as a curio (if that) associated with the Carolina and Georgia islands for the bulk of the twentieth century, new companies have arisen in the early twenty-first century to attempt what Hale and others recommended: putting yaupon on the U.S. stage. The new companies have been established within the growing range of *Ilex vomitoria* in the United States: Yaupon Brothers (central Florida), CatSpring and Lost Pines (both from Texas), and Yaupon Tea Company (Georgia). A standard nomenclature has at last begun to emerge—the preference for "yaupon" over "cassina" or "assí"—but notably none of these companies prominently feature the scientific name around which there might be some ambivalence. The newly formed American Yaupon Association highlights permaculture, an emergent eco-agricultural model that balances "profitability and environmental stewardship."[75] Permaculture, which prioritizes sustainability through mixed methods of cultivation, is but one of several agricultural and food movements that have arisen in response to climate change and resource scarcity, operating within the constraints of and modifying capitalism as an Anthropocene-mitigating strategy intended to improve the resilience of capitalist economics. These efforts have been rewarded with national attention: in October 2022, Whole Foods, Inc., predicted yaupon would be the number-one food trend for 2023.[76]

The new yaupon production model intentionally addresses both the labor excesses and the land impacts of extensive and intensive caffeine commodity production as part of the business model of yaupon companies, a distinguishing mark of elite coffee or tea products but now normalized across the bulk of yaupon manufacture. Much of the yaupon sold by U.S.-based companies is organic (as an endemic plant, it does not require fertilizers, herbicides, or pesticides) and foraged or grown on small plots of land (even in backyards in central Florida). CatSpring deliberately offers employment to people in workforce transition, the formerly incarcerated, and sex-trafficking survivors, suggesting that social and ecological responsibility is core to these new companies' messaging and mission.[77] Gone, too, is the anxiety about indigeneity. Instead, a Native past is prominently mentioned by all the companies. It is a marketing boon and, interestingly, there seems to be a transfer of indigeneity: "native" has moved from describing Indigenous people to describing the plant. The new production of yaupon redeems the mistakes of coffee, tea, and chocolate; consumption also renders a transformative effect on drinkers by committing them ethically, in right relationship with the land and with other people.

Guayusa

Whereas yaupon once circulated across the North Atlantic, *Ilex guayusa* had a more regional footprint, stretching at one point from Colombia to western Bolivia. By the time Spanish Jesuit Juan Lorenzo Lucero encountered the Jívaro on the Parosa River in 1682, both his order and the Spanish colonial government were very familiar with Indigenous use of yaupon ("caçina" in Florida) and yerba mate. Lucero promptly wrote the Spanish viceroy in Peru about the practices of Indigenous groups deep in the headwaters of the Amazon River. He said "to maintain themselves at their best, [the Jívaro] were accustomed to drink a decoction of an herb called *guayusa*, similar to laurel, several times daily. They were thus able to stay awake without losing consciousness for many nights, when they feared invasion by their enemies."[78] Lucero thus

FIGURE 1.5. *Ilex guayusa* leaves from Tiwanaku (Bolivia) burial.
Photograph by Beatrice Törnros. Image credit: Statens museer för
världskultur. Formerly in Gothenburg Ethnographic Museum, Coll.
70.19.20*b*. Creative Commons License. https://collections.smvk.se
/carlotta-vkm/web/object/74097.

clearly described the everyday practice of the *wayus* ceremony as
well as specific applications of the plant's psychoactive properties
to address exceptional circumstances.

Guayusa grows as tall trees on the humid slopes east of the
Andes; in the early twentieth century there were groves still standing in Colombia that had been planted in the early days of the
Conquest. Like yaupon and mate, the leaves are serrated-crenated,
with small teeth all along its edges, but guayusa has the largest leaf
of all three—the size of a hand. A remarkably well-preserved pre-
Incan archaeological find attests to guayusa's importance in both
ceremony and medicine. In the 1970s, a team of archaeologists and
historical botanists examined a medicine man's burial in Tiwanaku, a site just southeast of Lake Titicaca in highland Bolivia,
which included a carefully folded stack of *I. guayusa* leaves along
with a few other instruments including a snuff dish and what appears to be an enema tube (figure 1.5).[79] Radiocarbon dating placed

the packet of guayusa at 500 CE.[80] The fully intact leaves are just a little smaller than present-day guayusa samples and demonstrate trade in the leaf because the Bolivian highlands lie outside the growing range of the tropical plant.

Guayusa has a deep history of use by Indigenous groups in the continent and, perhaps more than its two cousins, reveals in its very physicality the evidence of long-term human intentionality. Guayusa has no seeds. And until recently, guayusa flowers had never been encountered by North Atlantic botanists (and the few that were located in a 1970s expedition to Ecuador were all staminate—all male).[81] The lack of seeds and the absence of flowers mean that guayusa cannot reproduce in the wild and that it depends exclusively upon human activity. Thus, all known samples of guayusa, either in laboratories or in the wild, are quite obviously domesticated and propagated by human cultivation in the form of cuttings. The lack of flower or fruit has long puzzled botanists, who rely on the flowers, fruit, and leaves of a plant to aid in identifying new or existing species. German botanist Theodor Loesener first scientifically described *Ilex guayusa* from a sample in Germany collected by Joseph Warscewicz, giving it its official scientific name in 1901, much later than either yaupon or mate. In his notes, he remarked upon the lack of flowers.[82] And he was not the first European plant enthusiast who had come across the leaf to make such commentary. English botanist and explorer Richard Spruce encountered it in his mid-nineteenth-century South American journeys, noting that he never saw either flower or seed and that it was always associated with villages or now deserted Indigenous sites.[83]

When Spruce ran out of coffee in eastern Ecuador, he decided to try his hand at making guayusa "tea," which he deemed "very palatable."[84] But he also described how his Jívaro hosts made a guayusa "infusion so strong that it becomes positively emetic" and that Jívaro men took the drink early in the morning daily in order to empty their stomachs of whatever remained of the previous night's meal. That is, as with yaupon, Indigenous practices around

I. guayusa prominently featured regurgitation as a form of purification. But because he had tasted the drink himself, Spruce knew that the plant was not normally emetic and his experience of guayusa was not dominated by a politics of disgust. Instead, he attributed the practice to learned behavior. Spruce wrote that Jívaro mothers taught their male children to regurgitate guayusa by giving them the drink and a feather with which to tickle their throats from a very young age.

More recent ethnographic research on guayusa usage supports this interpretation.[85] Ethnographers in the 1990s described how Achuar (Jívaro) men in the Peruvian and Ecuadorian Amazon regularly drink guayusa in the predawn morning, socializing and debating community life, after which they regurgitate the drink.[86] Among the Achuar, at-will vomiting is a learned skill, taught to prepubescent boys via the use of a feather or a finger. Blood samples from Achuar men who had partaken in the *wayus* ceremony show that vomiting helps modulate caffeine intake, allowing participants to drink guayusa for extended periods of time. Vomiting serves as a form of cleansing to meet the new day.[87]

Guayusa also features in a hallucinogenic complex of plant-based ceremony among Indigenous groups in South America. Although Jesuit Lucero wrote positively of guayusa in the quotation that opened this section, in that very letter he had strong words of condemnation for Jívaro usage of the plant: "They put together these evil herbs [*Datura, Banisteriopsis,* and other narcotic plants], with guañusa [*sic*] and tobacco, also invented by the devil."[88] Indeed, the hallucinogenic South American vine *Banisteriopsis caapi* so vociferously denounced by Lucero is a key ingredient along with the psychedelic shrubs chacruna (*Psychotria viridis*) or chaliponga (*Diplopterys cabrerana*) in the shamanic ayahuasca ceremony, which also sometimes incorporates tobacco in the boiled-down brew. Richard Spruce himself tried ayahuasca (sometimes called yagé) on his nineteenth-century journeys. The trumpet-flower tree *Datura arborea* and its close relative *D. sanguinea* were also used for their hallucinogenic properties in divination contexts among aboriginal groups in Colombia, Ecuador, and Peru. A more powerful narcotic than ayahuasca, *D. arborea* seems to have been particularly used by warriors, whereas *B. caapi* was favored by shamans.[89] Anthropologist Stephen Hugh-Jones makes an important distinction between foods and "non-foods" or "anti-meals" for the Indigenous groups of the western Amazonia with whom he worked for decades: foods like meat and cultivated plants nourish the body whereas tobacco, coca, ayahuasca, presumably guayusa, and so forth nourish the soul.[90]

The guayusa holly has been overshadowed by *Datura* and *B. caapi* in much of the historical botanical and travel literature about the region, but as Lucero himself noted, there are remarkable connections between them that illuminate important precolonial and ongoing plant practices. Guayusa plays a role in the ayahuasca ceremony, where it may be drunk both before and after imbibing the *B. caapi* drink to temper the bitter taste of ayahuasca and alleviate hangovers after the ceremony.[91] And some shamans even mix guayusa into ayahuasca as it is brewing.[92] There are gendered parallels between the ayahuasca and *wayus* ceremonies as well: early (male) writers asserted that women were not permitted to participate in either, though in the present these exclusions are not observed.[93]

Perhaps most telling, however, is the means of propagation. All three psychoactive plants are extinct in the wild and have only ever been found as cultivated specimens, testament to a long interspecies relationship rooted in time immemorial. And though *Datura* may be grown from a seed or cutting, *B. caapi* is traditionally grown from cuttings. That is, like guayusa, caapi is a clone of a particular plant carefully selected apart from all other caapi by unknown individuals in a distant past, with all living specimens connecting past to present.[94] In fact, the best-known stimulant of the region, Amazonian coca (*Erythroxylum coca* var. *ipadu*), is also propagated by stem cuttings by tribes on the Upper Amazon in Brazil, Colombia, and Peru.[95]

These shamanic linkages, so decried in the seventeenth century, have given guayusa new life as a socially responsible eco-commodity in the twenty-first. In their last semester at Brown University, Tyler Gage and Dan MacCombie developed a business plan to start RUNA, a company to commercialize and export fair-trade, organic guayusa beverages. According to Gage, RUNA grew out of relationships he had established with Kichwa communities in Ecuador as he sought to explore Amazonian shamanic knowledge during a break from his studies.[96] The company originally intended to straddle profit and nonprofit priorities as a social hybrid but grew into a for-profit entity that was acquired by premium beverage company All Market, Inc., with a corresponding separation from the nonprofit foundation and its eco-socio priorities.[97] Grown via agroforestry, which RUNA calls "rainforest gardens," the commercialized guayusa bears a strong commodity resemblance to the new yaupon companies that have arisen in the southern United States to find new markets for old products based on new environmental and social sensibilities.

Conclusion

Of the three *Ilex* beverages, guayusa resisted early moves toward commodification the most. And now that it has become part of international commerce, Indigenous ceremonial practice conducted by Indigenous communities themselves has remained central to the messaging and the branding since growing and harvesting guayusa are done by Indigenous people in western Amazonia. For yaupon, the move from *Ilex* as ceremony to *Ilex* as commodified caffeinated tea involved a rupture and a clear passage through a phase focused on *Ilex* as medicine.

Psychoactive New World plants destabilized accepted Old World science. The ancient Greek physicians Galen and Hippocrates thought that human health was a balance among four vital humors (bodily fluids): blood, phlegm, yellow bile, and black bile. For millennia, their medical schema was taken as scientific orthodoxy. But the discovery of New World plants and animals not described in classical literature was a theological and intellectual challenge to established Old World authorities. Because they were not mentioned in the authoritative medical literature, caffeinated drinks and other non-European plant substances superintended a shift in Western medicine and helped modern botany get its start.

Elements from the stories of yaupon and guayusa reappear in the story of mate: trade, ceremony, botanical puzzles, and more. But the question of what distinguishes mate from its lesser-known cousins is also partially a question of the creation and transmission of culturally induced ignorance. All three *Ilex* drinks enjoyed a heyday of colonial use, but guayusa and yaupon receded in popularity to the point that twenty-first-century marketers hail the "rediscovery" of lost beverages, found anew for cosmopolitan, culturally sensitive consumers and palates.

Only one persisted into the present: mate.

2

Jesuit Conspiracies, Colonial Jealousies

FORGERIES, BIOHACKING, jealous intrigues—the colonial history of yerba mate has it all.

Although it is the iconic national drink in Argentina, consumption of yerba mate remains lodged in the domestic sphere. Yet the country enjoys a thriving café culture where imported coffee, much of it from Brazil, reigns supreme. In 2008, the Argentine Chamber of Deputies solicited the executive branch to rectify the imbalance by encouraging the sale of nationally sourced yerba mate products in cafés, bakeries, and restaurants, an example of commodity nationalism.[1] As part of their argument, the lower house of congress recounted the glorious history of the important plant: Hernando Arias de Saavedra (Hernandarias), the creole Asunción-born son of a Spanish conquistador, first discovered yerba mate after an intense battle against a fearsome Guaraní tribe in 1592. As he and his comrades searched the hide bags of their vanquished foes, Hernandarias noticed strange dried leaves, which the Guaraní called "ca'a" (plant), and thus the mate habit transferred to Spanish colonial culture.[2]

Origin stories tell us about social priorities. This one valorizes the bravery of Spanish conquistadores while it simultaneously normalizes the violence of settler colonialism through the scholarly voice of history that makes it seem inevitable. Appealing to

Hernandarias as a founder understands Argentina as the heir, the descendant of Spanish colonizers. And like many others in its genre, this origin story is entirely fable, apparently invented whole cloth by nineteenth-century yerba mate merchants looking to enter the European market and who perhaps believed that a European public at a new high point of colonizing violence might find the account charming.[3] But, in fact, Hernandarias did not discover the drink in 1592. Rather, by that time yerba mate was already so entrenched in Spanish colonial culture across the River Plate region that in 1596, his first year as governor of the province of Paraguay, Hernandarias forbade the act of consuming mate, penalized with a fine and fifteen days' imprisonment.

Prior to the marketing hagiography of Hernandarias, a competing story about the origins of yerba mate circulated in South America for hundreds of years. Roman Catholic missionaries during the first few centuries of the Spanish Empire averred that the first-century Apostle Thomas himself taught the Guaraní and other Indigenous groups to use the plant during his missionary journeys.[4] Paraguayans still say "the first sip is for Saint Thomas" when drinking mate today. This origin story does different work from the Hernandarias fable. By asserting continuity between the hemispheres, this account highlights and legitimizes the religious dominance of Christianity in the New World. And, indeed, by insisting that Christianity had a deep historical footing in the New World, missionaries tried to neutralize the intellectual-theological threat posed by continents populated by people who do not appear in the authoritative scriptures of the Old World. Popular church teachings on mate were notably different from writings on guayusa. They sanitized, and even baptized, yerba mate. Yerba mate's two mythic origins have much in common: at their base, they both grapple with claims to power and claims to land posed by Indigenous groups and the existential challenge the existence of the "New" World posed to European and Catholic legitimacy.[5] To explain away settler-colonial violence, they attempt to wrest yerba mate from its Indigenous roots, a problem made unavoidably present by the material, embodied consumption of the native plant.

But as far as we can tell, the first moment of European contact with yerba mate is fully lost to history. The first written mention of yerba mate is very early and startlingly banal. And it isn't a story about discovery. It's a story about commerce, because even at the time of its first known mention by Europeans, yerba mate was already established as a full-fledged business. In 1567, Captain Juan Ortega sent a note to the de facto governor of the eastern Paraguayan region of Guayrá. In it, he mentions that Spanish colonists there were involved in trafficking yerba mate.[6] As with yaupon in North America, European settlers had encountered a society with a firmly entrenched *Ilex* habit and with what appears to have been a well-established trade in the leaf. Within a few decades, Spanish colonists not only traded but regularly enjoyed the drink themselves.[7] By 1580, visitors to the region noted that Spanish settlers as far as Buenos Aires commonly drank mate. And, of course, Hernandarias tried in vain to quash Spanish consumption. Colonial yerba mate followed this pattern: proscriptions against the use of mate, sometimes coming from secular authorities, sometimes coming as denunciations from the church, versus a thriving and expanding mate commerce even as its users grew steadily in number. Commerce and consumption won out.

This chapter traces commerce and consumption in the early colonial period from contact to the suppression of the Jesuit order in 1767 by unpacking two approaches, or perhaps two understandings of yerba mate: yerba mate as it unfolded in Spanish imperial political economy contrasted with the Jesuit mission experience.[8] As part of Spanish imperial economics, yerba was a leading agricultural commodity. At the Jesuit missions, yerba was a necessary tribute paid to the crown until the Spanish king expelled the Jesuit order from the entire empire on pain of death in 1767. For the more than two centuries from yerba mate's first contact with Europeans to the expulsion of the Jesuits from the colonies, yerba mate was a crucial touch point in a dizzying array of

competing forces: the economic development of commercial agriculture and mineral extraction, the legal and social structuring
of Spanish governance, the competing roles of crown versus
church, and the development of Jesuit medicine and scientific
knowledges as a complement to the scientific revolution. That is,
the plant sat at the intersection of economics, colonial governance,
and intellectual modernity. Its place in the Spanish imperial and
Jesuit missiological projects makes it part of major crises around
Native nations and part of the decision-making processes that
shaped the modern world.

Mate's entrance into the European economic order coincides
with the height of mercantilist capitalist principles. This timing
helps explain why, though it was a commodity traded by a European empire before either coffee or tea, mate did not become the
primary caffeinated drink of Europe. A key difference between
mercantile capitalism and classical liberalism is the role of the
government in actively coordinating economic activity. In mercantilism, the expansionist imperial state played a leading role in
directing investment, restricting foreign trade to protect national
interests, and mandating that colonies send unfinished goods to
the metropole and in return purchase finished products from the
colonial center. Underlying these activities was a belief that wealth
represented in precious metals should stay within the empire. To
that end, official houses of trade organized commerce, ensuring
that national-imperial priorities (rather than the wealth-building
of individuals) drove decision making. From our perspective in
the twenty-first century, mercantilism may seem like a quaint archaic phase through which the international economy passed en
route to modern (free-market) capitalism, but its logics successfully governed global empires for hundreds of years.

By comparing yerba mate's role in mercantile commerce to the
plant's role in a religious utopian experiment, we see a complex of
relationships that thrived for centuries. But we also see the development of New World identities around ethnicity and class. The
drink's colonial past provides insights into the workings and

limitations of mercantile capitalism that paved the way for subsequent capitalist experiments. In two understandings of value in yerba (Spanish commodity; Jesuit tribute), the struggle over yerba mate is a dispute for symbolic and political-economic dominance in the early Spanish Empire, and one fought not just between competing priorities of crown and cross but actually as a contestation over indigeneity.

Yerba Mate in the River Plate

Although Paraguay lacked the mineral wealth that became the backbone of the Spanish imperial project, yerba mate quickly became an integral part of the empire's extractive and extractivist project. Portuguese explorer Aleixo Garcia (d. 1525) first traversed Paraguay in the early 1520s, eventually making it across the arid Chaco region and into the Incan empire where he sought spoils before retreating southward, only to be killed by Guaraní allies. In 1537 Spanish explorer Juan de Salazar y Espinosa founded Asunción on the banks of the Paraguay River 270 kilometers north of its union with the Paraná River, which then winds southward to water the fertile Pampas and eventually joins the Uruguay River before spilling into the Atlantic as the River Plate (Rio de la Plata). Yerba mate territory lay hundreds of kilometers northeast of Asunción, in the vast Atlantic Forest expanse on both sides of the upper Paraná River, where wild *yerbales*—orchards—of *I. paraguariensis* could be found.

The unknown colonists who first encountered Indigenous yerba mate stumbled onto an acceptable substitute for the fortune-making mining in other parts of the empire. Yerba production took the place of gold and silver in meeting Spanish tribute requirements (the *mita*), and yerba even took the place of money in exchange.[9] This was not merely a convenient substitution. According to historian Thomas Whigham, because yerba sprang from the earth without human intervention, Spanish law treated it as a mineral.[10] At first, the quantities were small. In the early decades of the seventeenth century several hundred pounds a year were exported from the port of Asunción to Santa Fe, from which yerba was then taken to Buenos Aires or to Córdoba, and then over the Andes (figure 2.1). But as the century progressed, the amounts increased. A conservative estimate holds that, by the end of the 1640s, more than 3,000 arrobas (one arroba is about twenty-five pounds) of yerba reached Santa Fe, excluding another 1,000 arrobas of Jesuit production.[11] Two decades later, in the 1660s and 1670s, the numbers were closer to 30,000 arrobas of colonist production and 8,600 arrobas of Jesuit production. Contemporary writers claimed that 100,000 arrobas of yerba left Paraguay every year in the late 1600s, with 50,000 arrobas going southeast to Buenos Aires and 50,000 arrobas going northwest to Potosí.[12] Numbers could fluctuate widely depending on the internal political stability of Paraguay. The Revolt of the Comuneros (1721–22, 1730–35), which featured strong anti-Jesuit sentiment, destabilized production and pricing, for example. Nevertheless, by the middle of the 1700s, the yerba trade ran between 150,000 and 200,000 arrobas a year.

The botany of the plant presented certain difficulties in the expanding commerce. Unlike its *Ilex* cousins and unlike coca (*Erythroxylum coca*, from which cocaine also comes), yerba mate did not transplant or cultivate easily. The small dark seeds are encased in hard shells that are softened in the digestive tracts of birds for germination to occur in the wild. And so, the first written mention of mate describes commerce in the mate-rich Guayrá province 400 kilometers east of Asunción, the Atlantic Forest region east of the upper Paraná and north of the Iguazú River. In 1556, the Spanish encomienda labor system began in Paraguay, giving colonists a systematic way to extract yerba. Under Spanish law, Indigenous populations were commended (*encomendado*) into the ostensibly pastoral, Christianizing care of Spanish colonists in exchange for their unpaid labor. This paternalistic arrangement was originally intended as an improvement on the previous Spanish treatment of Indigenous groups who were worked to death in slave conditions without the benefit of evangelization. The encomienda system

FIGURE 2.1. Viceroyalty of Peru, location of Jesuit missions, yerba mate distribution, and yerba mate routes. Image credit: Juan Cristaldo and Silvia Arevalos, Exponencial S.A.

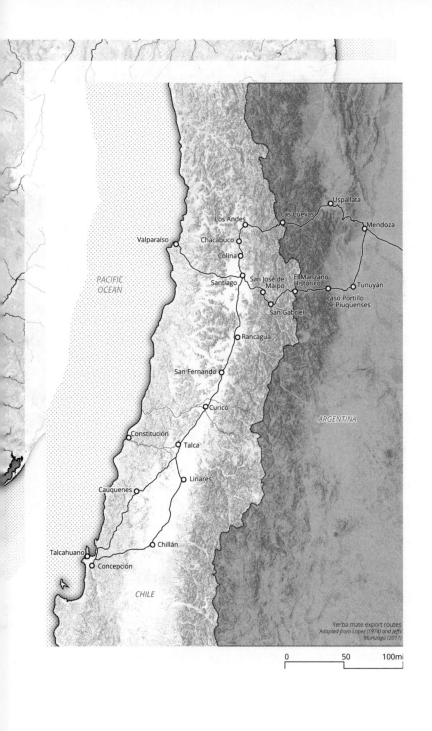

Yerba mate export routes
Adapted from Lopez (1974) and Jeffs
Munizaga (2017)

brought extensive plantation agricultural production to the best farmland in the Americas where both New and Old World crops were planted for tribute and trade (tobacco, wheat, sugar). But because the Spanish colonists could not grow yerba mate on plantations, groups of commended Guaraní were sent deep into almost impenetrable forests to gather and process the yerba.

The process was grueling and life-threatening.[13] Just as mine labor decimated the Native population, yerba harvesting disrupted Indigenous social systems as workers were coerced to leave their communities and relocate into the hinterland to collect it. They were even called *mineros* (mine workers). Carrying their equipment by hand, Indigenous laborers were forced into the forest to prune the leaves and branches of wild yerba trees thirty or forty feet high. At camp they gathered the pruned mate into a massive pile, which was flash-dried via intense direct heat (the processing step known as *sapecado*). Then, still in the middle of the forest, a wooden-framed dome (*barbacuá*) was built, over which the leaves and branches were spread, dried, and smoked (the *secado* step) via indirect heat for hours. The yerba was then coarsely ground (*canchada* or *mboroviré*) and packed into 150–200 pound bags and carried by the Guaraní, who brought it out of the forest on foot, later to be transported by mule or by boat to population centers (figures 2.2, 2.3, and 2.4). Commended Natives working at the yerba harvest would be gone for months. Contemporary chronicles described how many Guaraní perished in the wilderness due to hunger or exhaustion or because of wild beasts.[14]

Whereas for the Spanish, yerba mate quickly became a commercial object, Indigenous forms of consumption denote the crucial role for yerba in ceremony. Much of what we know about contemporary Indigenous practices comes from mission ethnographies, because many seventeenth-century Spanish government documents were more attentive to securing unpaid Indigenous labor for the harvest or to debates on the proper price of mate.[15] Writing in 1639, Spanish Jesuit Antonio Ruiz de Montoya described yerba harvesting and use in great detail:

FIGURE 2.2. "Process of Preparing the Yerba." John Parish Robertson and William Parish Robertson, *Letters on Paraguay*, vol. 2 (London: John Murray, 1838). Image credit: Acervo Milda Rivarola, Imagoteca Paraguaya.

FIGURE 2.3. Yerba mate harvesters, "Mensú," c. 1940. Image credit: Acervo Milda Rivarola, Imagoteca Paraguaya.

FIGURE 2.4. Freshly cut organic yerba mate, ready to be weighed. Itapúa, Paraguay, 2019. Image credit: author.

> With great care I have sought its origin among the Indians who are 80 and 100 years old. And I have discovered by verified fact, that in the times when these elders were young, they did not drink or even know [about yerba]. But a great wizard or mage, who treated with the devil, showed it to them and said that when they wanted to consult him, they should drink that yerba. And they did so. . . . And commonly, the sorcery that they do uses this yerba.[16]

Montoya's elderly interlocutors clearly describe a sacred, shamanic use for yerba consumption, akin to what colonial writers noted for yaupon and guayusa. Ca'a was not just any plant but a way to communicate with spirits and a way to receive wisdom. Montoya saw it as a competitor for Christianity.

Multiple colonial writers attest that yerba mate was frequently regurgitated in a ceremonial context, again, like guayusa and yaupon in a remarkable continuity among the *Ilex* beverages from

South America through the Amazon to North America.[17] The preparation of yerba mate also shows the extent and versatility of shared cooking techniques across the Americas. French anthropologist Claude Lévi-Strauss pointed out that smoking meats (and not just roasting them) was particularly important in Native American cuisine.[18] The temporary wooden barbacuá frame for yerba mate in South America is a kind of "buccan," a wooden frame used by Indigenous nations of the Caribbean and South America to smoke strips of meat and fish. That's where we get the word "buccaneers" for the pirates who sailed the Spanish Main. But among the Indigenous nations of Paraguay, the buccan was used to give the trimmed yerba mate its distinct smoky flavor.

For the Spanish, trade in mate was about commerce, the profit motive, and obligations to empire. But the precolonial trade indicated in the archaeological record and the earlier European writings suggests that Indigenous trade in the three *Ilex* drinks had a different rationale. The evidence of *Ilex* consumption outside its growing range suggests that trade was a way to reinforce the importance of ceremony and not just a means of wealth accumulation. Marcel Mauss's anthropology classic *The Gift* showed how the exchange and the circulation of goods among Polynesian islanders and Indigenous nations in the Pacific Northwest strengthened social ties. Similarly, trade facilitated and strengthened ceremony by making *Ilex* consumption possible beyond the botanical limits of the plants.[19] By extending the geography of cultural practices around all three plants, Indigenous groups who gathered them strengthened their external social bonds with other Native nations, which underscored the sacred nature of the *Ilex* plants within their own communities.

The distinction between trade for commerce and trade for ceremony also helps illustrate the importance of the former as a structuring principle for the Spanish imperial project. In the 1530s, Spanish jurist and Dominican friar Francisco de Vitoria penned two treatises that grappled with the legality of the Spanish conquest and effectively inaugurated modern international law and sovereignty theory: *De Indis* (On the Indians newly discovered) and *De iure belli* (On just war). Vitoria specifically addressed the question in terms of just war. He asked, in what situation would it be legal for the Spanish to make war upon the Native nations of the Americas and dispossess them? In other words, was colonialism *legal*? To build his Natural Law argument in defense of the Spanish, he first asserted that though the Natives were heretics in mortal sin because they did not practice Christianity, they were rightful rulers of their lands and owners of their possessions.

But according to Vitoria, Spanish aggression was justified if Native nations committed a natural offense against the rights of the Spaniards. Crucial among those rights was trade: "It is licit for the Spaniards to carry on trade [*negociar*] in the lands of the Indian barbarians, as long as they do no harm to their own country, importing the goods which they lack, etc., and extracting [*extraer*] gold and silver and other objects that abound; and their rulers cannot prevent their subjects from carrying on commerce with the Spaniards."[20] That is, conquest and dispossession were justified if Indigenous groups interfered with the Spanish rights to extraction and trade. To find that the first written mention of yerba mate is in the context of Spanish commerce reaffirms its fundamental role for the empire. The distinction between the two kinds of trade in yerba also illustrates how extractivism was an organizing logic for the Spanish Empire: via violence, extracting the labor and life of Indigenous bodies compelled to go ever deeper into the forest to extract the fruit of the land's fertility to enrich the pockets of colonial and imperial Spain.

Yerba in the Viceroyalty of Peru

Prior to the expulsion of the Jesuits in the 1760s, yerba mate's reach in the continent was much wider than the River Plate region. By 1616 trans-Andean traders could be found in the yerba mate–rich Mbaracayú region just west of Guayrá, and by the end of the 1620s the drink had a firm foothold in the Peruvian market.[21] Shipped down rivers in the skin bags of cattle that were slaughtered and eaten by the mineros themselves, yerba mate quickly spread throughout Spanish South America on a New World equivalent of the Old World Silk Road (see figure 2.1).[22] After reaching Santa Fe (Argentina) by boat and then being drawn to Córdoba on carts, the bags were carried on the backs of mules that trekked perilous paths across the Andes from Mendoza (Argentina) to Santiago (Chile) or up the Altiplano from Jujuy (Argentina) to Potosí (Bolivia) and Lima (Peru). Some of it even reached Quito (Ecuador) and ports of call much farther. At each stop on the trade route, yerba mate was taxed by the crown, raising the price. Despite the fact that Peru already had a stimulant habit in coca (or perhaps because of this), yerba mate also took hold.

Plants became part of the arsenal for European colonialism. Famous examples include the application of quinine as an antimalarial, enabling European troops to penetrate deeper into the Indian subcontinent and Africa in the mid-nineteenth century. Because of its stimulant properties, yerba mate was a linchpin biotechnology in the extractivist machine built by the Spanish Empire in Peru. As was coca. Prior to European contact, coca production was controlled and limited by the Inca, who restricted its use as an elite and ceremonial item, central in performing and consolidating Inca rule over the empire. When the Spanish dethroned the Incas, coca consumption expanded; demand increased dramatically in the sixteenth century. As (male) Indigenous workers were pressed into the silver mines of Potosí, their (meager) wages and rations flowed into a coca market that had newly developed around the mountain. Coca could be consumed in two ways: as a tea or, more common in the mines, as a wad of leaves combined with lime to be chewed and held in the mouth but not swallowed.[23] Though Indigenous women (*cocamamas*) retailed coca on the Potosí markets,[24] contemporary accounts describe how Spanish colonists grew wealthy by taking hold of the coca trade in the middle of the sixteenth century.[25]

Sidney Mintz coined the phrase "proletarian hunger killers" to describe the powerful combination of sugar plus tea or coffee in the nineteenth-century industrializing factories of the North Atlantic and the role of consumption in the expansion of capitalism.[26] Whereas both sugar and stimulating drinks had begun as luxury items in the North Atlantic, they were popularized and made accessible to the growing working classes through mass production in the nineteenth century. The combination gave a quick boost of energy (easily digested sugar), suppressed hunger, and increased alertness (via the caffeine), permitting factory owners to extend the working day without adding a full meal. Boiling water to make tea also seems to have had positive health impacts in Britain.[27] Thus Mintz connects the outdoor factories of sugar plantations in the Americas with the closed-door factories of northern Europe to paint a more complete picture of the origins of industrial capitalism. Under Spanish rule, coca no longer served only a ceremonial role. It doubled as a hunger killer in the mines, as a stimulant, and as an analgesic. But in the seventeenth century coca production and consumption actually dropped as a result of the population decimation wrought by disease and the conditions of colonialism. Fewer Indigenous workers for mines meant that they could demand higher wages and better food rations, decreasing demand for coca as a hunger suppressant.[28]

Yerba mate quickly came into the orbit of Potosí. In the mid-seventeenth century, Frenchman Acarete du Biscay snuck his way overland from Buenos Aires to Potosí, posing as the nephew of a Spanish gentleman because of Spain's prohibition against other Europeans visiting their holdings in South America. He described the agony of mine labor and how mate rehydrated exhausted workers: "the sulfuric vapors and minerals are so abundant that they dry out the mines in a strange way, to the point of impeding unrestricted breathing and for this they have no other remedy but the drink they make from the herb of Paraguay."[29] He added the interesting detail that mate also functioned as an emetic medicine, "to make them vomit and throw up whatever made their stomachs uncomfortable."[30] Du Biscay's account was quickly translated into English in 1698 and brought to light the inner workings of the

Spanish Empire to Europeans otherwise shut out of Spanish America. In du Biscay's telling, yerba mate was as necessary to silver production as were the mercury and the copper sulfate needed to extract and refine silver from the ore. That two stimulant hunger busters should be associated with the mine labor of Potosí testifies to the bitter difficulty of the work.

Both coca and yerba seemed to play a similar biohacking, body-enhancing role in the economic expansion of Spain from the sixteenth century onward.[31] In spite of the travel distance, in some ways yerba mate was a less complicated product for Peru: it came unencumbered with local meaning and production networks. Spanish writers recoiled at the common method of consuming coca by chewing and keeping an unswallowed wad in the mouth. Yerba mate, on the other hand, could be consumed in ways that signaled respectability in a European register: as a tisane or as a strained infusion. The unencumberment of yerba mate meant that a new ceremoniality, a creolized mestizo ceremoniality that reflected the cultural amalgamation of the Spanish Empire, could and quickly did arise.

Even the language around yerba mate reveals these shifts.[32] The Spaniards quickly called the plant and the product *yerba/hierba* (herb), the direct Spanish-language translation of the Guaraní *ca'a*. But *mate*, the word for the drinking vessel used for yerba, comes from the Quechua *matí* (meaning gourd or cup) and not the Guaraní *ka'ygua*. Moreover, "mate" is now often used for the drink itself. High-status accoutrements for consumption developed alongside the linguistic markers of a New World cosmopolitanism. The mates could be simple gourds or gourds decorated with silver or even intricate worked silver drinking vessels shaped like gourds. More surprisingly, it seems that it was in yerba mate's dispersal throughout the Spanish Empire that the most arresting visual emblem of the drink developed: the bombilla, the metal or wooden drinking straw that filtered the liquid from the leaves.

As evidence of the importance of American psychoactive plants in the Spanish Empire, in 1636 Antonio de León Pinelo wrote an extensive excursus, *Questión moral: Si el chocolate quebranta el ayuno eclesiástico* (Moral inquiry: Whether chocolate breaks the ecclesiastic fast), wherein he studied the moral economy of not only chocolate but other New World substances including coca, chicha, yaupon, and yerba mate.[33] The "moral question" he asked was whether chocolate (then taken as a liquid, following the Amerindian style) and any number of other consumables violated the weekly Catholic fast between midnight Saturday and the taking of the Eucharist at Mass on Sunday.

Born in the late 1580s to a Jewish converso (converted to Catholicism) family in Valladolid, Spain, Pinelo's parents brought him to Buenos Aires in the 1590s before moving to Córdoba, Tucumán province, and eventually to Lima, Peru.[34] Pinelo's status as a converso undoubtedly marked his experience and his outlook: Pinelo's grandparents were burned at the stake in Lisbon by the Inquisition, after being accused of being Judaizers in the 1500s, an event that precipitated the family's move to South America.[35] Other members of the extended León family were later caught up in anti-Jewish controversies and purges in seventeenth-century Lima.[36] Pinelo trained in Jesuit schools in Córdoba and Lima. From Lima, he returned to Spain to serve as a lawyer in the Council of the Indies in Madrid where he codified and organized the sprawling body of law known as the Laws of the Indies. Pinelo was employed at the Council when he wrote *Questión moral*.

Pinelo's description of yerba mate is firsthand; he doubtlessly had seen it in Córdoba, a major transit point in the trade, as well as in Peru, and he claimed that yerba had made its way to Spain (something he would know by his position of employment). He wrote:

> I finish [assessing] these liquors and drinks with one that doesn't even remove hunger nor temper thirst, but rather being medicinal has been converted into a vice. And, originating in the province of Paraguay, has extended through all of Peru and even sometimes has come to this Court. Behold that in that

Province there is an herb that has been given the name Yerba of Paraguay because only there does it grow and from there it is carried to other places. When ground it looks like sumac. This they toss into hot water and in a mate, which is a large gourd, they drink an azumbre's worth [2 liters], sometimes two or three or four times. Having had the stomach entertained with consuming tobacco or smoking coro[37] in the interim, they regurgitate it with ease. Its invention was a medicine . . . but now it has become a vice because there are people who drink it two and three times a day, and they get together just for this purpose.[38]

In the baroque style of the larger piece, Pinelo was thorough in describing the appearance of yerba, the use of a mate gourd, and yerba consumption (ceremonial and convivial) alongside tobacco and coro (a kind of wild tobacco) followed by regurgitation. Because it was a simple, non-nourishing beverage and because it was frequently vomited, Pinelo ruled that yerba mate did not break the ecclesiastical fast.

New World substances posed a fundamental challenge to the world detailed by Galen and therefore to Old World science and medicine. Pinelo's approach to New World psychoactive substances managed this tension by identifying and describing distinct categories of food, beverage, medicine, and vice that depended on the physical properties of the goods and on how humans employed those properties. Food assuaged ("removed") hunger; beverages tempered thirst. Medicine seems to refer to substances with psychoactive impact or which were not used primarily for nutrition (e.g., spices, sugar). Vice described inappropriate use that might be discouraged, whereas sin was categorically prohibited. Thus yerba mate was morally virtuous as a medicine but morally vicious when taken excessively (multiple times a day) and in a social context where people gathered explicitly for that purpose. In doing so, Pinelo set the early stage for a disenchanted, almost secularized read on psychoactivity.

And yet, in all his careful writing, Pinelo notably did not mention a bombilla. But Indigenous consumption practices—including vomitoria—continued for centuries. If Guaraní and other Native nations used a bamboo or some other wooden bombilla (the metallurgy for metal bombillas would have been developed in the mining strongholds of Peru), colonial writing could be expected to refer to it. But none of the texts consulted for this book make any mention of it. Writing in the late eighteenth century, Austrian Jesuit Martin Dobrizhoffer (who was fluent in Guaraní and other Indigenous languages, having lived among Guaraní and Abipón communities in Paraguay for eighteen years) described Spanish versus Indigenous mate consumption and explicitly wrote, "The Indians, who are not in the habit of straining it, often swallow unintentionally a quantity of the herb."[39] Again, no bombilla.

Much of the ceremonialized etiquette around yerba mate drinking as a form of classed distinction seems to have developed in the highly stratified colonial Andean mining societies of Peru, Chile, and Ecuador. All classes of Peruvian society, not just mine laborers, consumed the herb of Paraguay, with ingredients and implements that indexed wealth. Spanish military officer Antonio de Alcedo's late eighteenth-century cultural lexicon *Diccionario geográfico-histórico de las Indias Occidentales* (1789) contains multiple entries about yerba and its consumption in the Americas, including a noteworthy recipe under the entry "Mate" for its preparation in Peru: they take "a handful of the herb of Paraguay and a little sugar and toss in some embers so that it burns . . . then they pour in hot water" before drinking the beverage through "a small tube they call a bombilla."[40] The embers would caramelize the sugar and smoke the yerba even more until the water quenched the fire—a rustic recipe still employed today as traditional *mate cocido* in Paraguay. Whereas the Indigenous residents of Paraguay were not in the habit of straining yerba, consumers from Peru habitually used a bombilla.

Since the mineral wealth of the Andes caught the imagination of non-Spanish European writers, even many anglophone chroniclers recount the role of "Paraguay Tea" in the silver mines. John Campbell wrote in 1741:

> It is a great Mistake we are under in our Notion, that Negroes are employed in working these Mines, since it is certain that though they are much stronger and more robust than the Indians, yet they are not able to bear the Exhalations of the Mines, which stifle them as soon as they are let down; neither would the Indians be able to work, if they were not frequently refreshed with Paraguay Tea.[41]

The British were largely responsible for the sale of enslaved Africans in Spanish ports, perhaps a reason why anglophone texts so frequently remark on their presence. And sensing another market opportunity, part of the British attention to yerba likely arose from the fact that tea was prohibited from the Spanish imperial market.[42] British commodore John Byron stated in 1768 that yerba mate consumption was characteristic of elite Chilean women who were served the drink twice daily by enslaved African women and their descendants:

> Paraguay tea, which they call matte, as I mentioned before, is always drunk twice a day: this is brought upon a large silver salver, with four legs raised upon it, to receive a little cup made out of a small calabash, or gourd, and tipped with silver. They put the herb first into this, and add what sugar they please, and a little orange juice, and then pour hot water on them, and drink it immediately, through the conveyance of a long silver tube, at the end of which there is a round strainer, to prevent the herb getting through. And here it is reckoned a piece of politeness for the lady to suck the tube two or three times first, and then give it the stranger to drink without wiping it.[43]

Here at last are hallmarks of present-day yerba mate use: the metal bombilla shared between friend and stranger (figure 2.5). The use of the word "mate" for the hot beverage and then even the leaves themselves became entrenched outside of *I. paraguariensis* territory.[44]

Pl. XVI

Sketched by P.S. von Stone by G. Scharf.   *Printed by Rowney & Forster*

TERTULIA *and* MATE PARTY.

FIGURE 2.5. "Tertulia and Mate Party," Chile, c. 1820. From Peter
Schmidtmeyer, *Travels into Chile, over the Andes in the Years 1820 and
1821* (London: Longman, Hurst, Rees, Orme, Brown & Green, 1824).
Digitized by Google.

In spite of yerba mate's clear popularity in South America,
Spain apparently did very little to secure a European market for
the product, a detail European writers often mentioned.[45] Instead,
the mercantilist focus was internal to the empire, with a complicated tax scheme that encouraged smuggling and contraband. For
example, pre-independence Chile chafed at having to pay Buenos
Aires for yerba in coinage and precious metals.[46] The town council
of Santa Fe in Argentina complained that Chilean yerba merchants
eluded the town and instead traded with Buenos Aires directly
because the latter imposed fewer taxes on yerba.[47] Contraband
routes that avoided major population centers in Argentina arose,
pulling yerba down from Paraguay on tributaries of the Paraná or
Uruguay River and then seeking routes across the Andes.[48]
Though it was not sold in the Old World, yerba mate entered

Europe metabolized as the precious metals it was used to extract or for which it was exchanged.

Jesuit Yerba Mate

The tax resentments between the provinces did not compare, however, to the bitter jealousy between the Spanish colonists and the Jesuit order. Hernandarias himself as governor of Paraguay invited the order into Paraguay as a palliative against the brewing rebellion in the province due to colonist mistreatment of Guaraní and other Native nations. As part of the arrangement, Native nations "reduced" into Jesuit (but not Franciscan) missions were exempt from the encomienda labor requirement for a decade. This exception was later made permanent. They were also allowed to bear firearms, which proved necessary to the defense of mission populations against São Paulo–based slave raiders who ransacked their communities, forcing them to relocate from original settlements east of the Paraná to sites much closer to Asunción. The Jesuits famously established hilltop missions in the most fertile areas of the region, transforming the landscape into a planned utopian community and transforming yerba mate in the process. All the while, Spanish colonists blistered at Jesuit economic privileges and their perceived meddling in colonial social-labor arrangements.

When they first encountered yerba mate, Jesuit writers and other religious authorities decried it as demonic or, if the plant was benign, then its consumption led to moral decline. But quickly, as a combination of necessity and intellectual curiosity, the posture toward the plant radically changed. Jesuit missions were required to pay tribute to the crown and had to purchase ironware and other goods they could not readily manufacture in the Paraguayan hinterland. Without the mineral wealth of gold or silver, the primary specie of the province was yerba mate. The first Jesuit missions were in the heart of Guayrá, that *I. paraguariensis*-rich region where the first recorded mention of yerba was found. In order to meet this need, Father Antonio Ruiz de Montoya himself (who earlier had interviewed elderly Guaraní about the origins of yerba) petitioned the crown for permission to produce and export yerba mate in the missions. In 1645, the Spanish crown formally granted the request, but they may have already been involved in the trade since the 1620s.[49] And so, reduced Natives gathered yerba mate and processed it for the missions. In order to maintain a privileged status that allowed them to avoid many crown tax requirements, the Jesuits agreed in 1664 to cap their yerba exports at 12,000 arrobas annually.

It was in the missions of Paraguay that the Guaraní and the Jesuits together discovered how to cultivate the plant, supposedly a closely guarded secret lost to history when the Jesuits left the hemisphere.[50] Cultivation allowed them to plant yerbales just outside the walls of the missions and mitigated many of the worst challenges of the yerba harvest: workers did not leave families for months at a time, the trees were in neat rows, pruning was rotated and organized, and missions were not left unguarded and defenseless to the attacks of the Portuguese. The trees grew quickly; by the third year they were ready for the deep pruning that is the yerba harvest. With careful tending, each tree yielded abundant yerba for thirty years before having to be replaced. Harvesting yerba became part of the larger agricultural rhythm of the missions and the plant became part of the growing botanical repertoire of Jesuit science. Profoundly isolated from the materia medica of Europe in the Americas, the Jesuits were fully responsible for their own health care and that of the mission communities (see chapter 4). As such, they developed extensive pharmacological knowledge of local plants in the missions. Pragmatic and empirical, a Jesuit scientific tradition emerged out of necessity where, as historian Steven Harris asserts, they "were heavily engaged in the empirical and experimental aspects of early modern science while preserving (and transforming) traditional Aristotelian natural philosophy."[51]

Controlled cultivation also allowed the missions to perfect the product. The yerba from the wild yerbales included twigs with the leaves in a coarser mixture called *ca'a guazu* ("large yerba") or *de palos* ("with twigs"). But once *I. paraguariensis* was established in plantations, the Guaraní produced a more refined, higher-grade, and more labor-intensive yerba mate called *ca'a miri* ("little plant," where the diminutive also signaled affection) and more commonly written as *ca'a mini* by those unfamiliar with Guaraní and because the nasalized "r" in "miri" can sound like an "n." Ca'a miri included no twigs or branches, only leaves with the petiole and midrib painstakingly removed by hand. It commanded a much higher price.[52] And it was solely for export; the residents of the missions themselves drank ca'a guazu.

The price of ca'a miri—produced only in the missions—was double that of the ca'a guazu the colonists produced.[53] And the lucrative Peruvian market particularly preferred ca'a miri. Given the increasing needs of the missions, the 12,000 arroba export limit put additional pressure on the missions to produce the costlier blend. Predictably, colonists resented the reputation of mission yerba. They claimed that Jesuits ground their yerba finely in order to hide its origin, to which Jesuit José Sánchez Labrador retorted, "All the residents of Paraguay know the yerba tree. . . . It's a good secret, surely, a thing known in an entire province."[54] Spanish colonists also accused the missions of exporting more than the 12,000 arroba limit and of flooding the market. To defend themselves, the Jesuits demanded an independent audit of the years 1664–78 at Santa Fe (the entrepôt for Paraguayan yerba), which demonstrated that, indeed, their annual exports were below the 12,000 arroba cap. The audit did not, however, take into account the mission yerba rumored to have sidestepped Santa Fe control altogether by being shipped down the Uruguay River to Buenos Aires directly as the missions were by necessity constructed near waterways. The Jesuits insisted that their production of yerba was not profit-motive-based commerce but rather just to meet the order's tribute obligations (which had to be paid in specie) and to be able to purchase a few choice items they could not produce on the missions themselves.

The cultivation of yerba mate made the missions the envy of their neighbors. When the Jesuits were expelled from Paraguay in 1767, the planted yerbales fell to ruin as Guaraní abandoned the missions. Later writers lamented the loss of the mission technique or speculated that the industrious Jesuits must have figured out a mysterious way to patiently feed the seeds to birds to soften their shells.[55] But when the Jesuits were forced out of Paraguay, the thousands of Guaraní left in the missions surely knew the technique, though it seems no one asked them what it was. The loss of the knowledge is a form of colonial neglect, a form of ignorance. Yet Jesuit chroniclers themselves describe how they germinated and propagated yerba mate in the missions: a water bath. José Sánchez Labrador (1717–99) describes the same process as written in Martin Dobrizhoffer's account: "The seeds contained in the fruit, when washed in clean water release a frothy viscous material similar to soap lather. To remove this viscosity, they wash the seeds repeatedly; so the seeds are separated, dried, and kept to make seedlings. . . . When the seeds are dried without the washings and later planted, they do not germinate because the humidity cannot penetrate the casing and, little by little, they rot in the earth. If the fresh berries, recently plucked from the trees, are soon after sowed, they germinate because the resinous casing has not hardened and with the heat and humidity, they open and sprout."[56] This is the secret lost Jesuit technique: fresh berries could be sown directly into the soil; dried berries required soaking to remove the hard shell.

But colonists do not appear to have picked up either technique—perhaps because the mission communities kept it a secret or perhaps because the colonists were uninterested, choosing to continue to send bonded Indigenous labor into the wild yerbales. The difference in how the two groups produced the herb of Paraguay so popular throughout the Viceroyalty of Peru illustrates the complex of economic logics that operated simultaneously in the Spanish Empire. Colonists envisioned wealth-building as an extractive enterprise, one limited to the boundaries of the empire. Any competition threatened their position in a closed market. In contrast, cultivation in Jesuit missions was intended to bolster the independence and self-sufficiency of the utopian project. Neither was free-market capitalism. Tensions between the Jesuits and the Spanish colonists festered and the latter added their complaints and conspiracy theories about Jesuit secrets and intrigues to rising anti-Jesuit sentiment in Europe. By the late eighteenth century, Charles III of Spain had had enough. He ordered the suppression and expulsion of the Order from all Spanish realms on penalty of death in 1767.

Conclusion

After being kicked out of all Spanish possessions, the Jesuits retreated to Europe to write their memoirs, transcribe hand-penned manuscripts that had circulated between the missions, teach in universities, and serve in hospitals. In Paraguay, colonists eagerly seized mission territories even though some had been commended to the care of different religious orders, such as the Franciscans. But the thriving Jesuit missions and carefully planted yerbales fell into disrepair as the Guaraní withdrew from them, taking with them the knowledge of how to cultivate *I. paraguariensis*. Ca'a miri also vanished from the market. The yerba mate produced today is much closer to the ca'a guazu or yerba de palos described by the Jesuit fathers, although some yerba producers are experimenting with a leaf-only product that has a much more intense flavor.

Calling the path of yerba mate a "New World Silk Road" isn't exaggeration. On some of its longest journeys from Guayrá (Paraguay) to Quito (Ecuador), the leaf trekked more than 6,000 kilometers; the main east-west corridor between the start of the Silk Road in Xi'an (China) to Istanbul (Turkey) is 6,800 kilometers as the crow flies. Even as its use stretched far beyond its growing range, carried over mountains in hide bags hauled by mules, the herb of Paraguay integrated the distinct economies of the Viceroyalty of Peru. Just as yerba mate reflects important continuities in Indigenous America (trade, *Ilex* use in ceremony, smoking via a buccan), yerba mate in Spanish America interweaves the extractivism of the mine and of the field. Though the human history of mining is old, the global world market dependence on the extraction and circulation of minerals that came with Spanish colonialism in the Americas gave rise to a new method of building economies on minerals and the wealth of the earth. Extractivism took root in the Spanish Empire and has continued to the present.[57]

For the two hundred years from initial Spanish contact to the expulsion of the Jesuits, mate moved between Indigenous practice to a fully creolized one whose modes of production (extractive encomienda labor arrangements; mission-bound labor) and modes of consumption (recipes, accoutrements) reflected political-economic and social arrangements distinct to the Spanish Empire. Mate was almost everywhere in South America and even made it to Europe in small quantities. But though it was economically profitable commercial agriculture, because the mercantilist logic of the Spanish Empire kept products within the bounds of the empire, mate remained within that Iberian scope. The silver extracted from Potosí with labor fueled by mate, on the other hand, circled the globe.

PART II

Remaking the World of Mate

3

South American Cowboys and Nineteenth-Century Wars for Independence

A MAN STANDS to speak inside a rustic country home. The descendent of Spanish settlers, he is dressed in European military raiment but has covered it with a simple woolen poncho that reaches to his black leather boots. At the table before him sits a priest, clothed in a brown habit, writing on sheets of paper with a feather. A Charrua man wearing a bright red poncho stands ready to receive one of the envelopes. Seated near the fire is an Afro-Uruguayan man, also in a red poncho, with a kettle in hand as he readies to pour hot water into a mate as the warm light of the fire reflects off the bombilla.

The painting by Pedro Blanes Viale (figure 3.1) depicts one of the most iconic moments of Uruguayan history, when independence hero José Gervasio Artigas dictated a number of proposals that would be carried by delegates from what was then known as the Banda Oriental (the eastern bank) province to a congress in Buenos Aires on the other side of the River Plate in 1813. At issue was the question of what to do with the growing push for independence from Spain. Would all the provinces of the Viceroyalty of La Plata unite in one new country ruled from Buenos Aires? Or would those provinces enjoy more autonomy as a confederation

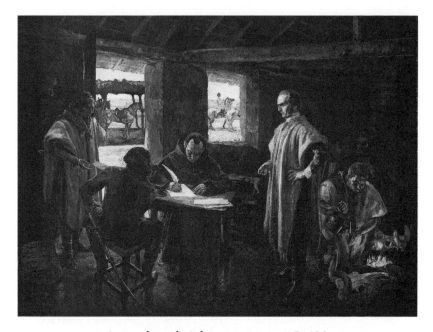

FIGURE 3.1. *Artigas dictando órdenes a su secretario José Monterroso en Purificación* (1919), Pedro Blanes Viale. Image credit: Museo Histórico Nacional de Uruguay.

of equals in the United Provinces of La Plata? The Instructions of 1813 emphatically called for independence from Iberian rule and for the autonomy of the federalist Banda Oriental from porteño (Buenos Aires) hegemony, insisting that a regional confederation have its capital *not* in Buenos Aires.

But when it was presented in Buenos Aires by the Uruguayan delegates, it was flat-out rejected and a bounty was placed on Artigas's head, unleashing a decades-long war for the province's independence. Neither the porteño elite, nor the Portuguese empire with its seat in Brazil, nor the United Kingdom wanted to acknowledge Uruguayan independence and, instead, took turns sending troops to occupy the maritime country. Artigas was eventually forced by Brazilian forces to flee inland with his troops, seeking asylum from Paraguay's ruler José Gaspar Rodríguez de

Francia in 1820. He lived in exile in Paraguay for the next thirty years until his death in 1850.

Independence from European rule in the nineteenth century both resulted from and exacerbated an identity crisis for the new South American nations. Two key questions demanded an answer. First was the question of national identity. What *people* made up the nations of Argentina, Brazil, Bolivia, Chile, Paraguay, and Uruguay? Only the descendants of Europeans? What about the many Africans and their descendants who had been trafficked as enslaved laborers? What about the Indigenous groups? What practices and customs demonstrated belonging in that national community? The second question was a political economic dilemma: How would a thriving, independent economy be formed? Both questions were answered by mate.

But *how* mate answered those questions differed depending on whether the country in question was primarily a consumer of yerba or also a producer. The world of mate shifted seismically in the decades following the expulsion of the Jesuits in 1767. The destruction of Jesuit yerba orchards left only native forests of *Ilex* in Paraguay and Brazil as sources for the leaf throughout much of the nineteenth century. But the growing populations of Argentina, Chile, and Uruguay were still eager markets for yerba even in the midst of revolutionary tumult. Murmurings of independence from European rule had circulated around the continent for years, but the Napoleonic crises of the early 1800s pushed them to the fore. The provinces of the Viceroyalty of Peru and of the newly formed Viceroyalty of La Plata (Argentina, Bolivia, Chile, Paraguay, and Uruguay) decided not just to reject the imposition of Napoleonic control over the Spanish throne but to assert full independence from Spain. Brazil, on the other hand, took a different tack. To flee Napoleon's advances, but also in recognition of the magnitude of Brazil within the empire, the Portuguese imperial throne decamped from Lisbon to Rio de Janeiro in 1808, where the emperor ruled until an 1889 coup dethroned him and ended the monarchy. The armed conflicts that ensued lasted almost the entire century as the new countries struggled to define their geographic borders externally and the national community within.

Consumption in the River Plate Countries Argentina and Uruguay

Cielito, cielo que sí
guárdense su chocolate,
aquí somos puros indios
y solo tomamos mate.—Bartolomé Hidalgo, ca 1810[1]

Little darling,
you keep your chocolate,
here we're all Indians
and only drink mate.

By the time Uruguayan poet Bartolomé Hidalgo penned that refrain on the eve of revolution, chocolate had so thoroughly conquered European palates that it was the sophisticated drink of choice for blue-blooded Spain-born elites. So, when Hidalgo saw Count José Antonio Joaquín de Flórez y Pereyra[2]—a Spanish emissary and military official who served as Spanish king Ferdinand VII's envoy to both Rio de Janeiro and Buenos Aires during the wars for independence—he knew just what to say. A poet *payador* (musician) *gaucho* from Montevideo, Hidalgo proudly declared that the proper drink of the River Plate was mate and its proper inhabitants rough, America-born, ethnically ambiguous "indios" contrasted, presumably, to Europeans such as Flórez. Part of the irony was that Flórez himself had actually been born in Buenos Aires during his father's diplomatic mission to the New World and grew up surrounded by mate.

The countries at the mouth of the River Plate, Argentina and Uruguay, became Argentine and Uruguayan through a love-hate relationship with the racially mixed South American cowboy, the cattle-rustling, knife-dueling, card-gambling, yerba mate–drinking

FIGURE 3.2. Ranch hands in Rosario, Argentina, c. 1895. Photograph by Samuel Boote. Image credit: Colección Dirán Sirinian.

gaucho (figure 3.2). Nation-building in South America was a dual boundary-making project: a matter of securing territorial boundaries and of defining the racial-ethnic makeup of the nation. For years, the former possessions of the Spanish Viceroyalty of La Plata (Argentina, Bolivia, Chile, Paraguay, and Uruguay) contested their borders militarily, culminating in the bloodiest international war in the Western Hemisphere, the War of the Triple Alliance (1864–70). In May 1810, the viceroyalty rebelled against Spanish rule. Argentina, under the centralizing vision of the Buenos Aires elite, sought to bring the outer provinces under porteño (from the Spanish for "port") dominance. Paraguay, more geographically distant from Buenos Aires, quickly declared independence in May 1811, but Uruguay had to face two close neighbors who wanted to annex the province on the eastern bank of the Uruguay River. Artigas and his troops revolted against Spanish authorities in 1811 and then expelled Argentine troops from Montevideo in 1815. In 1816, Portuguese forces invaded Montevideo, conquering it in 1817 and eventually annexing the province. A military insurrection by the rebel group Thirty-Three Orientals (*treinta y tres orientales*) began in 1825, drawing Argentina and Brazil into a war that was finally concluded in a peace treaty arbitrated by the British, which established Uruguay as independent of both Argentina and Brazil in 1828.

Uncertain geographic borders mirrored uncertain social borders. Many battles for independence focused on national and provincial capitals, but large swaths of the national territory lay sparsely populated, outside the control of the metropoles. Port cities like Buenos Aires, Montevideo, and Asunción were primarily populated by European immigrants (including, but not only, the Spanish-born *peninsulares* in government employ), their descendants born in the New World (notably, the *criollo*/creole caste from which many revolutionary military leaders came), mestizos of mixed Spanish and Indigenous ancestry, and enslaved and emancipated Africans and their descendants. On the other hand, the fertile pampas was occupied by Indigenous groups who defiantly resisted colonial rule, whether by European empires or newly independent settler nation-states, and by gauchos, a rural, ethnically mixed peasant and ranching (or rustling) class. Although today Argentina and Uruguay are imagined as white, European countries, on the eve of independence nearly 30 percent of Buenos Aires's population, 25–30 percent of Montevideo's, and 52 percent of Córdoba's were Black.[3] To the urban creole elite who sat at the hand-carved wooden desks in Buenos Aires where battle plans and constitutions were being drafted, it was clear which of these groups properly belonged in the national body.

Gauchos, Indigenous groups, and Black populations were all undesirable in the eyes of the urban creole elite. In North America, the frontier was imagined as a place of possibility, openness, and hope.[4] In South America, the frontier was a place populated by lawless, culturally and racially inferior groups who were obstacles to progress; though a fertile land, it was called a "desert" because of its perceived lack of civilization.[5] Argentine intellectual and future president Domingo Faustino Sarmiento expressed this spatial-social imaginary in the title of his book *Facundo; or, Civilization and Barbarism* (1845). For Sarmiento, Argentine dictator Juan Manuel de Rosas (1835–52) exemplified this danger in part because he had such sway over Argentina's Black population. In Sarmiento's words, they were "addicted" to Rosas and a "warlike race" in which even women acted like soldiers.[6] Sarmiento believed that "barbarism" posed an existential threat to "civilization" because barbarism was not just confined to the hinterland but always threatened to move in from the frontier to the metropole carried in the bodies and customs of any whose blood and culture were not sufficiently European.

The intention in Argentina and Uruguay was to create new nations based on European immigration, with Europeans as the founding fathers, adopting European customs, and dispensing with the cultural habits of the gauchos. "To govern is to populate," wrote Argentine intellectual Juan Alberdi in a draft of what would become the 1853 Argentine constitution.[7] So the plan for Argentina and Uruguay was to populate the new countries with people they saw as desirable via immigration, to only gradually end slavery, and to "conquer the desert" by launching genocidal extermination campaigns against Indigenous groups.[8] European families would then settle on the newly opened frontier, bringing progress to the nation (and outbreeding the remaining gauchos). To ensure this, Argentina was legally obligated by its 1853 constitution to promote "European immigration" and by the beginning of the twentieth century, three-quarters of the population of Buenos Aires was foreign born.[9]

But for all the hope for respectability to be brought aboard European boats, the practices and the bodies of Indigenous, Black, mestizo, and gaucho communities continued. In spite of efforts to vilify the gaucho and exalt Europeanness as the heart of national identity, another version of the founding national myth arose of begrudging admiration for the gaucho (figure 3.3). If Sarmiento's *Facundo* told the story of civilization's necessary triumph over the barbarism of Argentina's frontiers, Argentine José Hernández's bestselling epic poem, *El Gaucho Martín Fierro*, captured popular esteem for life on the margins. Among his many exploits, the poncho-clad Fierro deserts the (porteño-led) army on one of its "conquering the desert" campaigns, instigates a fatal duel by making lewd comments to a Black woman at a *pulpería* bar, and amuses crowds with his playing of payador music. Hernández's Fierro is derisive toward the new immigrants and positioned Hernández against the immigration policies of Sarmiento, Alberdi, and the porteño elite.[10]

Sarmiento saw Artigas as the epitome of the barbarous gaucho, wreaking havoc on the frontier.[11] The scene described at the beginning of this chapter, Artigas dictating the Instructions of 1813, has been painted, parodied, and turned into commemorative postage stamps, the definitive life-size version painted by Uruguayan artist Pedro Blanes Viale in 1919. According to popular accounts, the man pouring mate is military commander and poet Joaquín "Ansina" Lenzina (1760–1860), an Afro-Uruguayan born in Montevideo into slavery to parents who had been trafficked from Africa.[12] Ansina emancipated himself as a youth by escaping and embraced the life of a gaucho—whose traditional poncho both Artigas and Ansina wear in Blanes Viale's rendition—until joining a ship's crew. Accused of piracy, the ship was impounded by the Brazilian navy and Ansina was sold back into slavery in the Portuguese-speaking country.

COSTUMI DELL'AMERICA MERIDIONALE. — *I Gauchos*.

FIGURE 3.3. Gauchos. From an unidentified Italian magazine, c. 1860.
Image credit: Acervo Milda Rivarola, Imagoteca Paraguaya.

Years later, Artigas came across Ansina in Brazil and immediately emancipated him. Ansina joined Artigas for the rest of his life, as one of many Uruguayan troops who lived their last days in exile in Paraguay. After Artigas's death in 1850, an elderly Ansina moved in with the family of Afro-Uruguayan sergeant Manuel Antonio Ledesma in Guarambaré south of Asunción until his own death in 1860. Artigas and Ledesma were repatriated to Uruguay after their deaths,[13] lying honored in the national mausoleum. For decades, Ledesma's tomb and photograph were erroneously identified as Ansina's. Ansina's grave was never identified, but his loyalty to Artigas has been folded into the heroic narrative of Uruguay's founding, a way to grapple with the brutality and contradiction of slavery in the history of the republic. Although Ansina's mortal remains lie in an unknown mass pauper grave in a sleepy village south of Asunción, by law each cavalry unit in the Uruguayan armed forces must display a bust in his honor.[14]

Gaucho was more a way of life than it was a racial phenotype and in Blanes Viale's painting, three men from three distinct racial categories wear the signature poncho. Drinking mate, serving mate became signs of authentic belonging in the national body for the River Plate (see figure 3.2). Throughout the Americas, cuisine reflected the tensions between colonial powers and colonies. In the Central American country of Belize, there was a shift in culinary tastes around independence. Pre-independence, British prestige foods served as a sign of status. But after independence, local (national) dishes were prized as indications of the small nation's autonomy from the United Kingdom.[15] Something different seems to have happened for River Plate nations. At its core, the daily cuisine of what would eventually become Argentina and Uruguay came from the Jesuit mission-ranching/gaucho complex, a diet that consisted of abundant beef from the herds of semi-feral cattle that roamed the grasslands, along with the New World starches manioc and corn, and yerba mate.[16] Yerba was so central to the local diet that it formed, along with tobacco, part of salaries in the eighteenth century.[17]

As thousands of new immigrants arrived to the ports of the River Plate over the nineteenth century, they changed the demographics of the countries and brought with them cultural practices that would shift Argentina and Uruguay. Wheat in the form of pasta and bread became more important in the daily cuisine as the greatest number of immigrants in the nineteenth century came from Italy, Spain, and France. But despite other culinary shifts, the custom of mate was not replaced by coffee or tea even as groups that drank those beverages swelled River Plate demographics. The imposing Hotel de Inmigrantes, constructed in Buenos Aires in the early twentieth century to offer free lodging to more than seven hundred guests at a time, for example, served mate cocido (mate as a hot tisane) to its residents for breakfast.

A whole folklore and popular culture apparatus around mate matured in the River Plate. The very first documented tango lyrics were "Tomá mate, che"—literally, "hey, drink mate"—written by Spanish immigrant Santiago Ramos in 1853. The tango itself bears witness to the African and gaucho roots of popular culture in Argentina and Uruguay, in spite of military and historiographic attempts to erase the presence of non-white groups and configure the countries as essentially European.[18] In Montevideo newspapers of the 1830s, tango appears next to *candombe* as one of two dances performed by Afro-Uruguayans. In fact, the tango shares its rhythm with candombe and the Cuban *habanera*—musical styles with African roots.[19] The word itself is likely African in origin, perhaps a mispronunciation of the Yoruba thunder deity "Shango" or from the Congolese for "drum." Bartolomé Hidalgo's four-line "cielito" poem was just the tip of the mate folklore iceberg. Hidalgo, Martín Fierro, and even the versed "Tomá mate, che" tango point to a larger musical tradition in the River Plate known as the *payada*. Payador (troubadour) gauchos were esteemed poets and improvisational guitar players; *payada* songs were often composed in a call-and-response or as a contrapuntal musical duel between payadores. Mate consumption became part of the cultural complex of the new nations.

Consumption beyond the River Plate

By contrast, the Andean countries of Bolivia, Ecuador, and Peru developed coffee cultures. Chile, an Andean country that was part of the Viceroyalty of La Plata, was a curious outlier. It saw a growth across the board of all three major stimulating drinks in the nineteenth century: coffee, yerba mate, and black tea. With the dissolution of the Spanish Empire, important changes affected mate's former commercial circuit. The political break between Spanish America and Spain resulted in an economic rupture as trade no longer followed the contours and imperatives of the empire. The British could at last bring tea from Asia to new markets in South America. As we saw in the previous chapter, mate was wildly popular throughout the viceroyalty; coffee and tea arrived to palates that already had well-developed caffeine tastes and a social, creolized consumption ritual. Yet, writers in eighteenth-century Peru celebrated the arrival of the café and coffee culture as a modernizing force associated with Enlightenment and Liberalism, contrasting it with mate, the latter a supremely domestic drink.[20]

Even so, caffeine dependencies are notoriously hard to break. Although Peru played an influential role in mate's creolized ceremony, coffee came into Peru both as the urban institution of the coffeehouse and through the rural institution of the coffee plantation, which moved southward from Guayaquil (Ecuador). Peru eventually produced enough coffee not only to meet national demand but for export in the nineteenth century. That is, coffee firmly established its place on both the consumption and production sides of the commodity chain and thus displaced yerba mate. Transportation also played a key role for markets that did not produce yerba mate. It is one thing to send hides of yerba mate on rafts down the Uruguay and Paraná Rivers to Montevideo and Buenos Aires; it is quite another to pack them on mules up the altiplano or over the Andes on roads no longer even poorly maintained by one central imperial government.

Political turmoil in the region affected mate prices. In Chile, the price skyrocketed by 2500 percent from a colonial average of three pesos per arroba to about seventy-five pesos during the wars of independence.[21] Balking at these numbers and the loss of precious metals to the yerba trade, Chilean liberator Bernardo O'Higgins encouraged the substitution of *naranjillo* (a local citronella) for *I. paraguariensis*.[22] Naranjillo proved a poor surrogate. Over the next century, yerba mate imports to Chile grew tenfold, but at the same time tea and coffee imports grew at an even faster rate, eventually eclipsing the South American stimulant.[23] While tea came from afar, coffee benefited from proximity as plantations spread across the continent. Some of the best could be imported from the coca-producing Yungas region of Bolivia.

A U.S. visitor to Chile in the 1830s remarked that mate, which had been "everywhere in Chile, previous to the [1810] revolution, was substituted for the more costly tea of China" and that "since that period, the old ladies only adhere to the practice, while the young ones, more refined in taste, prefer sipping young Hyson or Bohea [Chinese teas], from a gilt edged China tea cup."[24] To help understand why tea and coffee were able to displace mate in Chile and its neighbors (and perhaps why mate was not able to displace coffee and tea in North Atlantic markets until recently), the distinction Benjamin Orlove and Arnold Bauer make between "the allure of the exotic" and "the allure of the foreign" is useful.[25] Nineteenth-century Europe, with its fascination with Chinese porcelain and silks from the Orient, imported the exotic as a way to consume, possess, and even subdue the Other. Latin America, on the other hand, sought distance from the exotic Other in the form of Indigenous and African-descended communities by importing foreign goods and practices from Europe. Orlove and Bauer argue that the rising popularity of French wine-making styles, the preference for coffee and tea rather than mate, and even the architecture of homes in Chile reflected aspirations for a Europeanized lifestyle.[26]

By the time of independence, mate was solidified enough as a creolized custom across the Spanish Empire that it did not register as *indigenous* but rather as a local custom. Even as new national borders were being drawn in the old viceroyalties, the coffee/mate line became a new kind of boundary. Early Europeans in the region, as historian Rebecca Earle has observed, imagined Native consumption as "unfood," grotesque, and not fitting for proper Christian (European) palates. But centuries of use by colonial Iberian America had so thoroughly transformed mate into a creole custom that even new immigrants to the River Plate picked it up and celebrated it. Mate consumption marked the consolidation of two distinct geographical-cultural units, post-independence, in Spanish America: the Viceroyalty of La Plata as distinct from the Viceroyalty of Peru.

Production

Paraguay

Aspects of the story of Paraguay's founding can sound like something out of a magical realism novel. Like Uruguay, Paraguay sought autonomy from the Buenos Aires elite. The small country defeated Argentine troops led by porteño General Manuel Belgrano, who was sent to "liberate" the country from European rule in March 1811. The revolutionary junta in Asunción then rejected an offer of two hundred Portuguese troops from Brazil to support the Spanish royalist cause in May 1811, thus effecting the country's independence.[27] When Paraguay declared independence, almost no one in the new country had a university degree, even among the elite. Universities had been discouraged in Paraguay by the Spanish authorities the century before as a way to tamper revolutionary and independent tendencies in the province after the pro-autonomy Revolt of the Comuneros (1721–35). The charismatic lawyer and skilled administrator José Gaspar Rodríguez de Francia, who had studied at Córdoba in Tucumán province, was one of the few university graduates in the country at the time (figure 3.4). Though Francia had read Montesquieu and knew of new models

FIGURE 3.4. José Gaspar Rodríguez de Francia drinking mate, cigar in hand. John Parish Robertson and William Parish Robertson, *Letters on Paraguay*, vol. 2 (London: John Murray, 1838). Image credit: author.

for the triumvirate separation of powers into executive, judiciary, and legislative branches, he apparently kept the information to himself as Paraguayans debated how to form an independent government.

An 1813 Paraguayan Congress made up of a thousand male representatives drawn from across the country set up a new government following the non-Spanish model they knew: imperial Rome.[28] Two consuls who were to take turns leading the nation were appointed, Francia and military leader Fulgencio Yegros. According to popular legend, two chairs were prepared for the consuls—one labeled Caesar, the other Pompey for the two rulers of the Roman Empire—and Francia quickly sat down on the Caesar throne, leaving Pompey for Yegros.[29] Predictably, Francia (Caesar) had Yegros (Pompey) removed from power in 1814 and then had himself voted "Supreme Dictator of the Republic" for perpetuity by a national congress. Any resistance to Francia's centralizing power was met with swift punishment; in 1820, Yegros was caught up in a failed Good Friday Conspiracy that tried to overthrow Francia and was executed a year later. Francia was famously paranoid about dissent or conspiracy. He ejected foreigners who crossed him, incarcerated rivals, and governed with complete control until his death, bolstered by an extensive system of secret informants.

To protect Paraguay's independence, Francia embarked on a fiercely isolationist, anti-imperial policy. He closed the country to most international trade as a way to foster local economic independence. By the same token, Francia extended the first case of political asylum in the Western Hemisphere when he welcomed Artigas. Whereas Montevideo and Buenos Aires policy encouraged European immigration to whiten the national bodies, Francia suspected European and creole elites as not sufficiently loyal to the new nation and outlawed marriage between whites. Instead, by law, creoles and Europeans had to marry individuals of racially mixed ancestry. Slavery, however, was not abolished.[30] Like other port cities in the region, Asunción had a considerable Black population and according to census records, on the day of independence nearly 50 percent of the city's residents were Black.[31] Francia's primary concern for Paraguay was to maintain its autonomy from its large neighbors (and to safeguard his own power) while developing a thriving, independent economy. Under his watch, yerba production and exports remained in private hands, but the government limited sales and set yerba prices in the 1810s and 1820s on the lower end of the historical price range. This kept a basic necessity inexpensive for locals while encouraging Paraguayan agriculturalists to move from mate to other products.

In 1806, fourteen-year-old Scot John Parish Robertson sailed out of Greenock to seek his fortune in South America. He witnessed the British siege of Montevideo but had to return to Scotland when the Spanish retook both Buenos Aires and Montevideo. With an eye for trade, Robertson returned to the continent in 1808, stopped briefly in Rio de Janeiro, and then sojourned in Buenos Aires for two years before trekking inland to Paraguay to reach Asunción. Sometime later, Robertson contracted Payaguá sailors, an Indigenous nation renowned for their canoeing skills, to navigate a barge loaded with yerba mate and other wares down the Paraná River to Buenos Aires. In complete silence, they steered past a Spanish blockade while the Spanish troops napped, never knowing they had been evaded. So successful were his commercial (ad)ventures that he invited his younger brother William to join him. Together, they witnessed the rise of Francia. The first time John met Francia, the Paraguayan leader had a cigar and a mate in hand (see figure 3.4); William was actually at the congressional convention that elected Francia as dictator. But the brothers lost Francia's good graces when they could not acquire the military armament he desired and were banished by the dictator in 1815. Decades later, they composed a multivolume book series, *Letters on Paraguay* (1838), their firsthand accounts of the revolutions and the Francia regime, books that were simultaneously published in London and New York with subscribers in Buenos Aires, Montevideo, and the Portuguese consulate in London.

And so, in spite of the country's isolationism under Francia, news about Paraguay—as a place of potential, languishing under tyranny—spread.[32] In one of the most reprinted sections of the books (published in magazines and newspapers across the anglophone world) John, who had made a small fortune trading yerba, recounts a visit to a wild yerbal 150 miles northeast of Asunción. After an arduous trek, wrote Robertson, "we emerged . . . into a beautiful country, richly adorned with all the finest specimens of Paraguay scenery. . . . We were in the midst of an extensive valley, well-irrigated, and closely shut in, on all sides, by wood of every description, from the shrub and the orange tree, to the most gigantic timber of the forest."[33] With painstaking detail he described how, once having found a thicket of trees, harvesters built corrals for the bulls whose hides would be used to bundle the yerba and whose flesh would feed the workers. The animals thus cared for, multiple small *tatacuás* (firepits) were constructed to provide the intense heat of the *sapecado* (flash dry) first step and then much larger domed wood frame *barbacuás* on which leaves would be slowly smoked (see figure 2.2). Finally, the leaves were pounded and then sewn into the new hides. Each hide sack contained anywhere between 200 and 220 pounds of mate (eight or nine arrobas). As the hide dried and tightened in the sun, Robertson recalled it became "a substance as hard as stone."[34] Setting up the camp took three days.

Robertson went deep into the forest with several experienced yerba harvesters who showed him how to hatchet-prune the trees, which ranged in size from shrub to fully grown. "The smaller the plant, the better is the tea which is taken from it considered to be," he wrote.[35] The whole endeavor could last up to six months with workers capable of producing some two hundred pounds (eight arrobas) of yerba a day. A mate-processing camp operated something like a coal-mining or factory town. Workers purchased their harvesting tools via credit extended by the yerba master, ate food purchased on credit, and slept in hammocks purchased on credit, leading to a kind of debt peonage. Even so, wages for what John

Parish Robertson called "peons" (later called *mensú*) ran higher than those for similar agrarian or domestic work.[36] Grueling labor conditions went along with profit; the processing was entirely manual in Paraguay and each step required a differently developed expertise. The technique witnessed by Robertson was strikingly similar to what had been recorded by Catholic missionaries centuries before.[37] It had likely changed little over hundreds of years.

By the time John and William Parish Robertson published their memoirs, Europe already had a strong appetite for news about Paraguay's curious ruler because of his dealings with (read: incarceration of) French botanist Aimé Bonpland. The Paraguayan leader captured the attention of European writers as a tropical despot who openly embraced the title of "dictator," eschewed personal wealth, and did not care one whit about the opinion of leaders or publics outside Paraguay. But all leaders, even perpetual dictators, die. At his passing, Francia left no apparent successors. Carlos Antonio López (1844–62), an Asunción-born lawyer who some writers claim was Francia's estranged nephew, was named consul in 1841 and then president in 1844 under the country's first constitution, which reproduced many of the authoritarian structures of Francia's administration.[38] Lopez's new government, however, undertook a different economic model.

Unlike Francia, Lopez saw free-flowing trade and comity with other nations as key for growth. For example, he sought U.S. recognition of Paraguay's independence (which Francia had not) and Brazil formally recognized Paraguay's independence in 1844.[39] He similarly fomented cotton production, at first to reduce Paraguay's dependence on imported cotton for military uniforms and then as an export-oriented cash crop.[40] And in 1846, he declared a government monopoly on yerba exports. As under the time of Francia, production primarily lay in private hands, but Lopez conscripted the military to harvest yerba for the government.[41] To increase government income, the Lopez administration granted concessions to Paraguayan entrepreneurs to commercialize and export yerba to River Plate markets and beyond.[42]

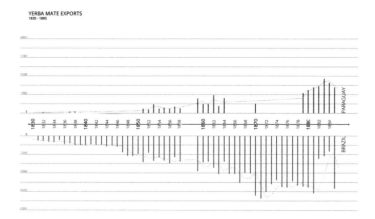

YERBA MATE EXPORTS
1830 - 1885

FIGURE 3.5. Brazil and Paraguay yerba mate exports (tons), 1830–1885. Sources: Vera Blinn Reber, "Commerce and Industry in Nineteenth Century Paraguay: The Example of Yerba Mate," *The Americas* 42, no. 1 (1985): 47, table 5; Fundação Instituto Brasileiro de Geografia e Estatística, *Estadisticas Historicas do Brasil, 2a edição* (Rio de Janeiro: IBGE, 1990), 351 (for Brazil yerba mate exports, 1831–1987). Image credit: Juan Cristaldo and Silvia Arevalos, Exponencial S.A.

Carlos Antonio López and his oldest son, Francisco Solano (1862–70), opened trade relations with the United Kingdom and the Continent, attempting to put yerba on the European market. They simultaneously imported European industrial technology, building a railroad and a significant metalworks at Ybucuí, south of Asunción. Whereas yerba exports had fallen after the expulsion of the Jesuits and the Francia regime, during the two Lopez administrations, numbers began to rise (figure 3.5). After 1852, these numbers got a boost when a rebel army overthrew Argentine leader Juan Manuel de Rosas, who had refused to recognize Paraguayan independence and who had restricted trade on the Paraná River. For Francia, a robust Paraguayan economy ought to be built via independent agricultural production to ensure the country's self-reliance. The Lopezes, on the other hand, sought to jump-start industrialization by purchasing advanced technology and know-how from abroad. And their program to transform the nation was paid for by yerba exports.

Brazil

The turmoil of the Francia years with uncertain exports opened the door for a new player to enter the mate trade. Argentine Francisco de Alzagaray stepped off a boat in the Brazilian port city of Paranaguá in 1820 to look for yerba, reasoning that there must be untapped mate potential in the southern forests of the country where the oldest Jesuit ruins lay. The cultivated yerbales were a distant memory, Paraguay's yerba supply was uneven because of Francia's internal policies, and authorities in Buenos Aires levied taxes on whatever did manage to make it out of Paraguay for the use of the Paraná River. But although demand for yerba had declined in Lima and Potosí, in the River Plate countries it only grew. The southern region that eventually became the Brazilian states of Rio Grande do Sul (bordering Argentina and Uruguay), Santa Catarina, and Paraná had an entrenched mate-drinking gaúcho culture more in common with the River Plate than with northern Brazilian cities like Bahia and Rio de Janeiro. Like other entrepreneurs both foreign and Brazilian, Alzagaray envisioned an economic opportunity if a new supply of mate could be found.

The nineteenth century is known as Brazil's coffee century when the South American country rose to prominence as the world's top coffee producer and exporter, a distinction it still holds today.[43] But it might also be thought of as Brazil's mate century. Brazil entered the international yerba business relatively late, but when it did, it became the world's largest producer and exporter of the leaf for nearly a hundred years.[44] Coffee was introduced to Rio de Janeiro in the 1760s. Dutch immigrant John Hopman is generally credited with being the first to export coffee, grown from his plantation in Engenho Velho on the outskirts of the city a decade later.[45] Operating with European and North American capital, Brazilian coffee producers transformed landscapes first in Rio de Janeiro and then westward to the plateau of São Paulo.[46] Forests were cut down and replaced with vast plantations of the East African plant.[47]

The burgeoning international demand for coffee reinvigorated the transatlantic African slave trade, which was made technically illegal in Brazil in 1831 to little avail. Not only were the coffee plantations cultivated and harvested by unpaid Black laborers, the infrastructure, ships, routes, docks, insurance policies, and financial tools developed to move coffee to North Atlantic markets depended upon and stimulated the traffic of bonded bodies.[48] And so, both the coffee and the sugar that sweetened it in European and North American cups were produced at the hand of the transatlantic slave trade. Coffee interests even kept competing local caffeinated products like guarana out of northern markets.[49]

Alzagaray was right. The old yerba region of Guayrá east of the Paraná River where Spanish colonists had been recorded commercializing the leaf now lay under Brazilian-Portuguese control.[50] And indeed, southwestern Brazil had vast, untouched yerbales throughout the Atlantic Forest in what are now the states of Mato Grosso do Sul, Paraná, Santa Catarina, and Rio Grande do Sul. First called *congonha* ("that which gives sustenance") from the Tupi and later *chimarrão* from the Spanish *cimarrón* ("brown" and "untamed"), mate had already caught the attention of the Portuguese as a potential commodity prior to Alzagaray.[51] A royal missive as far back as 1721 had directed the captain general of São Paulo Rodrigo César de Meneses to send a box of yerba along with "the recipe for how to use it" to Lisbon.[52] But little happened. When Alzagaray began his search at the beginning of the nineteenth century, mate processing in Brazil was still hyperlocal and rudimentary.

But Alzagaray and others had larger markets with precise mate palates in mind. The artisanal Brazilian mode of production changed with two key innovations brought from the exterior. Alzagaray constructed the first mate *engenho* (literally, "machine") in Paranaguá, a mill to grind dried yerba and prepare it for export. The technology quickly traveled inland to Curitiba, where Brazilian colonel Caetano José Munhoz established Engenho da Gloria in

1834, the first of dozens of milling factories.[53] Munhoz's company changed hands a few times, but it still operates today to produce the brand Mate Real. Water-powered and then steam-powered mills reduced labor inputs, making mate processing more efficient.[54]

The mills became hubs to which carts and barges of trimmed leaves were brought from what would eventually become the state of Paraná; their owners amassed great fortunes from the 1830s onward even though yerba mate production was just a fraction of coffee production. In 1831, Brazil exported thirty-two times more coffee than mate; but mate exports grew steadily through the nineteenth century (see figure 3.5).[55] On the strength of the yerba mate industry, the state of Paraná with its capital at Curitiba successfully petitioned for independence from São Paulo in 1853. The economic dynamism attracted a new wave of immigrants from central and eastern Europe who joined, intermixed with, and partially displaced the Indigenous and Lusophone groups that had previously inhabited the region. Yerba harvesting and exports built the physical and political infrastructure of the southernmost states of Brazil. And today the states of Paraná, Santa Catarina, and Rio Grande do Sul are among the wealthiest in the country, with a per capita GDP higher than the national average.

The second technological innovation that spurred the success of the yerba industry was the importation of Paraguayan barbacuá-processing techniques to roast the leaves, giving them a distinctive smoked flavor. These steps were necessary to convert Brazilian raw material into a product desirable for the Argentine, Chilean, and Uruguayan markets. Like the newly established coffee regions to the north, mate in the south was developed for foreign consumers.[56] If history doesn't repeat itself, it rhymes. During the Spanish Empire, the Jesuit mission–produced ca'a miri enjoyed international repute as a premium yerba compared to the more common yerba de palos marketed by envious Spanish colonists. In spite of its larger scale compared to Paraguayan mate, Brazilian mate—which was called "mate paranaguá"—contended with higher-quality Paraguayan production, though the latter was harder to come by.[57] As early as 1829, Brazilian producers were accused of substituting other *Ilex* leaves for *I. paraguariensis*.[58] The growing importance of yerba in Brazilian culture and commerce is clear from one of the initial acts of the first governor of the state of Paraná in 1853: prohibiting the mixture of other plants with yerba mate.

As luck would have it, French botanist Auguste de Saint-Hilaire was traveling through southern Brazil, Argentina, and Uruguay to gather botanical specimens just as the mate trade took off in southern Brazil. He wrote, "Because political circumstances at that time rendered communications between Paraguay proper and Buenos Ayres and Montevideo almost impossible, people came from these towns to seek mate at Paranaguá, a port near Curitiba."[59] In Curitiba Saint-Hilaire observed the source-plant for congonha/mate paranaguá. The drink produced from it was considered so inferior to Paraguayan mate that residents of Buenos Aires and Montevideo thought it must come from a different tree. But Saint-Hilaire compared a few samples of yerba from the Jesuit missions and the ones he gathered in Curitiba to declare that they were scientifically identical; the only difference was how they were prepared. And, in an 1822 article on his journeys in the *Mémoires du Muséum d'Histoire Naturelle*, Saint-Hilaire gave yerba mate its scientific name *Ilex paraguariensis*.[60]

It was an emblematic irony of Francia's foreign relations strategy compared to Brazil's that mate was officially described in Brazil while being given a name that recognized its roots in Paraguay. For decades to come, the two countries competed to dominate the mate trade. The export numbers during this period (see figure 3.5) tell an important story. In the first comparative year from these records (1832), Brazil exported 1,478 tons and Paraguay exported 376 tons, which meant Paraguay accounted for 20 percent of all yerba mate exports in that year. Nineteenth-century statistics can be notoriously fickle; the Paraguayan ones sourced here come from many different documents. And the Brazilian numbers, though they are from a single government report, combine years from 1833 to 1887 (i.e., 1833/1834, 1834/1835) without clarifying whether the amounts listed are for twelve or twenty-four months. Nevertheless, the mid-century numbers on Brazilian and Paraguayan yerba mate exports illustrate notable changes.

Twenty years later, in 1855, a representative year of exports for the decade, Paraguay's exports reached 1,483 tons under the policies of Carlos Antonio López to foment the commercialization of yerba mate as a way to bring in foreign exchange. After the closed Francia years, Paraguay's exports were finally near their highest colonial outputs once more. In that same year, Brazil's published statistics were either 5,973 tons (for 1854/1855) or 6,873 tons (for 1855/1856). If those numbers or their average of 6,423 tons is accurate, Brazil had effectively doubled its yerba mate exports with each decade. And Paraguay would have still accounted for about 20 percent of all yerba mate exports for that year. If, however, the Brazilian numbers are for two years, then the numbers of yerba mate exports for 1855 are somewhere between 2,987 and 3,418 tons, and Paraguay would represent nearly one-third of yerba mate exports (exporting about half of what Brazil had exported). Paraguay's growing yerba exports and the desirability of its higher-quality product imperiled Brazil's industry.

Conclusion

Unfortunately, nations are built not only from shared economic progress or cultural practices but also from the battlefield. War broke out between River Plate neighbors. Just as Argentina and Brazil had fought over possession of what would become Uruguay in the first half of the century, in the second half of the century, armed conflict with Paraguay engulfed the region. The War of the Triple Alliance (1864–70), fought between the combined forces of Argentina, Brazil, and Uruguay against Paraguay, devastated the landlocked country.[61] The bloodiest international war of the

Western Hemisphere ended only when Francisco Solano López was killed by Brazilian troops in 1870 in the hills of Cerro Corá in Amambay—in the heart of yerba mate territory.

Before the end of the war, more than two-thirds of all Paraguayans lost their lives; as much as 90 percent of the male population (including children) was killed on the battlefield.[62] The children who survived were taken as trophies of war to Buenos Aires and Rio de Janeiro and the entire country was politically and economically restructured while the victorious Alliance troops occupied Paraguay. Although the conflict resides in dusty history books for the victors, for Paraguay, memory of the "Great War" (*la guerra guazu*) remains ever present. The Paraguayan media make mention of it every day, and in casual conversation ordinary Paraguayans refer to it as "la Guerra del Setenta" (the War of '70), as if it were the war of 1970, not 1870. On August 16 every year, Paraguayans observe the Día del Niño (Day of the Child), just as they celebrate Mother's Day and Father's Day. The date marks the 1869 battle of Acosta Ñu, where thousands of Paraguayan child soldiers as young as six, wearing fake beards, faced better-equipped Brazilian troops. While their mothers watched from the sidelines, their sons' pleas for mercy were ignored and they were slaughtered on the spot. Whatever hope of a United Provinces or confederation between Argentina, Paraguay, and Uruguay had existed was dashed. And just as mate was becoming an economic force in the region, large swaths of lucrative contested yerba mate territory were definitively transferred by the war into the hands of Argentina and Brazil.

4

Botanical Imperialism and the Race for Plant Knowledge

WHEN THE FRENCH PHYSICIAN-BOTANIST Aimé Bonpland turned in for the night on December 7, 1821, in the village of Santa Ana, he went to bed believing that he was on the cusp of a great triumph: the rediscovery of how to cultivate yerba mate for mass production in Argentina. But as Bonpland slept on the outskirts of the ruined Jesuit mission, hundreds of Paraguayan troops silently crossed the Paraná River and made their way through the wooded hills to the quiet village where the botanist and his guides took their repose. Just before daybreak, the Paraguayans attacked. Nineteen men were killed and Bonpland was arrested on the orders of Paraguay's ruler José Gaspar Rodríguez de Francia.

With no warning, Bonpland was hauled across the Paraná River to Paraguay, where he was confined for nine years. The French botanist was cut off from international communication and forced to live in small Paraguayan villages in the rural hinterland surrounding the former missions. During his time in Paraguay, Bonpland raised cattle and grew local crops, fashioning the agricultural implements himself by hand. He learned to speak Guaraní and rumor has it that he started a second family, but because pen and paper were scarce, he was unable to continue his work of scientific notation. Prior to his imprisonment, Bonpland was already famous in Europe, but the controversy in Paraguay garnered public attention across the Atlantic World. Bonpland's former traveling partner, German naturalist Alexander von Humboldt, Latin American revolutionary Simón Bolívar, and many others wrote entreaties to Francia for the better part of a decade, begging for clemency, to no avail. Francia did not even bother to open many of the letters, though he did write back to rebuff Bolívar in 1823.[1] Bonpland was finally permitted to leave Paraguay in 1831. He never returned to Europe and spent his remaining years conducting botanical research expeditions (including yerba mate) in Argentina, southern Brazil, and Uruguay, and even visited Paraguay in late 1856.

Bonpland's crime was suspected botanical espionage and biopiracy. His attempts to establish new yerba mate orchards in disputed territory (identifying precisely which trees produced the highest-quality beverage and incorporating knowledge from residents near the decimated Jesuit missions) ran afoul of a Paraguayan government suspicious of attempts to steal the secrets of Paraguay's wealth and set up a competitor. Before finally granting him permission to leave the country, Francia himself described Bonpland as having intended to "take hold of territory and yerbales that belong to Paraguay . . . just like one of those spies that came to these countries with other Frenchmen."[2] Not only was yerba an important financial concern, but the area south of the Paraná where Bonpland had planned his cultivation experiment was simultaneously claimed by Paraguay, the United Provinces with its seat in Buenos Aires, and the breakaway republic of Entre Rios. Bonpland's presence encroached upon Francia's interests territorially and, with the potential to revitalize mate cultivation, monetarily. His detention in the South American country was certainly more adventure than Bonpland had planned on, but there was more than a grain of truth in Francia's worries.

Bonpland was an experienced bioprospector by the time he visited the contested border with Paraguay. Along with Alexander von Humboldt, he had taken a five-year journey to the Americas (1799–1804) where they had collected and classified thousands of plant specimens and returned home to international acclaim.

During their travels, the two European explorers paid particular attention to medicinal and psychoactive plants as well as those with industrial potential. They meticulously documented the growing ranges of different species of cinchona, the tree from which quinine comes. Quinine was key in developing the antimalarial that allowed European penetration into South Asia and Africa only decades later, opening a new phase of European colonialism.[3] Bonpland and Humboldt also witnessed and described the making of deadly *curaré* arrow poison from *Strychnos toxifera*, which now has clinical uses as a muscle relaxant in low dosages and even as an antidote to strychnine poisoning convulsions.[4] After a years-long hiatus in Europe, Bonpland returned to South America to botanically study and exploit mate's medicinal, psychoactive, and financial potential.

Nineteenth-century scientific exploration was both the vanguard and the buttress of European imperial expansion in South America, Africa, and Asia. In the name of science, expeditions gathered botanical, anthropological, and geographic information that later served military purposes in colonial incursions. Although the first European botanical gardens got their start as open-air medicine cabinets in the sixteenth century, by the nineteenth century, botanists in Europe gathered samples of plants from around the globe, inventing taxa, isolating compounds, and attempting to grow tropical species in climate-controlled greenhouses and then in tropical colonies.[5] Anthropologist Lucile Brockway points out how botanical gardens within the British Empire served as nodes, gathering and distributing knowledge in service of empire.[6] For the bioprospecting botanists in the field, observing local expert use of plants was invaluable to help them find medically or commercially useful species. But many communities recognized the threat posed by the loss of intellectual property or a plant monopoly. This was, after all, the century during which tea was secretly smuggled out of China and rubber out of Brazil, both to be replanted in British colonies in Asia.

The story of how the Dutch (and neither the Bolivians nor the British) came to dominate quinine production is paradigmatic.[7]

The bark from the various cinchona species that grow across South America has been used for medicinal purposes by Indigenous peoples since time immemorial and quickly transferred into the early colonial materia medica of Catholic missionaries as a fever reducer. Centuries later, English alpaca trader Charles Ledger collected cinchona seeds from select trees in Bolivia with the guidance of Aymara bark and seed hunter Manuel Incra Mamani.[8] Although the British had already established cinchona plantations in British India, Ledger sold those seeds to the Dutch government in 1865 to be planted in Java. The seeds gathered by Ledger and Mamani yielded a cinchona species with a much higher concentration of quinine; by the end of the nineteenth century, Dutch cinchona came to command 80–90 percent of the global market. Bolivia's quinine exports plummeted. The cinchona species was named after Ledger in his honor; Mamani was arrested for illegal exportation of cinchona seeds and then beaten to death.

Had Bonpland not been detained by Francia, he would have likely won the race to scientifically name yerba mate. But another French botanist, Auguste de Saint-Hilaire, preempted him while Bonpland was imprisoned without access to the outside world. The inextricable links between the history of yerba mate and the history of multiple empires show us how science and empire build one another. But they also highlight the differences between institutions of science within opposing empires. Mate was a psychoactive stimulant grown and commercialized in the context of European empire for European colonial consumption, like coffee and tea; in its original habitat, unlike coffee and tea. Carl Linnaeus himself proposed the genus *Coffea* and gave the binomial name *Coffea arabica* in the original 1753 edition of his *Species Plantarum* (coincidentally on the same page where he also scientifically described *Cinchona officinalis*, from which the antimalarial quinine comes).[9] The Swedish naturalist also gave the name *Thea sinensis* to Chinese tea and identified the genus *Camellia*, to which all the *Theas* were transferred by British botanist Robert Sweet in 1818.[10]

Mate plant science can be viewed as the staging ground for imperial dramas and contests between political economic philosophies specifically through the lens of European scientific exploration and travel writing. That impulse elicited strong local South American reactions, some supportive, some suspicious. Although coffee, tea, chocolate, and even its *Ilex* cousin yaupon were cultivated in European botanical gardens, yerba mate was not. In spite of its economic importance in the Spanish Empire, it was not even grown in the royal gardens of Madrid—which only possessed a dried sample of the leaves. Thus, mate was the last of the three great commercial stimulant beverages to be scientifically identified.[11] If this is a book about the worlds made by mate, this is a chapter about mate as scientific practice, which can be expressed in various questions. Why was it that the French and not the Spanish scientifically identified the species? What is mate in science that it is not in commerce? What do we learn about Western science as a set of practices and networks and priorities from mate? And, ultimately, for all his reputed anger and his unquestioned control of Paraguay, why didn't Francia do anything worse to Bonpland?

Mate Science in the Spanish Empire and Jesuit Materia Medica

As we saw in chapter 2, Spanish administrators and Catholic missionaries produced a large body of literature on yerba's botanical and cultural characteristics for centuries. That is, the first Europeans to study and write about yerba mate did not think of themselves as professional scientists working for institutions dedicated to scientific knowledge (though many of them were trained physicians), unlike Bonpland and those who followed him. But of course, the knowledge of mate that circulated for centuries before self-consciously styled scientific explorers arrived on the scene was the foundation upon which professional botanical work was built. Thus, one of the important distinctions between the botanical scientific and economic approaches of modern European empires has to do with the vector for botanical knowledge. European tropes of discovery and scientific description emphasized individual genius and distorted how important communal work is in the production of knowledge.[12] Taking seriously early approaches to mate requires writing back into the story of science those who have been written out of it, including bureaucrats and religious workers in a European empire that often gets branded as less modern than its northern counterparts (more on this later).

The New World encounter changed Spanish (and European) approaches to knowledge about nature as the search for new products for commerce drove the expansion of the imperial frontier. The existence of previously unknown lands, full of new people, plants, and creatures, forced the hand of the Spanish, making them aban don earlier scholasticism and requiring the creation of new techniques to learn about and study the things they encountered.[13] As a result of the day-to-day pressures of life in a new context with unfamiliar flora and fauna, empiricism as a way of knowing became the dominant approach to science in the Spanish Empire. Practical knowledge was drawn from observations in the field, asking the questions "what does this plant do?" and "how do people use this plant?" During this time, Spanish approaches to science were principally pragmatic rather than theoretical, standing in marked contrast to later northern European approaches, for example, Linnaeus's binomial naming system. Perhaps this is why the scientific name of a plant so well known in the Spanish Empire for centuries was given by a French botanist.

The difference in approaches between empires is well illustrated by the institutions developed to house and propel scientific knowledge. Scientific exploration in the Spanish Empire was institutionalized through the Casa de Contratación and the Consejo de Indias, which were primarily government administrative entities, not scientific museums or universities. The Casa de Contratación (literally, "House of Trade") was founded in 1503 to regulate trade in the Atlantic with broad powers over all Spanish activity. In addition to collecting all colonial taxes, every trip on the oceans had to first be approved by the Casa, which functioned as a storehouse for the empire's maps. Maps were the prized intellectual property of the sixteenth century and the Casa's cartographic enterprise, drawing cosmographic, geographic, and navigational knowledge from and for explorers, was famously secretive and extensive. The Council of the Indies (the Consejo) was founded in 1524, just a few years after the Spanish took the Aztec Empire, to administer Spanish holdings in the Americas, advise the monarch, and supervise the Casa.

Reports and samples of flora and fauna from the Americas entered the Casa as a matter of course. From the Casa, critical plants made their way to important pharmacies (*boticarios*) also established in the sixteenth century and consolidated under the Royal Academy of Pharmacy in the eighteenth century. Spanish cures circulated beyond the Iberian empire, smuggled within the Americas from Spanish holdings to the British and French Atlantic empires and then to Europe, the Ottoman Empire, and as far as Japan (via the Dutch East India Company).[14] European colonialism allowed for an increasingly uniform global disease environment, which coincided with the globalization of medical remedies as well as other commodities. But as the humoral theory of medicine fell out of favor and was gradually replaced by a germ theory of disease, some of the cures in the Spanish pharmacy eventually descended into irrelevance while others (like cinchona) took off.

Yerba mate made it to the Council of the Indies multiple times, asserted jurist Antonio de León Pinelo in his legal-theological treatise *Questión moral* (see chapter 2), when he declared mate properly consumed a form of licit medicine, as distinct from beverage, food, or vice. For Pinelo's legally informed, Inquisitionally inflected botanical inquiry, plant science was not so much a way to think about the general biology of plants but rather a focused attention on those properties that affect humans. In the case of mate (and chocolate, chicha, yaupon, and coca), Pinelo sought to understand the plants' psychoactive properties by their actions upon human bodies. Scrutinizing the New World plant drinks was actually a way for Pinelo to think about the *human* body and the *human* mind and the way they could be influenced by different stimuli. Just as early Spanish interest in how Indigenous communities ate was a way of thinking about the body and an early form of race-thinking, so too was the theological analysis of psychoactive plants based on their bodily effects a way of thinking about the mind.[15] Spanish botanical pharmacology can be seen as a way to practice an early modern psychology.

But of course, Spanish colonists were not the only Europeans who studied yerba mate. Handwritten copies of *On the Property and Virtues of the Trees and Plants of the Missions, Book 1* (1711) by Jesuit father and physician Pedro de Montenegro can be found in archives on both sides of the Atlantic, testament to its circulation and impact in the Spanish Empire.[16] On pages slightly yellowed with age (figure 4.1), a chronicler has drawn the crenelated leaves and berry clusters alternating on branches radiating from the thin trunk of a female *I. paraguariensis*. Below the image are the names for "ca'a miri tree" in both Spanish and Guaraní ("Ybira caamiri"). Ybira or, as it would be written today, *yvyra* is the Guaraní for "tree."[17] Ca'a miri was the name for the special mate blend only produced in the Jesuit missions.

The detailed entry on yerba mate starts, "The Almighty has raised in these distant lands of America this tree, so beautiful and pleasant to the eyes as it is tasty and useful to its residents," and goes on to describe medical uses as a purge (an "infusion made with hot water" and sugar) in the morning as well as more social uses, such as the custom of taking it cold on hot days ("taken in times of heat with cold water, as the Indios do").[18] Montenegro adds, "The leaf fresh, or dried into a powder, (or fresh leaf pounded) cures new wounds and aids damaged nerves. . . . Taken before drinking, it prevents inebriation. By ancient tradition, in Paraguay and Misiones, Saint Thomas taught its use to the Indians."[19] Thus Montenegro's description, obtained while he lived in Paraguay, includes Indigenous medicinal uses as a liquid, crushed and powdered, Catholic theologizing, and recipes for the beverage.

FIGURE 4.1. Sketch of the yerba mate tree ("Arbol de la yerva caãmini") from Pedro de Montenegro, *On the Property and Virtues of the Trees and Plants of the Missions, Book 1* (1711). Image credit: Biblioteca Nacional de España.

The Jesuits who interacted with mate as a plant and as ritual came to the New World with a set of practices and predispositions toward knowledge that shaped how they saw plants. The Society of Jesus was an intentionally scholarly order, prizing rigorous academic work in theology, philosophy, law, astronomy, mathematics, and more. Historian of science Steven Harris points to what he calls a Jesuit "ideology" (a complex of institutional structures encompassing Jesuit life) as part of his argument that Jesuits practiced an early modern scientific tradition based on empiricism and experimentation. Harris is part of a move to position Jesuit science as properly belonging to the larger Western scientific revolution, asserting that "forms of science that developed and thrived within the Society were those that resonated with the basic apostolic values of the Society and were useful in achieving the goals of its ideological program."[20] Embedded in this analysis is a critique of the assumption that scientific knowledge that comes at the impetus of secular or commercial values based on a profit motive is more properly value-neutral compared to the kind of science that arises from apostolic values.

The notion of "habitus" from Marcel Mauss and Pierre Bourdieu might also be useful in understanding how Jesuit science unfolded in relation to mate. Simply put, habitus refers to social practices that we learn so deeply we begin to embody them without realizing how much they have shaped us. Classic examples are the physical predispositions necessary to play an instrument or a sport—the "proper" way to hold a guitar or a tennis racket. But habitus is more than just the physical. Even more importantly, habitus describes our mental psychosocial predispositions. For example, the unwritten curriculum for how to participate in and graduate from a liberal arts college in the United States includes much more than learning to raise one's hand to ask a question or how to use a pincer grip to hold a pencil but rather how to organize a research paper or a study schedule, and even the desire to finish university and have a degree. For Bourdieu, habitus is an almost unconscious acculturation process, but for Mauss, habitus can be deliberate. One could intentionally develop dispositions, practices, habits, and ways of viewing and moving in the world. And Mauss's framing of the concept lends insight into practices of piety, in which individuals cultivate their spiritual personhood through moral action.[21]

Jesuit habitus, built in the European colleges and cloisters where the first members of the order were trained and took their vows, shaped how they experienced mission across the world and how they engaged plants. When seventeenth-century Jesuit missionary Antonio Ruiz de Montoya and others met Indigenous groups in Paraguay who used mate in shamanic rituals to communicate with spiritual forces, they apprehended this knowledge as believers in a spiritual world. Recall that Montoya wrote disparagingly about "a great wizard or mage, who treated with the devil," and yerba mate sorcery (chapter 2).[22] And yet he himself petitioned the Spanish crown for permission to commercialize the leaf and shortly thereafter colonial yerba mate cultivation went into full swing. Was this just hypocrisy or economic expediency? Neither. Rather, the deeply Thomistic orientation of the Society of Jesus framed their interactions with plants and plant knowledge. Dominican friar Thomas Aquinas (1225–74) reintroduced Aristotelian thought to much of Europe, but in dialogue with theological concerns and with a deep belief in the Christian faith. He asserted that God had created the realm of nature (one distinct from the supernatural) with order and rules that could be discerned through human reason. His teachings heavily influenced the Jesuits, including the great Jesuit philosopher Francisco Suarez (1548–1617), who taught at Salamanca and then multiple Jesuit colleges.

Reason and faith worked together for the Jesuits who ventured into unknown lands with new flora and fauna. Far from familiar surroundings and the pharmaceutical resources of Europe, the Jesuits built an extensive materia medica using local plant knowledge in the Americas and in their travels in Asia. As Jesuit physician Montenegro's text shows, they learned from both local use and their own empirical observations about the curative properties of plants, shared in manuscript writings with illustrations that circulated between missions. With this knowledge, they planted extensive pharmaceutical gardens for their colleges and missions.[23] These gardens were sites of experimentation (e.g., attempting to acclimatize Old World plants to New World contexts as well as cultivating New World plants) and thus a crucible for the combination of plant knowledges from around the world.[24]

Rather than conceiving of scientific study as threatening to or divorced from their faith, Jesuits practiced medical botany as a form of survival and as a form of apologetic defense of the faith, as proof of God's existence, provision, and character. To convince congregants to convert to Christianity, they needed to counteract the healing power of traditional practitioners by showing themselves as true healers. When the Jesuits encountered mate, even though they took the supernatural valence of plant practices seriously, they also sought to understand its natural properties granted by God without fear of spiritual contamination.

And so, mate quickly moved from cultural curiosity to foraged commodity to agricultural product that circulated across a continent under the tenure of the Jesuits in Paraguay. Other medicinal or psychoactive substances underwent a similar transformation as Jesuit cures became popular in Europe. Samir Boumediene, a historian studying the cultural worlds of the order in the Americas, argues that the substances that became part of the world-famous Jesuit pharmacopeia moved between gift and curiosity and ultimately became commodities.[25] Often, the purported origin stories of how Europeans came to learn about an Indigenous cure featured a moment of gifting. One of the stories Boumediene recounts for the discovery of Jesuit powder (cinchona bark) includes a gift of the substance—emphasizing peaceful conviviality and not the violence of colonialism. Because text and object circulated within the religious order, rare samples then appeared in curio cabinets and collections in Europe as a way to index the Jesuits' global presence. As recipes were written for the use of these cures (and circulated in printed or manuscript texts), they became officialized, spurring a robust trade. That is, the recipe gave form to the demand.

Anthropologists are keen to carefully distinguish between a gift and a commodity, the social obligations that each entails (reciprocity for the former; payment for the latter), and how something changes when it used to be a gift and is now exchanged as a commodity.[26] But in Boumediene's weaving of Jesuit medicine and history, the circulation of a written recipe in a recipe book also played a decisive role in the commodification of a cure (and in accruing prestige to the Society of Jesus). Inspired by the Greek physician Dioscorides's first-century *De materia medica* pharmacopeia, Pedro de Montenegro assembled observations by previous Jesuit physicians, Indigenous testimony, and his own observations in the Paraguayan missions. The resulting ethnobotanical text circulated as meticulously handmade copies in the eighteenth and nineteenth centuries (even after the expulsion of the Jesuit order). Though it advocated a now outdated humoral view of medicine (including purges, bloodletting, and other ways to rebalance the liquid humors of the body), it set forth a worldview that was simultaneously sacred and empirical.

But the text does more than just reveal a curious past. Though Hippocratic and Galenic thinking on humors might not be on the syllabus in medical schools today, these ways of thinking linger in popular medicine across Latin America.[27] Scholars of Latin American science and botany from Argentina to Mexico argue convincingly that the Jesuit materia medica found in pharmacopeias in the Americas not only circulated in the past or influenced European scholars who read the texts or studied under Jesuits in the many colleges. Instead, as Argentine plant specialists Gustavo Scarpa and Leonardo Anconatani write about the impact of Pedro de Montenegro in the River Plate region, these historical texts reveal ethnobotanical continuities with "creole and Indigenous ethnomedicine today" that is humoral.[28] Specifically, the "hot-cold syndrome" (e.g., whereby something "cold" is taken to combat "heat"—as Montenegro reported for Indigenous medical uses of yerba mate) and the emphasis on leaves as the prototypical source of curative power are well-documented humoral influences in present-day medical ethnobotany and ethnomedicine in Argentina and beyond.[29]

Rather than becoming primarily a cure in the Jesuit arsenal, mate's medical botany quickly also incorporated commercial agriculture;

both were taken as a sign of divine blessing. As part of an embodied apologetics for the faith, all of mission life was ordered, including and especially agriculture, which was evidence of the successful extension of Old World Catholic living. Agriculture itself was a way of thinking about community. And the cultivation of mate, even and especially because it was so difficult for others to accomplish, and sedentary living were marks of civilization, a way of life that was legible to European Christians as properly European and Christian. In addition to depicting health and the human body, the plant science in Montenegro's and other Jesuit texts was a way of thinking about nature, creation, and community. Montenegro's mate recipes presented medical uses for a plant that both he and his readers knew was also used in a social recreational way at that point. And so, whereas in Pinelo plant science was something akin to psychology, in Jesuit writings, it was a form of sociological thinking.

The Race to Name Mate

By all accounts, Bonpland had achieved the apex of fame and influence as a scientist when he returned to Europe after his 1799–1804 journeys with Humboldt. He found favor in Napoleon's court and was soon appointed botanist and general manager of the gardens at Empress Josephine's Château de Malmaison. Josephine had secretly negotiated the purchase of the château while Napoleon was away on campaign in Egypt. He returned to find a bill of purchase that needed to be paid. Josephine's ambitious plans for the gardens as a premier site of experimentation, which contained a world-leading collection of roses and where emus pranced and kangaroos leapt across the lawn, were imperial testament of France's expansion. In the gardens' heated greenhouses, rare plants and exotic flowers were cultivated and acclimatized to Europe for the first time, including eucalyptus, hibiscus, and camellia.[30] Even after their divorce because the empress could not produce an heir, Napoleon conceded ownership of Malmaison to Josephine. But although Bonpland was comfortable in France, he longed for the pace of discovery and exploration in South America.

When Josephine died in 1814, Bonpland was present at her deathbed.[31] Shortly afterward, Bonpland returned to South America, receiving a hero's welcome when he arrived in Buenos Aires in 1817 where he was named Professor of Natural History. He made his way to the region of Corrientes, just south of Paraguay, in 1820. From there he started a colony in Santa Ana, close to the old Jesuit missions where yerba had once been cultivated and where knowledge of the technique might yet linger. In the missions, Bonpland found remnants of the old yerbales still growing and determined to restore them and send the mate down to Buenos Aires with help from French merchant house Roguin & Meyer Company.[32] The French botanist counted on local knowledge from the *correntinos* who even then worked the post-Jesuit yerbales. Paraguayan supreme dictator Francia watched these developments and Bonpland's closeness with Francisco Ramirez, governor of the short-lived Republic of Entre Ríos, with unease.

While Bonpland languished in Paraguayan custody, his compatriot Auguste de Saint-Hilaire rushed to publish an 1822 advance of his lengthy botanical notes from the expedition in southern Brazil and Uruguay in the prestigious *Mémoires du Muséum d'Histoire Naturelle* in Paris.[33] Steering clear of Francia, Saint-Hilaire had traveled to the old Jesuit missions to confirm his suspicion: mate paranaguá and the herb of Paraguay were one and the same.[34] At the end of his teaser, Saint-Hilaire announced to the *Mémoires'* readership that he could determine that mate belonged in the *Ilex* genus. "Until now, writers have had little agreement on the genus," he triumphantly declared. "Having found it with flowers and fruits, I was able to analyze it, and in a memoir which I propose to submit to the Academy on the plant in question, it will be easy for me to demonstrate that it belongs to the genus *ilex*."[35] And then a footnote specified "Ilex Paraguariensis." Two years later, Saint-Hilaire attempted to change the name to *Ilex mate*, but it was too late.[36] Saint-Hilaire's holotype specimen, the example of a single organism used to identify a species,

FIGURE 4.2. *Ilex paraguariensis*, holotype. Collected by Auguste Saint-Hilaire. Muséum National d'Histoire Naturelle, Paris (France). Collection: Vascular plants (P). Specimen P00631854. Image credit: MNHN-Paris, Museum National d'Histoire Naturelle, JS-2008, http://mediaphoto.mnhn.fr/media/1443109068717QMTpwY4TuZgQvYVc. The MNHN gives access to the collections in the framework of the RECOLNAT National Research Infrastructure.

came from a tree near Curitiba, Brazil; the name *Ilex mate* would have regionalized yerba's identity, instead of maintaining its colonial branding as the "herb of Paraguay." As figure 4.2 shows, the *Ilex paraguariensis* holotype in France's Muséum national d'histoire naturelle has the flower, leaf, and seed—the classic attributes botanists use to identify species.

Saint-Hilaire wasn't the only botanist who tried to rename *I. paraguariensis* after his assignation.[37] When he was finally allowed to leave Paraguay, Bonpland donated a mate specimen to the British diplomat Henry Stephen Fox with the name *Ilex theezans* in 1832, a species name that eventually was assigned to a different *Ilex* (one with smooth leaves) with a similar growth range that sometimes was used to adulterate yerba mate. It seems that Bonpland had actually given that name to yerba mate during his years in Paraguay, only learning of Saint-Hilaire's achievement later, but he insisted upon using his own notation. If anything, the contest over naming (which also occurred with *Ilex vomitoria* as the more pleasant name *Ilex cassine* was preferred by users of yaupon) shows that it took years for science to be settled.

Plant samples circulated through botanical gardens in the nineteenth century across imperial boundaries with more ease than economic goods, a sign that mercantilism as a political economic philosophy with its injunctions against extraimperial trade was being challenged by a new form of liberalism, or at least that science was somehow above imperial boundaries. The samples British diplomat Fox received from Bonpland ended up in Kew Gardens; although the holotype of *Ilex paraguariensis* remained in the Muséum national d'histoire naturelle in Paris, samples gathered by Saint-Hilaire also made it to Kew Gardens. Bonpland also sent specimens from Argentina to the Botanical Garden in Rio de Janeiro for British engineer-turned-botanist John Miers, who had previously toured the region.[38] Science simultaneously transcended empire and served it.

Unlike other explorers, when John Miers embarked on his South American expedition in 1819, he did it in the company of his very expectant wife, who gave birth prematurely in a posthouse in Mendoza, on the foothills of the Andes. She and the infant survived. His memoirs of the 1819–25 journey were speedily published in 1826 to great readership in both his native Britain and North America. But selections of Miers's *Travels in Chile and La Plata* were only translated into Spanish in 1968 in Argentina and in Chile in 2009.[39] According to Chilean historian Gonzalo Piwanka Figueroa, the text was too "critical" and exaggerated to the point of falsehood.[40] Indeed, in its descriptions of daily life in the former viceroyalty, Miers employed colorful language. A trained engineer, Miers set out for Chile from England with a speculative plan and the machinery to construct a copper refinery, a project that foundered because of the difficulty in acquiring legal rights for his plant. His flour mill was much more successful, but he accused the Chilean government of luring foreign investors with the promise of cheap raw materials and then taxing them to ruin.[41] The family then settled in Argentina, relocated to Rio de Janeiro a few years later, and only returned to Britain permanently in 1838. All the while, Miers collected thousands of plant samples.

During the initial overland journey from Buenos Aires to Santiago in 1819, the British team repeatedly came across yerba mate, which Miers described in a vignette early in the first volume of his memoirs. Miers's party awoke before dawn on April 11, Easter Sunday, in the small town of Mercedes, west of Buenos Aires. Only Miers and his wife had shelter in a "miserable hovel"; the rest slept under the open sky.[42] In the chill of the early morning light, their Argentine hosts in Mercedes prepared mate over the fire, Miers reminisced:

> The matesito was handing round from one to another, each in his turn taking a sup through the long tin tube of the infusion of yerba, out of the little calabash, or matesito. The whole scene and circumstances of the time led me almost to imagine that we were bivouacking among the Indians, or among some of the savage outcasts of society.[43]

Miers detailed the morning yerba ritual, including drawings of the mate and bombilla. He seemed fixated on the sharing of the bombilla, which he repeatedly emphasized: "These people never hesitate to receive into their mouths the tube which but an instant before was in the mouth of another. In the most polished society, the same tube will pass round in the same manner from one to another."[44] In Miers's *Travels*, the shared bombilla was read as lack of civilization. Similar to the politics of revulsion in the ritualized regurgitation with yaupon in North America, the mode of consumption of mate violated British notions of hygiene.

On the very same page, Miers switched from his description of mate to his assessment of Argentine customs. Although they were in a highly Catholic country on Easter Sunday, arguably the most sacred holy day in the Christian calendar, he criticized their hosts as deceitful and lazy for waiting until after sunset to produce a change of horses for his team to use. He added:

> I could discover no regular employment that any of the people here followed; true it is that this was Sunday; but from all I could see, and all I could learn, there was no sort of regular employment; I could not make out from them how they contrived to live. During by far the greatest part of the day the women were basking in the sun, and conferring on each other the mutual favour (for it is their great delight) of picking the vermin from their hair. They were shamefully dirty.[45]

Unfavorable descriptions like this litter the entire two-volume text, framing Latin Americans as morally and physically vicious. In asking why it is that mate was unable to find a market in the anglophone world, this kind of aghast description of shared bombilla use likely played a role.

Miers's later botanical writings are less incendiary. He held Bonpland's yerba mate samples as authoritative but thought that Saint-Hilaire erred in thinking that plant samples from Curitiba trees used to produce mate paranaguá demonstrated that these were one and the same with yerba mate.[46] He was not able to find the holotype specimen (figure 4.2) in the Muséum national d'histoire naturelle in Paris and wondered whether it had been mislaid or lost during the Great Exhibition of 1855—and so he based his assessment of Saint-Hilaire's purported error on his own impression of trees used for mate paranaguá (recall the many rumors of adulteration against which Brazilian production had to contend).[47] For his contributions to botanical knowledge, Miers was inducted into the Linnean Society of London and then the Royal Society.

Though Bonpland and Miers evidenced very different responses to life in the River Plate, literary scholar Mary Louise Pratt considers them exemplars of what she calls the "capitalist vanguard." Travel literature allows Pratt to study "contact zones," which she describes as "social spaces where cultures meet, clash and grapple with each other, often in contexts of highly asymmetrical relations of power, such as colonialism, slavery, or their aftermaths."[48] Travel writers in the nineteenth century, per Pratt, reframed Latin America as in need of European industry. They believed Latin America was fundamentally not capitalist because of what they perceived as indolence, but also because of what they saw as a greater failure to rationalize production. "Europe" here was *northern* Europe. Miers and Bonpland both embody the European attitudes Pratt describes. Miers explicitly criticizes a lack of industry in Argentina and Chile; Bonpland, of course, went to Latin America to restart rationalized yerba mate cultivation. In spite of New World agriculture and sedentism, lack of industry and lack of proper science were both evidence of want of rationality and proof that the Spanish had failed to civilize the Americas.

In addition to attempting industry, the capitalist vanguard advanced North Atlantic penetration into Spanish South America by doing important work of the imagination. Edward Said famously explained orientalism not so much as the study of or fascination with things orient but a process by which the West came to imagine, know, and justify itself through a discourse of the Other.[49] Similarly, northern Europe and its empires distinguished themselves as rational, scientifically and economically fit through distinction from decadent southern Europe and its tattered empires. The well-known "Black Legend" of Spain, begun out of eyewitness descriptions and denunciations of sixteenth-century Spanish colonial cruelties committed against Native nations in the Caribbean, gave rhetorical and ideological legitimacy to (particularly) British incursions on territory claimed by that other European power. But by the nineteenth century, the Spanish Empire offered northern Europe two Others. One group was proximate: the Spanish in the desultory Iberian Peninsula; another was distant: creoles, mestizos, Black, and Indigenous residents of Spanish America. Together, the two groups offered a double justification for the benevolence and necessity of northern European empire.

Paraguay's ruler José Gaspar Rodríguez de Francia reacted immediately and forcefully to the incursion of northern Europe's capitalist vanguard. Bolívar's letter in defense of Bonpland contained the barely veiled threat, "I would be capable of marching to Paraguay solely to liberate the best of men and the most celebrated of travelers," but Francia rebuffed the great liberator of the continent.[50] As he did, he pointed to Bonpland's surveillance work (and that of other French explorers) as an affront to Paraguay's sovereignty. Still, he held Bonpland rather than kick him out of Paraguay's orbit as he did with other foreigners, including the Robertson brothers we met in chapter 3. This may indicate that it was not so much Bonpland's physical presence or his person but the activity he was conducting that was a threat.

As absolute ruler, Francia could have had Bonpland executed, but the French botanist was not physically harmed—and neither was Francia's regional political rival Artigas, now in asylum. News of Bonpland's captivity whetted North Atlantic imaginaries of Francia as a tropical dictator (a Latin American version of Oriental despotism). But when free to leave, Bonpland remained in the continent. In fact, it was the opinion of the usually very critical John Miers that Francia was kind to Bonpland. Miers wrote: "The

Dictator received him with every demonstration of respect and kindness. . . . The best proof that Bonpland was satisfied with the treatment he received, is that he never protested against his captivity, and that he refused (I believe, for a period of two years) to avail himself of the liberty given to him."[51] Rather than evidence of Francia's caprice, the benevolence toward Bonpland might be taken instead as a sign of respect.

The response in Brazil took a very different form. While Pratt attends to the narrative imposed by North Atlantic scientific exploration, historian Teresa Cribelli complicates that analysis by noting how the Brazilian empire reacted to and incorporated the same scientific, imperial, and economic impulses.[52] Emperor Pedro I decreed the formation of the Sociedade Auxiliadora da Industria Nacional (Society for the Promotion of National Industry) with its seat in Rio de Janeiro in 1825 in order to foment Brazilian industry and economic development through scientific discovery and technological development. Modeled after the French Société d'encouragement pour l'industrie nationale (Society for the Development of National Industry), the Sociedade advised the state and published an important scientific journal, O Auxiliadora. With the latest findings in applied science, the Sociedade served as a conduit for Enlightenment ideals from Europe while straddling the internal contradiction of an economy built on slavery. The Sociedade disseminated information about the latest scientific advances with attention to agricultural improvement to transition away from enslaved labor to free, waged labor.[53]

In her close reading of O Auxiliadora, Cribelli highlights the influence of the cameralism of Carl Linnaeus, among other European scientists, in the Sociedade's economic botany. Cameralism is an economic philosophy akin to mercantilism; in cameralism, protectionist measures are used to make domestic economics self-sufficient.[54] Linnaeus advocated for the substitution of domestic plants in place of imported exotics and the acclimatization of foreign plants to Swedish soil. Within Brazil, cameralism led to an impulse to identify native products that could be substituted for foreign imports. The Sociedade also advocated for using Brazil's "industrial forests" to source products that could be manufactured and exported, such as yerba mate. With members who stepped into and out of government administrations and who served on the boards of Brazilian corporations, the scientific findings published by the Sociedade in *O Auxiliadora* translated into policy recommendations.

While Brazilian scientists focused on their forests, elsewhere the locus of economic botanical work expanded from the greenhouse to the laboratory as the latter took center stage. Mate science grew rapidly in northern Europe after Saint-Hilaire's identification. Though they lacked territorial holdings in the Americas, German scientists contributed to stimulant chemistry through their laboratory work. Caffeine was first isolated in coffee (hence the name for the chemical compound) by German scientist Friedlieb Ferdinand Runge in 1819.[55] Less than a decade later, in 1827 French chemist M. Oudry extracted the alkaloid theine from *Camellia sinensis*.[56] Shortly thereafter, in 1838, Dutch chemist Gerrit Jan Mulder and German chemist Carl Jobst simultaneously and independently established that theine and caffeine were identical.[57] German chemist and pharmacist Johann Trommsdorff performed a number of experiments on *I. paraguariensis* in 1836, though it was in 1843 that British scientist John Stenhouse identified theine in the plant.[58]

Conclusion

Mate science in flux reveals how different imperial regimes— Spanish, Portuguese, French, British, Brazilian—had different botanical economic philosophies, reflected in differing botanical scientific priorities and practices. Mate in European science intertwined with mate in European commerce, but science and commerce had different aims: in the former, discovering the plant's components, properties, and their usefulness to people; in the latter, finding a better position in the market. Because mate commerce and mate science developed side by side, they provide incentives and insights that influence one another. Lab chemistry lay one step further removed from field exploration and ethnobotany, dearticulating the product from its cultural context and allowing it to be accommodated into another. But the scientific identification of *I. paraguariensis* and all the advances in the lab science that followed failed to fulfill Bonpland's original intention of finding a way to cultivate the herb of Paraguay.

5

New Ventures in Green Gold

IN 1886, Aryan supremacists Elisabeth Förster-Nietzsche (the sister of Friedrich) and her husband, Bernhard Förster, landed in Paraguay to start a German utopian colony in the yerba mate–rich hinterland. But they were not the first foreigners drawn to postwar Paraguay with a vision of building a prosperous future on a blank slate. Two decades prior, Tomas Larangeira saw his first glimpse of the forested expanse that would become the world's single largest transnational mate company, as he accompanied Brazilian troops during the War of the Triple Alliance. Larangeira, a "sulista" businessman from southern Brazil, was one of a veritable army of suppliers for the war effort. When Paraguay's president Francisco Solano López was killed in 1870 and hostilities formally ended, Larangeira joined the demarcation commission assigned to scope out and define Paraguay's northern border with the Brazilian state of Mato Grosso. The dense thicket of Atlantic Forest in Mato Grosso (literally, "great forest") lay far from imperial metropoles like Rio de Janeiro and São Paulo and was populated primarily by Guaraní-Kaiowá Indigenous groups. The Paraguay River, which wound south between Mato Grosso and Paraguay, provided easier communication with the outside world than did arduous overland journeys. Prior to the war, Paraguay heavily limited traffic along the river as a matter of national security, but the destruction of Paraguay's defense and political institutions opened up access to Mato Grosso.

News of the massive conflagration of the War of the Triple Alliance found an eager public in the North Atlantic, and not merely because British banks financed both sides of the war effort.[1] Known for taking firm positions on the most controversial issues of the day, the anti-slavery, pro-Union (against the Confederacy in the U.S. Civil War) British weekly magazine *The Spectator* published numerous articles on the "Paraguayan War." In 1869, before the war had ended, regular (and anonymized) correspondent "J.M.L." described it as a contest over yerba mate territory. Despite purported claims to respect Paraguay's sovereignty and territory, wrote J.M.L., the purpose of the secret Triple Alliance treaty between Argentina, Brazil, and Uruguay "really aim[ed] at its hopeless dismemberment, by tearing off from it to the north, for the benefit of Brazil, the *yerba maté* districts" after which the rest of Paraguay would become yet another "province of the Argentine Republic."[2] Thus would the greatest wealth of Paraguay be absorbed by its ready neighbors.

In the wake of the devastating war, Paraguay was left depopulated. A quarter of its previously claimed national territory, much of which was yerba mate regions, was assigned by peace treaties to Argentina and Brazil.[3] The bloodiest international war of the Western Hemisphere had many causes, but mate played a crucial role both in the conduct of the war and in its aftermath. Paraguay's mate exports, and thus its foreign exchange and ability to finance the war efforts, were interrupted as the conflict went on. Brazilian soldiers from across the country were exposed to the beverage consumed by Argentine and Uruguayan troops in the alliance.[4] Perhaps most importantly, the war marked a definitive change in the political economy of mate. The postwar years saw the rise of corporations (privately and publicly held), instead of government-led production, as the key players in the mate trade. And in a curious twist of history, the "rediscovery" of mate cultivation arose from the ashes of the Nietzsche-Förster colony.

But as we know, the mate trade was centuries old; what was new was free-market capitalism. Long an export-oriented agricultural commodity, mate was reorganized for regional consumption in a series of economic experiments that incorporated the latest capitalist financial and production techniques. Colonial mate had been governed under a mercantile capitalist logic for centuries and even after independence yerba mate responded to the political-military agenda of Paraguay's leaders. The incipient mate industry in Brazil experimented with new models of production, but the postwar environment gave rise to full-fledged liberal capitalist yerba mate. The active role of the state receded from its mercantile capitalist high point. Factory owners and bankers became the new protagonists of economic policy as the means of production (factories, fields, mines, etc.) were privatized. Trade across imperial boundaries was encouraged because wealth was understood to come from commodity exchange rather than the amassment of gold and silver bullion.

Capitalism is about controlling plants, not just managing labor. As the dominant economic logic metamorphosed from imperial mercantilism to liberal capitalism, the natural landscapes where mate grew were transformed into industrial forests, a source of agro-commodities to be extracted for commercialization on a global market. The story of yerba runs counter to the story of caffeinated capitalisms in the North Atlantic world, where, in the case of coffee and tea, the product was grown on plantations distant from the consumers and the headquarters of those companies. Production of tropical goods for North Atlantic consumers resulted in the spatial reorganization of colonies in the Americas, Africa, and Asia as agro-export-oriented enclaves in the Global South. And, of course, this very process was underway just at the same time in northern Brazil. But in southern Brazil and in Paraguay, the mate industry unfolded through a very different process.

The Rise of the Mate Giants

Whether or not territorial appropriation of lucrative forests for their mate potential was a guiding motive, the movement of Brazilian troops through the remote recesses of the region inspired dreams of wealth. Traveling along the Paraguay River (as had John Parish Robertson decades before on his own journey to the wild yerbales) after his stint surveying the new border between Brazil and Paraguay, Tomas Larangeira eventually settled in the Paraguayan port city of Concepción, an important transit point which, like Asunción, had been occupied by Brazilian troops during the war. As the principal Paraguayan port in the yerba mate–rich regions of Amambay and San Pedro, Concepción housed yerba mate processing companies where Larangeira could learn the trade.[5] Although he started his company in Paraguay, Larangeira had his sights on Mato Grosso, the area north of the Apa River border between the two countries, which he had explored in 1872 as part of the demarcation expedition. While the yerbales east of Concepción were well known, the ones north of the Apa were relatively untapped. Larangeira was a close contact of the new governor of the new state of Mato Grosso, and he petitioned the Brazilian government for permission to explore and extract yerba in the region. Beginning in 1882 Larangeira received a number of land concessions that at their largest totaled about five million hectares[6] (an area greater in size than the country of Denmark) to develop a transnational mate giant (figure 5.1). With exclusive rights to the yerba and the land, he started Empresa Matte Larangeira.

The subtropical woodlands and wetlands that made up Mato Grosso were home to isolated Indigenous Guaraní-Kaiowá groups who were not incorporated into the Brazilian administrative body. No matter. Because Indigenous communities had no written title to the lands they lived on, their ancestral territory was declared state property. The concession of land also presumed rights to the labor of residents on the land. Some were pressed into Matte Larangeira as bonded labor. Others were cast off during land seizures because, as Guaraní-speakers, they were rebranded as Paraguayan nationals (most Paraguayans even to this day speak Guaraní as their first language).[7] From the perspective of the Brazilian government, developing the mate potential of the region was more than just a way to bring wealth to the country. It was a way to exert new territorial claims and to build ties from newly incorporated land to established metropoles via the construction of infrastructure and the movement of populations to new cities. Perhaps the best-known example of this strategy was the twentieth-century construction of the planned capital Brasilia. Constructed in the 1950s, Brasilia was the conclusion of a debate dating to the early nineteenth century over whether to relocate the Brazilian capital to a city intentionally built at the center of the country, beyond the influence of traditional power centers.[8]

Early Brazilian yerba exports had utilized proximity to the ocean to move the product to its consumers—Paranaguá, after all, was a port on the Atlantic. But Mato Grosso lacked these connections and so Matte Larangeira itself oversaw the construction of numerous ports and railroads in Brazil, all to transport the mate. Even in the 1940s, the fastest way to get from Guairá to Porto Mendes on the Paraná River was to take the private Matte Larangeira train.[9] Infrastructure built around the budding mate industry also provoked the migrations of people, drawing workers from across Brazil. The company constructed entire cities, Porto Murtinho (named after Brazilian finance minister Joaquim Murtinho, who invested in the company) on the Paraguay River, Campanario in the thick of the forest, and Guairá on the banks of the Paraná River, to facilitate the processing and transport of its foraged mate.[10] The old Matte Larangeira locomotive stands as a relic today in an open-air museum in a public plaza in the heart of Porto Murtinho.

The Brazilian government itself underwent significant changes in the last years of the nineteenth century. A military coup overthrew Brazil's monarchy in 1889, after which the victors declared the country a republic, necessitating a transformation of the governing apparatus. But not all were pleased. The Federalist Revolution (1893–95), a failed insurrection starting in the southern state of Rio Grande do Sul, sought greater regional independence but instead consolidated the new Brazilian republic and sent waves of gaúcho migrants (with mate drinking habits and harvesting experience) to Mato Grosso to claim newly accessible land.

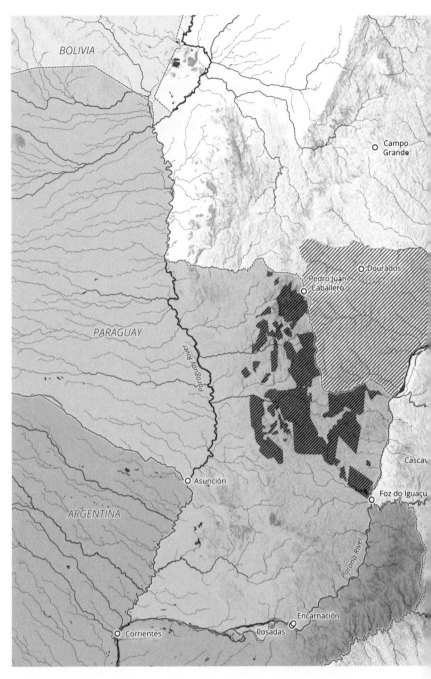

FIGURE 5.1. Holdings of Matte Larangeira and La Industrial Paraguaya in Argentina, Brazil, and Paraguay. Image credit: Juan Cristaldo and Silvia Arevalos, Exponencial S.A.

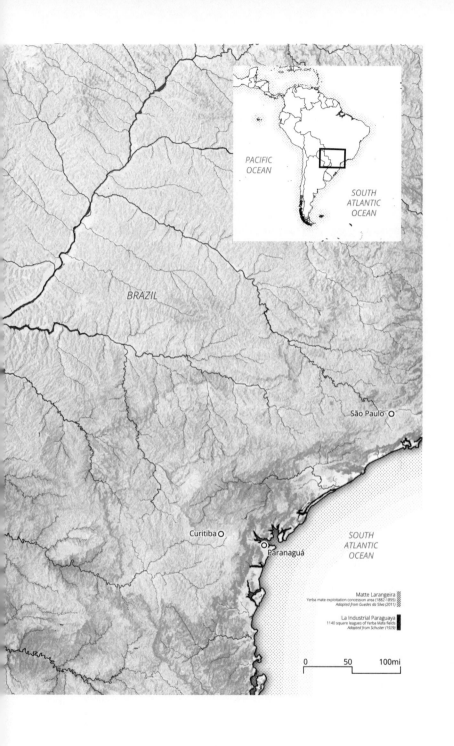

PACIFIC
OCEAN

SOUTH
ATLANTIC
OCEAN

BRAZIL

São Paulo ○

Curitiba ○
○
Paranaguá

SOUTH
ATLANTIC
OCEAN

Matte Larangeira
Yerba mate exploitation concession area (1882-1895)
Adopted from Guedes da Silva (2011)

La Industrial Paraguaya
1140 square leagues of Yerba Mate fields
Adopted from Schuster (1929)

0   50   100mi

The presence of white Brazilian settlers affirmed Brazilian possession of territory that was embroiled in legal disputes over ownership of the land. Eliza Lynch, the Irish consort of Paraguayan president Francisco Solano López who had followed him to the very end of the war and buried him and their fifteen-year-old son on the same day in graves excavated with her bare hands, returned from Europe in 1875 after five years to assert claims to property granted her by López. But she was promptly banished from Paraguay in perpetuity. One of their surviving sons, Enrique Solano López, who was allowed to remain in Paraguay, was similarly unsuccessful in validating Lynch's title to the yerba mate land north of the Apa River now under Matte Larangeira control.[11] The territory wasn't just defended by military fortifications. It was also held through the power of private enterprise and demographics.

The new yerba industry in Mato Grosso differed notably from previous developments in the southern Brazilian states of Paraná, Santa Catarina, and Rio Grande do Sul. In the southernmost states, mate processing was decentralized. There, independent mills (*engenhos*) were established as privately owned enterprises, leading to the enrichment of a small number of families. Matte Larangeira, on the other hand, was vertically integrated. It singularly commanded all the harvesting and processing through its monopoly concession, leading to the enrichment of a single company. Whereas mate in the Brazilian south was a family affair, Matte Larangeira held a public offering in 1891 through a new regional development bank, O Banco Rio e Mato Grosso. More than 14,000 individuals bought shares in the company.[12] In fact, it was Matte Larangeira's initial public offering that created the first bank in Mato Grosso, which was then liquidated in 1902 in a moment of national economic restructuring that attempted to offset fiscal crises caused by coffee dependence in the new republic. The publicly held company became like a state within the Brazilian state of Mato Grosso—answering to local politicians who invested in the firm, employing a private police force to assist in seizing Indigenous territory, and forcing Indigenous residents to work (often unpaid) in the company yerbales.[13]

Remnants of the company Larangeira founded exist to this day not because he took it public in Brazil but because he took it to Argentina. Tomas Larangeira entered into an agreement to commercialize mate in the River Plate countries with Francisco Mendes Gonçalves, a Portuguese businessman he had met during the war while they both did business to supply Brazilian troops. Mendes relocated to Buenos Aires after the war. Because of the bargain the two men struck, yerba mate from Mato Grosso traveled down the Paraguay River, stopped at the entrepôt of Concepción, and continued south to the confluence with the Paraná River at the border with Argentina and then further to Buenos Aires. Later, to avoid the taxes imposed by the Paraguayan government in Asunción for use of the Paraguay River, the traffic moved eastward to Porto Mendes on the Brazilian side of the Paraná River south of the majestic Guairá cataracts.

On the Paraguayan side of the border, a similar story unfolded. The war definitively shifted the economic model of development in Paraguay.[14] Albeit under tight control from a self-declared dictator and then a hereditary presidency, prior to 1870 Paraguay practiced a policy of internally guided development and possessed an autonomous economy. Industrialization and infrastructure were financed and directed at the guidance of the Paraguayan government with an ever-present preoccupation to secure and maintain Paraguay's independence, especially vis-à-vis its neighbors. And these initiatives were headed and controlled by Paraguayans.

The war transformed the focus of Paraguay's economy from prewar independence to international entanglement. Paraguay was saddled with unpayable war reparations to the victors: USD$200 million to Brazil, USD$35 million to Argentina, USD$1 million to Uruguay, and an 1872 loan in London of USD$7.3 million.[15] But all of its exports in 1876 only totaled USD$392,887—orders of magnitude too small to make a dent in its debt.[16] There was nothing to be done but sell something of greater value: the soil and the future. To meet these obligations and those incurred to finance the war, government bonds and vast tracts of the best agricultural land and forests were auctioned off to foreign investors in Latin America and the North Atlantic. An 1871 national decree forbade "abandonment" of yerbales to assure a steady labor force, declaring that workers were not permitted to even temporarily leave the wild yerbales without written authorization from the foreman or the owner of the yerba establishment, on penalty of incarceration and bonded labor in that very yerbal.[17]

In this context La Industrial Paraguaya was founded in 1883 to commercialize beef, cotton, tannin, and, especially, yerba mate. Paraguay's elite and British foreign capital were the initial investors and important Paraguayan politicians (all men) composed the board, including Bernardino Caballero—a war hero and the founder of the hegemonic Paraguayan Colorado Party. La Industrial (as it was known) took control of more than 3.5 million hectares of land (see figure 5.1).[18] Its workers, debt peons like those of Matte Larangeira, had to purchase all their work materials and food from the company. They labored in the sweltering natural yerbales west of the Paraná River, processing the mate much as it had been done during colonial times. Venturing into the wild yerbales to process the yerba was dangerous work. Paraguayan workers were called "mensú," a guaranization of the Spanish term "mensualero" (monthly employee), as they were ostensibly paid monthly but in practice once every three or four months and lived on credit otherwise.

La Industrial was frequently accused of mistreating workers and failing to pay local obligations, and stories of privation of the mensú abound.[19] To bring these abuses to light, Spanish anarchist and journalist Rafael Barrett published a series of articles in 1908 denouncing labor conditions and the inescapable debt peonage in La Industrial and Matte Larangeira's yerbales as nothing less than a continuation of slavery, writing that "the extraction of yerba mate rests on slavery, torment, and murder."[20] Labor in the wild yerbales depopulated Paraguay as youth were drawn in to replace older workers who perished, a peacetime parallel to the popula-

FIGURE 5.2. La Industrial Paraguaya Headquarters, Asunción, c. 1911. From Alexander K. Macdonald, *Picturesque Paraguay: Sport, Pioneering, Travel; A Land of Promise* (London: Charles H. Kelley, 1911). Image credit: Acervo Milda Rivarola, Imagoteca Paraguaya.

tion loss of the War of the Triple Alliance. Three hundred men had left Villarrica in Paraguay to work yerbales in Brazil in 1900, Barrett asserted.[21] But not even twenty of them returned. His articles circulated widely throughout the River Plate and, although Barrett died of tuberculosis in 1910 in France, he had a lasting impact on local anarchist politics and on many of the region's great writers, including Jorge Luis Borges and Augusto Roa Bastos.

Forced labor was nothing new in mate regions, of course. The debt peonage described by John Parish Robertson in the time of José Gaspar Rodríguez de Francia began earlier. Prior to the War of the Triple Alliance, Carlos Antonio López had used soldiers to harvest yerba. Anthropologist Richard Reed holds that, while Matte Larangeira pressed Indigenous workers to harvest the wild yerba, La Industrial depended more on mestizo populations because Ava Guaraní in Paraguay preferred to work for smaller producers and fled from La Industrial because when the company's yerba producers came across Indigenous groups they sexually assaulted and massacred them and pillaged their homes.[22] Today SEA, a new Paraguayan yerba company created to sell agrochemical-free mate gathered by the Ava Guaraní, proclaims on its packaging that the mate is prepared by "those free from the factories of the ex-Industrial Paraguaya." The word loosely translated as factory is *obraje*, which has imperial resonances, referring specifically to factories and workshops in the Spanish colonial era where Indigenous workers were compelled to labor by hand.

Less than two decades after the war, half of Paraguay's mate exports were in the hands of just one company. In 1887, La Industrial declared a credulity-defying dividend of 62 percent for its shareholders. That year, it exported 4,777,335 kilograms of yerba.[23] By 1902, its dividend had settled to a handsome 15 percent.[24] Market returns of these kinds raise concerns; for comparison, the U.S. stock market averages 9 percent annual growth only when calculated across many decades. As Paraguay rebounded from the demographic catastrophe of the war, much of La Industrial's mate was consumed internally, but in 1903, the firm exported 3,200,000 kilograms. Total sales that year were 4,267,712 kilograms.[25] The large quantities of mate sold by Matte Larangeira and La Industrial notwithstanding, the two companies frequently faced financial crises. Their politicized boards often changed hands and both companies reincorporated themselves in Argentina to expand their access to the desirable River Plate market.

La Industrial quickly came under the control of Anglo-Argentine financial interests. The Farquhar Syndicate, headed by U.S. industrialist Percival Farquhar, purchased La Industrial in 1912. The magnate had a plan to consolidate ownership of an international railroad network linking the southern part of the continent via which to transport yerba mate, cattle, timber, and other goods.[26] In the span of a few years, the syndicate quickly bought up railroads in Argentina, Bolivia, Brazil, Chile, Paraguay, and Uruguay and acquired control of vast expanses of terrain for timber, cattle ranching, and quebracho extraction (the quebracho tree provides vegetal tannin for leather curing and the wine industry). In Paraguay alone the syndicate controlled five million hectares of land—more than twice the size of the state of New Jersey. The company was almost entirely financed by capital from Europe, but because Farquhar registered the railroad companies in the United States, suspicions arose that the interconnection would be a foothold for U.S. interference in the southern part of the continent.[27] After all, the country of Panama had been carved out of Colombia in 1903 with U.S. support in order to secure U.S. access to the thin strip of land that would become the Panama Canal. The entire scheme in Paraguay collapsed in 1914 when capital tightened (British railway interests were queasy about the competition), the Brazilian and Argentine companies went into default, and ownership of La Industrial and the railways once more changed hands.

To foster its own nascent yerba industry, Argentina set import limits by placing higher taxes on fully milled mate than on yerba *canchada* (mate that has been smoked and only roughly ground). Thus, Paraguay moved from providing Argentina with the finished product to a semi-finished one. In addition to an imposing headquarters building in Asunción, La Industrial (figure 5.2) opened three mills—one in Asunción, one in Corrientes (Argentina), and one in Buenos Aires—where mounds of partially processed yerba would be sent to be finely ground and packaged. These value-added steps meant that money from the transactions concentrated in cities, rather than in the rural hinterland. More importantly, wealth concentrated in Argentina, not just Asunción. Matte Larangeira also constructed mills for its product in Argentina. The Brazilian yerba giant shipped their yerba down the Paraná from Porto Mendes on the east bank of the river; La Industrial shipped from Puerto Flor de Lis on the west bank of the Paraná a little farther south. At the turn of the century, the Paraguayan multinational La Industrial controlled some 60 percent of the yerba trade in Paraguay. Two other companies, headed by new immigrant capitalists, controlled other large quantities: Domingo Barthe with 15 percent and Boettner, Gautier & Co. with 10 percent of the trade in Paraguay.[28] But the real rivalry lay between Matte Larangeira and La Industrial.

Perhaps most distinctive of this new phase in mate's economic journey was the rise of branding and marketing. Large companies sold their yerba under trademarked names in stylized packaging—Cruz de Malta and T. L. (both from Matte Larangeira), Flor de Lis (La Industrial), Asunción (Barthe). Although the financial architecture of the companies was new for the era, many of the harvesting and rudimentary processing techniques themselves were the time-tested methods recorded in the Robertsons' and in Jesuit writings. In previous centuries, the brand identity of mate was based on general preparation methods (the pricey leaf-only ca'a miri of the missions versus the more common yerba de palos), but the new mate transnationals took up lessons learned from coffee to create specific marketing strategies based on flavor profiles, advertisements, and packaging. Like wine, mate has terroir. The taste of the beverage depends on factors like the soil where the tree takes root, how old the leaves are, and whether the trees are grown under shade. Older leaves exposed to the sun for years have a stronger and less desirable flavor than newer leaves. The kind of wood burned for smoking via barbacuá imparts a particular essence. Through distinctive paper, metal, and even glass packaging, the companies were able to distinguish their mate for consumers who then became accustomed to a specific flavor and even caffeine intensity. Magazine advertisements displayed mate drinking as authentically local to the River Plate, invoking images of national identity, the gaucho, and the legacy of the Spanish Empire (figure 5.3).

Yerba mate traveled on an international circuit of fairs and expositions in the late 1800s as postwar Brazil and Paraguay actively sought new markets for it. Direct interactions with potential customers offered producers important lessons. Brazilian mate

FIGURE 5.3. Advertisement for Flor de Lis yerba mate (manufactured by La Industrial Paraguaya) in Argentine magazine *Caras y Caretas* 16 (792), December 6, 1913, p. 50.

vendors, for example, learned that a Parisian public recoiled with horror when presented with yerba mate still in the animal hides (with protruding legs and feet) that were used to bundle the mate after roasting. In response to these French tastes, Afro-Brazilian engineer and abolitionist André Rebouças pleaded that mate instead be sent to a European market in pine boxes.[29] One visitor to the Argentine section of the 1876 Grand United States Centennial Exhibition in Philadelphia noted the abundance of hides, skins, and the "disagreeable odor of departed animal life."[30] He went on to comment that yerba mate was "packed in the skins of animals killed for that purpose, the legs serving as handles for these queer looking bags."[31] Matte Larangeira, listed as a Paraguayan company rather than a Brazilian, was one of only two yerba mate companies present at the Exposición Universal de Barcelona in 1889 where there were dozens of coffee and hundreds of wine companies present.[32] La Industrial won the Grand Prize at the Food and Health International Exposition in Paris in 1909.[33] Awards at international competitions, as proof that yerba mate in general and the specific company in particular were palatable to foreign publics, featured prominently in the advertising strategies.

Visitors to the World's Columbian Exposition in 1893 saw yerba mate displayed alongside samples of the coffee for which the South American country was famous when they entered the Brazil exhibition in Chicago.[34] The catalogue of the Brazilian section extolled the beverage: "Matte is an excellent drink, agreeable to the taste, and very healthy. . . . It is considered better than tea and coffee by the greatest part of those who become accustomed to it."[35] Interestingly, the catalogue entry also highlights that mate possessed "theine," underscoring that "this alcaloide [sic] is exhibited together with matte to show that the latter is a true substitute for Chinese tea."[36] Readers at the time might not have known that theine was the name for caffeine extracted from tea rather than coffee (though the Brazilian organizers of the exhibit knew). But to defend coffee interests, the Brazilian exhibition positioned mate as comparable to and thus substitutable for Chinese tea.

Marketing professionals assert that value creation takes place not just at the point of manufacture but also in the carefully tended relationship between consumer and company. Advertising companies do more than convince a buyer to spend in a certain way;

they also cultivate identity through connection. As mate was branded, consumer identities were no longer tied just to the ritual practice, the community of mate drinkers, or even a particular flavor profile. Now, by their choice of mate brand, they could connect their identity to a specific corporation. With registered trademarks of Cruz de Malta, Flor de Lis, and Asunción came branded mate accoutrements: gourds or guampa drinking vessels with the company name etched on the side, stylized tins just large enough to hold a bag's worth of mate. Even though mate had been an export-oriented commercialized commodity for centuries, the marketing push of the late nineteenth century was characteristic of new capitalist strategies.

Although it may seem that mate debuted in U.S. markets only recently, the transnational mate giants endeavored to gain footholds in North America in the nineteenth century. To reach a U.S. public, Matte Larangeira was incorporated in New Jersey under the anglophone-friendly name Yerba Maté Tea Company and published a glossy pamphlet with the tagline "Hebe herself could serve no dantier cup."[37] Journalist William Mill Butler, the U.S. writer who penned the booklet, emphatically stated that the goal of the piece was "to make known to the American people the excellent qualities of *Yerba Maté Tea*" before detailing an orthographically questionable account of the history of the drink. Photographic sketches of phenotypically European mate consumers in Victorian dress drinking out of porcelain cups pepper the document (figure 5.4), decidedly different from contemporary accounts of mate consumption in travel literature (recall Miers's description in chapter 4). While the advertising of mate for a South American public emphasized national notions of authenticity through iconic images of rural life, Yerba Maté Tea Company rendered mate respectable to a North American public by positioning consumption as fully Europeanized, though the drink's production and origins were acknowledged as Indigenous.

Well into the twentieth century attempts to open the North Atlantic market continued, but strong headwinds prevailed and

South American Maté Reception.

FIGURE 5.4. "South American Mate Reception," as depicted in William Mill Butler, *Yerba Maté Tea: The History of Its Early Discovery in Paraguay* (Philadelphia: Yerba Maté Company, 1900), 6. Image credit: author.

neither coffee nor tea was displaced by mate. Analyses of caffeine commodity histories point to the important role coffee and tea had in the formation of working classes in industrial centers as wage laborers who moved to industrializing cities provided the linchpin demand that triggered a massive transformation in caffeine production. To meet that demand, export-oriented enclaves were created in (former) European colonies where the tropical plants could grow on monoculture plantations. Paraguayan historian Herib Caballero points out that there is something neocolonial about structuring the relationship between the mate-producing regions of South America and the U.S. public as a mate enclave.[38] And, indeed, a 1900 diplomatic report presented to the House of Commons in the United Kingdom explicitly said the target market was the U.S. "labouring classes."[39]

Consumers in the North Atlantic world were spatially distanced from the production of the caffeinated commodities increasingly consumed by the growing proletarian populations, but mate consumption and production were compressed. Not only did the mensú consume the mate that they themselves gathered, urban industrial workers in Asunción, Buenos Aires, Curitiba, and Montevideo had an awareness of the labor conditions in the agricultural hinterland of the yerbales and workers from yerba mills in those very cities formed a key part of urban labor movements. But the weight of political elites favored the large mate transnationals.

In many ways, the mate giants illustrate historian Peter Eisenberg's thesis about "modernization without change."[40] Eisenberg writes about the sugar industry in Pernambuco (Brazil) and argues that modern, industrial production did not always bring with it social or economic transformation. Sugar was modernized from 1840 to 1910 through technological advances, the reorganization of the industry, and the gradual abolition of slavery. But social and economic arrangements of inequity endured, even after the fall of the monarchy. Late nineteenth-/early twentieth-century yerba was modernized along the lines of what Eisenberg describes for coffee: technological improvements, the legal abolition of slavery in Paraguay and Brazil, economic reorganization (liberalization of trade, the creation of publicly held transnational yerba giants), marketing, and even constitutional reorganization of states (the first Paraguayan republic was formed and then demolished and then a new one formed; the Brazilian empire was replaced with the Brazilian republic). And yet, the trappings of modernized production and governance did not necessarily bring economic or social change. In fact, mate elites maintained and solidified their power; the legal nature of forced labor changed (prisoners, debt peonage, Indigenous slavery); and the labor experiences remained brutal.

Cultivation Rediscovered

Elisabeth Förster-Nietzsche and Bernhard Förster exaggerated the comforts of Paraguay to convince dozens of German colonists to decamp to the South American country as part of an Aryan utopian experiment. Fiercely German nationalist and antisemitic, the two were introduced to each other by Richard Wagner's wife, Cosima, and later married on the composer's birthday in 1885. Bernhard had first visited Paraguay in 1883, scouting a site for a future German colony. With a promise of land from the Paraguayan government if he brought 140 German families to help repopulate the country, Förster returned to Germany to wed and recruit emigrants. The Försters arrived in Asunción in 1886 and were joined by fourteen families before setting out through snake-, mosquito-, and piranha-infested rivers to make their way deep into the San Pedro countryside to found Nueva Germania in 1887.

The Aryan paradise did not go well. Keeping the details of his arrangement with the Paraguayan government secret, Bernhard Förster mismanaged the finances of the venture and struggled to settle debts. It seems that he and his wife held out hope that Friedrich Nietzsche might be induced to join the experiment, or at least help fund it, but Friedrich despised the German nationalism and antisemitism that undergirded the project. The philosopher had actually broken with his former close friend Richard Wagner, whose antisemitism had become more pronounced.[41] In a letter to his sister just before her departure to Paraguay, Friedrich described himself as an "inveterate Europeanist and anti-antisemite" and asked her to abandon the endeavor.[42]

Once in the South American country, Elisabeth's entreaties to her brother described the weather, which alternated between torrential rainfall and blazing heat, as "The best weather in the world, always dry with a cloudless sky: Italy is nothing in comparison."[43] Elisabeth's description notwithstanding, the rains made European-style agriculture difficult in San Pedro. The unfamiliar terrain, hot and humid, was unlike Germany and even those colonists who had agricultural backgrounds struggled to farm in their new domain; the landscape of northern Paraguay was less forgiving than they had been led to believe.

Moreover, Elisabeth herself remained comfortably ensconced in Asunción for the first two years, while the German colonists contended to clear the settlement. Her grand entrance to Nueva Germania in March 1888 was accompanied by flowers, gunshot salutes, a banquet, and celebratory songs in German.[44] In spite of the Försters' efforts to quelch them, rumors circulated that the situation of the colonists was desperate and Bernhard failed to fulfill his contract to bring 140 German families. When he was unable to obtain a loan in June 1889 to cover the costs of the colony, Bernhard Förster fell into despair and took his own life in a hotel room in the German settlement of San Bernardino on the banks of the Paraguayan lake Ypacaraí. The German press reported that he drank strychnine poison; Elisabeth insisted he'd had a nervous attack and died of natural causes.[45] By the end of that same year, Friedrich Nietzsche descended into madness. Elisabeth eventually returned to Germany to care for her brother until his death in 1900 (and to edit his writings into an apology for German nationalism and antisemitism, despite his contrary stance). It was Elisabeth Förster-Nietzsche who enthusiastically greeted Adolf Hitler at the footsteps of the Nietzsche-Archiv in Weimar, which he visited multiple times, and Hitler himself attended Elisabeth's funeral in 1935.

The colonists she left behind in Nueva Germania had to find a way to survive in the new land.[46] And necessity gave rise to invention. They began to work with local agricultural knowledge and some intermarried with Paraguayan locals, abandoning the racial purity espoused by the Försters. One of the original colonists, Friedrich ("Federico") Neumann, figured out how to germinate *I. paraguariensis* seeds in 1896. And in 1901 Nueva Germania harvested the first crop of cultivated yerba mate since the eighteenth century. News of the rediscovery of mate cultivation rocketed beyond South America.[47] As early as 1900, even before the first harvest, U.S. consul John N. Ruffin sent word that a stock company had been organized in Paraguay to cultivate yerba.[48] Ruffin saw in cultivated yerba mate an agribusiness with growth potential, writing that "it is a business that is bound to increase, as the supply in the Yerbales will give out in time, while the consumption is continually increasing."[49] The only other mention of Paraguayan products of potential interest to the United States that year was Ruffin's report on the artisanal knitting and intricate lacework of the country, which he deemed "too small to command attention."[50]

Ruffin included details from a recent site visit to the German colony about the technique used by Neumann: "In the first place, seeds are passed through an acid bath. This is necessary, because each kernal is surrounded by a hard shell."[51] A keen observer of their new environment, Neumann began to develop his mate-cultivation technique when he hypothesized that the birds that ate the bright red seeds of yerba mate played a key role in the propagation of the species. And so he sought to imitate the condition of avian digestive tracks. Like the Jesuit missions centuries before which used a water bath to soften the hard shell of *I. paraguariensis* seeds over several days, Neumann mimicked the work done by birds via an acid bath of charcoal and sulphuric acid that promptly removed the covering. The seeds germinated quickly and the seedlings had to be transplanted within a few months. Five years later, when the young trees were sturdy enough, came the first thorough pruning.

Mate cultivation spread throughout the region, especially once it was shown that the trees withstood the harvest (figure 5.5). Chance would have it that at the same time that Neumann was conducting his experiments in Paraguay, Franco-Argentine landscape architect Jules Carlos Thays also developed a technique for seed germination. In 1903, a large mate plantation was established in San Ignacio, Misiones (Argentina), signaling an important change in that country as it began to produce its own yerba. Though Nueva Germania was quickly eclipsed by other mate-growing regions (especially to the south in Paraguay and in Corrientes and Misiones provinces in Argentina), the successful rediscovery revolutionized the business.

FIGURE 5.5. Pulverizing cultivated yerba ("sapecado") in Brazil, early twentieth century. Photograph by Vladimír Kozák. Image credit: Museu Paranaense.

Modernization and Change:
The Denouement of the Mate Giants

Mate cultivation disrupted the dominance of the large transnational yerba companies that used state power to gain control of wild yerbales through government concessions. Instead, local producers were able to grow the crop and control its harvest; cultivation moved mate away from feudal-like privilege to private enterprise. As plantations grew, the need to venture ever deeper into wild yerbales and climb dangerously high trees vanished. Competition from cultivation improved the labor conditions for yerba mate harvesting, though it took decades before Matte Larangeira and La Industrial lost their vast territorial concessions from the Brazilian and Paraguayan states.

Not all technological or financial infrastructural innovations result in social transformation, but Neumann's rediscovery of mate cultivation did. With its planted orchards, Argentina was no longer just the world's leading consumer of mate. It dethroned Brazil as the world's leading producer. Brazil retaliated by raising tariffs on Argentine wheat to little avail. Brazil still held onto its market in Uruguay and to this day is the lead supplier for its southern neighbor.[52] In addition to satisfying its national demand, Argentine mate companies sent their product to the well-established market of Chile and across the ocean to new markets in the Middle East.

PART III

Mate Culture Goes Global

6

Mate in the Middle East: Fatwas and Finger Puppets

AS THE NATIONAL ANTHEM of the Soviet Union intones in the background, a mustached finger puppet named Goon (*shabiha*) in Syrian military uniform takes a sip out of a silver-plated mate gourd. Then the "Top Goon" finger puppet himself, Syrian president Bashar Assad, comes in. It is 6 p.m., time for a very important video conference. But just before he Skypes Russian president Vladimir Putin on the bright pink toy laptop, the Assad finger puppet also takes a swig from Goon's bombilla and mate.

"Hello? Boss?" says Assad in Arabic to Putin on the open laptop. "I'm calling you to talk about the plan we're implementing."

Putin's offscreen response is a series of unintelligible high-pitched squeaks. Encouraged, Assad continues to elaborate their plans to suppress the uprising that threatens revolution.

"Let's talk about our strategy to mislead the international community," he says while Goon takes another sip of mate. "We started with terrorist bombings to remind the international community of 9/11 and its nightmare, Al Qaeda. We're also working on turning the Free Syrian Army into armed Salafi militias, which is easy because of their battalions' Islamic names."

Just then, the call to Putin drops. Goon has accidentally cut off the palace internet in addition to that of the protestors. Enraged, the Syrian president strikes Goon and yells at him, "Idiot!"

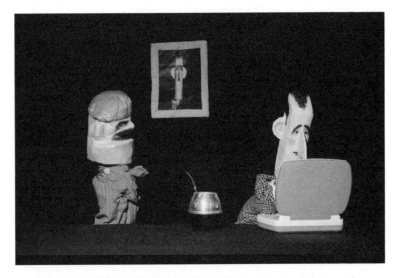

FIGURE 6.1. Bashar Assad speaks to Putin via Skype while Henchman watches in the background. Note the ornate mate gourd.
Still from "Skyping Putin," episode 6, season 2, *Top Goon* (2012).
Massasit Matti, YouTube Channel. Creative Commons Attribution
license (reuse allowed). https://www.youtube.com/watch?v
=jTAq6jtQD3Y&t=2s. In addition to the Arabic-only version,
Massasit Matti has a version with English-language subtitles to the
spoken Arabic and which includes an English-language final screen
of the episode.

To calm himself while the connection is reestablished, the
Assad finger puppet takes another drink of mate. "Yes, Putin. Before we lose connection, what happened to the new arms delivery?"
he asks once they are able to speak again.

Putin's high-pitched rapid squeak responds and then Assad ex-
claims, "Fantastic, fantastic, bravo! You are a great partner," as he
dances with joy.

"Warm greetings to [Russian prime minister Dmitry] Medve-
dev. Kiss him for me," the Assad finger puppet says to end the
Skype call. Then he complains, "Oh, Goon, talking over Skype is
really tiring," before disappearing from the stage.

Alone again, Goon has one last sip of the mate before the Soviet Union's national anthem plays once more. The screen turns black, red letters proclaiming a message to Vladimir Putin (and the international community) in English:

> The functions and powers of the Security Council are to maintain international peace and security in accordance with the principles and purposes of the United Nations

The line is a direct quotation from the UN Charter and is meant to call out the hypocrisy of Putin and the Russian Federation's military support of the war in Syria in spite of Russia's seat on the UN Security Council.

From the so-called "hummus wars" to biblical consumptive laws and the way dietary restrictions within ethnoreligious identities shape culinary landscapes, food is a powerful force in the Middle East. Prohibitions on pork and alcohol have led to culinary creativity in Jordan's capital, Amman, for example, where alcohol-serving bars are "Christian" and Korean restaurants that serve pork are semi-underground. Disagreements over not just the right recipe for but whose culture was responsible for inventing hummus have regularly flared up for nearly a century: some claim the chickpea dish was an Israeli creation, others assert it was more properly Arab (and thus inclusive of the region).[1] Even within a country, intense differentiation between communities can be marked by cuisine. For the rice-preferring northern Iranian region of Gilan, saying "Go and eat some bread!" functions as an insult.[2] As the cuisines of the Americas dispersed after Contact, the Middle East adopted culinary elements from the New World that were ignored by Europe. Allspice, a New World ingredient that did not enter the daily European spice-scape, has become an important flavoring component in Lebanese meat dishes where it neutralizes the fetid *zankha* overtone associated with eggs and meat.[3] Mate, too, made it in the Middle East. Decades of trade show visits, pamphlets written in English, and locally incorporated holding companies failed to win over North American consumers in the early twentieth century. But in a very different market, a remarkably unforced approach succeeded: *migration* gave rise to both mate's market and its meanings in the Middle East.

Perhaps more than elsewhere in this book, the story of how mate found a foothold in the Middle East illustrates the complex process of transculturation. Cuban anthropologist Fernando Ortiz coined the term in his masterwork *Cuban Counterpoint*.[4] In it, he compared tobacco and sugar, two great commodities that dominate Cuba. Through their differences (one masculine in Spanish, one feminine; one native to the Americas, one hailing from the Old World; one mass produced, one processed artisanally), Ortiz illustrated the cultural complexity of Cuba as a site of ever-unfolding transculturation. Ortiz specifically rejected the term "acculturation," meaning the acquisition (or imposition) of another country's culture, because it obfuscates or ignores a complex process including the loss, the "uprooting of a previous culture."[5] For Ortiz, the process of transculturation acknowledges the violence and asymmetry of colonialism as, for example, the enslaved Africans brought to Cuba were "snatched from their original social groups, their own cultures destroyed . . . like sugar cane ground in the rollers of the mill."[6] But for Ortiz, transculturation also points to the unmoored experience of disadjustment-readjustment, deculturation-acculturation (all terms he uses) that all residents of Cuba underwent. Indeed, in narrating how mate made a new home in the Levant, it may be helpful to think of transculturation as at least four distinct but interrelated trajectories, all of which appear in mate's journeys in the Middle East: (1) direct transfer, (2) translation, (3) substitution, and (4) resignification.

Migrations

In the nineteenth century, thousands of predominantly Christian Arabs, mistakenly (and sometimes pejoratively) called "Turcos" because the Ottoman Empire governed the Levant at the time, disembarked at ports throughout the Western Hemisphere.[7] Their ranks were joined by migrants across the confessional divide from what are today Syria, Lebanon, and Palestine: Shia, Sunni, Druze, Alawite, Ismaili. Many settled in Argentina, despite attempts to curtail immigration from the Orient, and were seen as inferior to the desired immigrants from western Europe.[8] On the streets of Buenos Aires, they encountered mate use as part of everyday life. Like other newcomers incorporating into River Plate society, the Arab immigrants took up the mate habit. And from the metropole, they moved westward, south, and north, some even laboring in the cultivated yerbales newly planted after Neumann's rediscovery of *I. paraguariensis* germination.

But unlike European migrants to the region, the Arab diaspora brought the mate habit back to their place of origin. As merchants with an economically incentivized practice of circulating between New World entrepôts and, perhaps, as cultural heirs to seafaring Phoenicia, the Syrian and Lebanese diaspora stayed mobile even while settling in the Americas. Remittances from family members in the Americas became a vital source of income. Syrian migrants in Argentina alone sent 24 million Argentinian pesos to their families in 1913.[9] These numbers are staggering. One Argentinian "paper peso" was about $0.43 at the time; one Argentinian "gold peso" equaled $0.965 (like today, Argentina ran multiple exchange rates with the U.S. dollar).[10] Even at the lower end of these ratios, remittances from Argentina were more than $300 million a year in today's dollars. Bolstered by these economic ties, migrants from the Levant would travel back to the Middle East to visit family, to wed, or even to retire.[11] And in the early years, they brought mate in their personal luggage.

Arab immigrants wanted to prove their place in the new nation, especially because they faced anti-Arab sentiment in Argentina. Arab Argentine writers in the mid-twentieth century argued that Arabs were the original gauchos and thus the source of founding identities for the nation: skilled horsemen, fearless, independent.[12] Another way they showed their true Argentineness was by wholeheartedly consuming mate. When they continued to do it in their returns to the Levant even when they were surrounded by

Country	1936	1937	1938	1939	1940	1941
Australia	2,991	5,848	4,593	3,791	4,162	750
Bolivia	39,918	59,451	68,458	55,183	64,418	86,721
Canada	980	382	1,836	0	0	0
Chile	12,035	4,660	19,011	14,252	15,788	26,890
France	3,773	15,933	4,712	4,343	0	62
Germany	205	510	6,005	245	0	0
Peru	1,554	2,784	3,087	1,588	3,100	6,326
Spain	8,769	0	0	0	0	0
Syria	39,639	18,373	44,539	30,650	12,400	0
Turkey	3,136	0	0	0	0	0
United Kingdom	6,548	6,188	8,475	5,626	12,761	4,996
Uruguay	0	1,160	972	875	920	1,640
United States	18,239	13,181	7,195	11,090	10,627	11,015
Others	1,857	1,886	13,749	9,337	6,260	2,871

FIGURE 6.2. Argentina yerba mate exports (1936–1941, in kilograms). Elaborated by author from Comisión Reguladora de Yerba Mate records.

other stimulant options, their proper belonging in the River Plate was underscored.

By the late 1930s, the Middle East was a major market for Argentine mate (figure 6.2). Yerba mate exports from Argentina to Syria (encompassing Lebanon as well) were higher than any other market outside of Latin America. On the cusp of World War II, only Bolivia bought more yerba. Today, the Syrian and Lebanese markets represent the vast majority of Argentina's mate exports, Chile is the regional import leader in Latin America, and Bolivia no longer ranks as an important market. If mate came in bags, bottles, or tins carried by hand in the early 1900s, a hundred years later, shipping containers filled with sturdy fifty-kilogram sacks take the journey to ports on the eastern Mediterranean. A few brands dominate Argentina's exports: Amanda, Piporé, and Cruz de Malta (of Matte Larangeira fame), among others. While some imports come in ready-for-sale packages, several importers have set up processing plants in the region where they package the milled mate or produce blends tailored for Middle Eastern customers. El Kureshi Company, a yerba importer in Mersin (Turkey), for example, sells its packaged mate under the brand name Yabroud Yerba Mate. Yabroud is the name of the Syrian village where former Argentine president Carlos Menem's (1989–99) parents were born.

Mate Takes the Stage

Food was at the symbolic and catalytic center of the Arab Spring protests of 2011 whose touchpoint was the self-immolation of Mohamed Bouazizi, a fruit and vegetable vendor brought to the brink of despair by Tunisian police harassment and the rising cost of food. Bouazizi's death in January 2011 triggered uprisings throughout the region. Reflecting on the protests at Tahrir Square, one young Muslim Brotherhood activist in Egypt explained the movement as, in part, "a mobilization for democratic control over food production and food distribution."[13]

Starting in 2012, the Syrian political theater group Massasit Matti began posting their finger-puppet series *Top Goon: Diaries of a Little Dictator* to YouTube, satirically rendering the violence of the Syrian Civil War and the impotence or even self-interested complicity of the media and international community in the face of efforts to overturn the Bashar Assad regime. To reach as wide an audience as possible, Massasit Matti produced two versions of each *Top Goon* episode, one fully in Arabic, one with English subtitles and text. A decade later, millions of displaced Syrian refugees live in camps in neighboring countries or have tried to make their way to safety in Europe or beyond. The anonymous Massasit Matti members also had to flee. Bashar Assad remains in power and the would-be revolutionary offshoot of the Arab Spring in Syria appears on its last legs. Massasit Matti, through their high-contrast lighting/low-tech finger puppets, stand in a long line of Arabic political theater, using art and humor to articulate their quest for freedom. The last episode of the second of three seasons ends with a quote from Syrian playwright Saadallah Wannous (1941–97): "We are condemned to hope and what takes place today cannot be the end of history."[14]

Massasit Matti uses a bare-bones stage with only the simplest props to depict place and identity. Significantly, in several of their skits, a real mate drinking vessel and bombilla serve that role. Although the drink comes from South America, yerba mate has been so thoroughly transculturated to the Levant that it has become an iconic part of Syrian life. Syrians from all walks of life drink the beverage, as shown by Assad and his henchman Goon but also by another *Top Goon* episode, "The Women of the Revolution," in which heroine Um Hussein shelters (male) protestors in her home as the sounds of gunfire rage outside. She sends the security forces at her door away and then calms the cowering protestors with the offer of mate. "Have some Mati tea to relax," she says.[15] At the end of the episode, another woman, Hurria, returns with medication to treat a badly injured youth (wounded, presumably, at a protest) in hiding. She takes several sips of the mate and then says to her male relative, "This is not just your revolution, it's also my revolution."

Among the many salient details in the five-minute video, the mate and bombilla become almost characters in themselves, linking scenes and the passing of time. As the characters share the same mate across gender boundaries, the physical object and the act of drinking itself indicate familiarity and solidarity between the characters. But as anthropologist Arjun Appadurai found in his work on the "gastro-politics" of eating in Hindu communities, food can simultaneously express connection and differentiation.[16] By gastro-politics, Appadurai means "conflict or competition over specific cultural or economic resources as it emerges in social transactions around food,"[17] revealing what he calls food's powerful "semiotic virtuosity."[18] Because food can mean so many things to so many people at the same time, it is the site of political and social dramas. Massasit Matti's Goon and Top Goon drink mate with enthusiasm, fulfilling a common stereotypical association between the Alawite community (from which Bashar Assad and his close associates come) and mate. It's an association that holds up under scrutiny: recent ethnobotanical research among Syrian residents and the diaspora has found that although mate consumption is present across the religious sectarian divide, mate use is highest among the Alawite and Druze communities.[19]

And what of the gastro-politics of mate in Massasit Matti? Not only did the troupe show the protestors drinking mate, Syrian president Assad and his soldiers did as well—a common drink on opposite sides of a profound divide. But it is a mistake to think that Massasit Matti used mate to create a moral equivalence or social solidarity between them. Instead, the consumption of mate by the finger puppets sets the drama squarely in Syria by using a beverage that has become iconically Syrian, as a mode of distinction from other Arab and Middle Eastern countries.

So tied to Syrian identity is yerba mate that the very name of the troupe Massasit Matti comes from the name of the drink. *Matti* is "mate" and *massasit* (literally, "lollipop") is the Arabic for the bombilla drinking straw. For nearly a hundred years, Syria (and then Lebanon and Syria following independence) has been the largest market for yerba mate outside South America, in spite of the marketing attempts to enter the North Atlantic we saw in chapter 5. In fact, for many years, one of the only ways to get loose-leaf yerba mate in the United States in communities without a substantial presence of immigrants from South America was at Arab grocery stores. Now mate use even follows the movements of Syrians in the Civil War and the ensuing refugee crisis. Large burlap bags of yerba and mate drinking accoutrements have appeared in the souk of Amman (Jordan) where, years before the influx of Syrian refugees, they were not present in that city's great market.

The process of transculturation meant that some aspects of mate practice in South America transferred to the Middle East, but others did not. And some of those that did make it were inflected in new ways, while others remained intact. The practice of sharing the same bombilla passed from mouth to mouth does not seem to violate notions of hygiene and personal space for consumers in the Levant who might be used to sharing a narghile (the hookah) smoking pipe—in contrast to British travel writers who observed the practice in South America. But to ensconce the bombilla in Levantine households might mean using an Arabic word for it (*massasit*), though the Spanish-language term "bombilla" is also commonly used. Similarly among Druze in Lebanon, the Arabic for gourd (*qar'a*) and not just the arabicization of "mate" is used for the drinking vessel. And the practice itself has shifted in key ways in the Levant, like the introduction of wiping the mouth of the bombilla with a piece of lemon between each user, as a way to give it flavor and to clean it.

Leading Druze politicians and public figures often pose for photographs with their mate drinking vessels and hot water thermoses in hand.[20] Just as spices and herbs like orange peel and chamomile are commonly mixed with tereré (cold) and mate (hot) beverages in South America, distinct recipes for mate have developed over the years in the Levant. Ginger, hyssop, wormwood, rosemary, thyme, and cardamom are added, in various combinations, to mate for Middle Eastern palates. And so, the transculturation of yerba mate in the Middle East included direct transfer (as happened to yerba mate itself), translation (the name "mate" remains, but the words "massasit" and "qar'a" are used), substitution (as with the tweaked recipes of herbs mixed with mate), and, lastly, resignification.

Mate's New Meanings

As it spread beyond Middle Eastern communities with diasporic ties to South America, mate was *resignified*, by which I mean not just that what mate signals has changed but that it is newly meaningful among many already established signals. At its base, resignification indicates that the link between signifier and signified has been broken and a new link formed. An everyday example is the @, the "arroba." The @ appeared in Spanish-language colonial manuscripts for hundreds of years as the abbreviation for "arroba," an archaic unit of measurement common in the Spanish Empire. The word "arroba" comes from the Arabic *al rub'* (عربا) for "quarter" to mean a quarter of the hundred-pound quintal unit of measurement, that is, twenty-five pounds. Yerba mate exports were measured and recorded in @ (arrobas) in the colonial and early national periods; over the course of the nineteenth century, pounds and kilograms displaced the old form as units of measurement. But in the past thirty years, the @ has been popularly resignified to mean "at" in email addresses worldwide—and now in contexts far beyond email addresses.

Islamic scholars issued a fatwa religious ruling on mate in 2008, reminiscent of Pinelo's seventeenth-century theological treatise on the Catholic fast and psychoactive New World drinks.[21] The fatwa is an example, par excellence, of mate's resignification in the Middle East. For most of the twentieth century, mate consumption in the Middle East was concentrated in the Levant, where communities had frequent and direct contact with South America. But mate-importing merchants have now successfully turned their attention to untapped markets in the region. Kabour Group, based in Yabroud (Syria) and Misiones (Argentina), sells an unnamed but famous (so they assert) brand of mate under the private label Kharta al Khadra. A quick glance at the red four-leafed vegetal motif at the center of the bag, reminiscent of the red four-pointed cross on Cruz de Malta's package, suggests that the company started by Tomas Larangeira in Paraguay just after the War of the Triple Alliance has entered the Middle East without the Christian iconography of the cross, perhaps making it more acceptable to consumers of other confessions. Note that Cruz de Malta is also sold by name in the Middle East.

Residents of the Gulf have recently been exposed to mate both at home and abroad in the region. Prior to a Covid-19 pandemic forced closure, summer vacationers escaping the heat of the Persian Gulf encountered the beverage next to narghile tobacco pipes for rent in the Maté Factory Café in the Mount Lebanon town of Aley (figure 6.3). The Saudi Arabia–based "Dr. Mate" website ships products imported from South America to consumers in the kingdom and its neighbors. To help potential customers understand the

FIGURE 6.3. The Maté Factory Café peddling mate next to rent-your-own narghile pipes in Aley, Lebanon. Image credit: author.

benefits of drinking mate, the Dr. Mate site has published a ninety-page Arabic-language downloadable guide that explains (with images) the history, health benefits, and processing of yerba mate as well as step-by-step instructions for how to prepare the hot beverage. And just in case all of that isn't inducement enough, the website and guide are littered with photos of Argentine soccer stars like Diego Maradona and Lionel Messi drinking mate.

As mate has grown beyond a diasporic community with personal connections to the cultural landscape of South America and to the production of yerba mate, doubts have arisen. The inquiry that drove Islamic scholars to render an online decision was "Is mate halal to drink, some say it is food for pigs?" The fatwa team who reviewed the query and enunciated the nonbinding yet authoritative decision was drawn from scholars and graduates from

Islamic institutes in Mauritania, Saudi Arabia, and Yemen.[22] They ruled that mate was acceptable under Islam, declaring that "[mate] is not intoxicating or unclean, as such, there are no objections to it."[23] Like Pinelo's declaration on the spiritual acceptability of mate in Catholic practice, the fatwa on yerba mate came a century after popular consumption and commerce in Muslim Middle Eastern communities. Rumors that pigs, ritualistically defiling in Islam but not in Christianity, grazed among *I. paraguariensis* would only be imaginable in a milieu with no visual referent for the Atlantic Forest that shelters the trees nor familiarity with the beef-centric diet in the River Plate. Moreover, price-sensitive farmers would not feed "green gold" to swine.

Although mate contains psychoactive substances, consumption was deemed permissible (halal) though inebriation is prohibited (haram) in Islam, per a history of fatwas on coffee, tea, and other beverages that contain caffeine and other stimulants. Coffee, especially, has a long history of treatment under Islamic jurisprudence because of its presence in the Ottoman Empire and the Middle East.[24] In Ottoman Turkey, coffee and the coffeehouse were banned, then permitted, then banned again multiple times, starting in the 1500s. At least two issues arose regarding coffee. First, it clearly has a psychoactive effect on the human body. Sufi mystics, for instance, famously used coffee to aid in the extended fasts for prayers. This raised the question of how to properly understand the moral valence of coffee's effects.

But it seems that the real sticking point was the way in which coffee was consumed: in the coffeehouse, a gathering place in the 1500s where men from different social classes and professions mixed, shared ideas, and at times developed revolutionary fervor (or so the regime feared). The sultan decreed a ban on coffeehouses in 1578, stating that "coffeehouses, the gathering place for the sinful, should be banned. . . . At the present, people gathered with young boys, took *macun* (hashish), *beng* (marihuana), and *afyon* (opium), drank wine . . . with the pretext of coffee drinking, play backgammon, chess . . . gamble, and spend their time with these illicit behavior[s]."[25] In their study of how Ottoman coffee-house culture helped form the identity of consumers in the six-teenth and seventeenth centuries, Emınegül Karababa and Gülız Ger note that the fact that coffeehouse bans and fatwas had to be reissued regularly points to how ineffectual those prohibitions were. Moreover, they argue that the very experience of defying the state and religion by consuming coffee in a coffeehouse trans-formed both the Ottoman state and religion, as well as the coffee drinkers themselves. Ironically, the bans may have done as much to produce revolutionary fervor as the content of conversations at the coffeehouses. Stimulant consumption, especially because it was deemed illicit, changed the relationships to institutions of power.

The fatwa decision, Dr. Mate's guide, and online forum answers to questions like "Islam + mate" mark mate's accommodation to a fuller Middle Eastern context. With the resignification of mate, it became not just a souvenir acquired in journeys abroad or an index of transatlantic diasporic identity. Now it rests amid other region-defining symbolic systems. More than just a mere transla-tion of terms into Arabic or a substitution of familiar ingredients for others, as it has been transculturated, mate has assumed an agentive role within a wider Middle Eastern cultural context. And with the fatwa, mate has settled into the religious valences of Islam as it did with Christianity centuries before.

Conclusion

In the spirit of a counterpoint, the other stimulants consumed in the Middle East offer enlightening comparisons to mate. The Middle East was traditionally a crossroads for traders of coffee and tea as those drinks moved from the East to the West on the Silk Road. But mate must be imported from afar with the Middle East as a destination rather than a point of transit. Although mate is a relative newcomer to the region, black tea was consumed in the Middle East for at least a millennium before it made it to European teacups. The common story about coffee is that it was first brewed by Yemeni Sufi mystics in the fifteenth century before spreading through the region.[26] Yemen is also the only place in the Middle East where khat (*Catha edulis*) consumption is legal, where its use actually predates coffee.[27] Similar to coca in South America and the betel nut in Southeast Asia, the leaves of the East African khat plant are chewed to release its amphetamine-like stimulant cathinone. Interestingly, psychoactive plants that are chewed tend to be more illicit (socially unacceptable) and even illegal (unacceptable per the purview of the state) than stimulant plants that are used to brew a beverage.

Rather than displacing these other stimulants, mate carved out its own space. Cuban anthropologist Fernando Ortiz's original notion of transculturation suggests that the symbolic system receiving mate has also been changed by mate's presence. The fact that mate is now a stand-in for and even an intensifier of Druze identity in Lebanon illustrates this point. The tight association with certain confessional or ethnic communities within the Middle East is what allows Massasit Matti to repeatedly work mate over, like hands molding clay, into an exploration of Syrian identity. Mate, which used to index connection to South America or Levantine identities within the region, is now being given new meanings in the Middle East. What those are remain a new chapter that is still to be written.

7

The New Postindustrial
Hipster Mate

IT'S A SMALL DETAIL, easy to miss if you're not purposefully looking for it. But a diminutive red-white-and-blue Paraguayan flag on a brightly colored bottle, just one of many festive decorations on a label in North America, made headlines in the South American country in 2020: premium Paraguayan yerba mate was going to the United States. Organic, fair-trade yerba artisanally crafted by a group of Indigenous and mestizo farmers living on the outskirts of the remote Mbaracayú Nature Reserve would soon appear in North Atlantic supermarkets as Guayaki brand yerba mate.

Nestled in northeastern Paraguay where the Atlantic Forest meets the savannah ecosystem of the Cerrado, the Mbaracayú Nature Reserve encircles a biodiversity hotspot of 64,405 hectares covered by thick canopy, lagoons, and waterfalls. The history of nature parks in the United States, from Yellowstone to New York City's Central Park, includes the forced removal of Indigenous and other marginalized peoples to create romanticized wild spaces.[1] But in the case of the Mbaracayú Nature Reserve, the Indigenous Aché and Guaraní communities who make their home in the reserve's area of influence were recognized as critical forest protectors from the very start. And so, rather than attempt to remove Indigenous people from their ancestral land in the name of conserving nature, the reserve established a model where cultural, environmental, and financial sustainability are inextricably linked.

The Mbaracayú Nature Reserve's leadership envisioned conservation work as extending beyond the technical borders of the protected area, and they realized that impoverished farmers might surreptitiously enter the park for firewood or to plant Paraguay's rising and illegal cash crop marijuana. As part of its mission, the reserve distributed *I. paraguariensis* seedlings and technical assistance to hundreds of farmers living around the park to raise organic, shade-grown (*bajo monte*) yerba mate in 2015. Fair-trade certification took more than a year because of the remoteness of the community in eastern Paraguay and because of the lack of data on the part of the Paraguayan government. But the effort paid off. Amid the economic and public health devastation of the Covid-19 pandemic, the Guayaki Yerba Mate Company paid producers 52 percent more per kilo than the market price in Paraguay for their first harvest in 2020.[2] And the yerba was carted off to North Atlantic markets.

Walk into almost any major grocery chain in North America—not just the Whole Foods or Trader Joe's of the world that cater to publics self-consciously prioritizing the eco-friendly, organic, or exotic in their shopping—and you can find yerba mate products for sale. Anglophone-friendly CLEAN Cause, GoMate, EcoTeas, and Guayaki peddle mate in cans and bottles as well as in teabags or loose-leaf for the gourds and bombillas they also advertise on their websites. Or perhaps visit a swanky café in New York's SoHo with decorations meant to evoke Morocco and order a "maté latte" off a menu that extols the benefits of the South American find, asserting that "it does not contain caffeine," instead possessing a smoother stimulant called "mateine." This is pure marketing. Mateine is chemically identical to the compound caffeine; the difference is it comes from mate, not coffee. To satisfy another need, Sephora, Ulta, and Shen carry beauty products "rich in yerba maté extract" to exfoliate the skin and "reveal radiance." The last time I went to my neighborhood Costco before writing this chapter, a yerba energy drink was on the shelves—a sign perhaps more than any other that mate is now mainstream in the United States. No longer consigned to "ethnic" Latin American or Arab grocery stores, yerba came into its own in the North American market in the twenty-first century.

Yerba mate finally has made headway as an earthier caffeinated drink with promises of a better buzz and a more authentic, spiritual connection to place. In recent years, a flurry of new mate products have been created specifically for North Atlantic markets, distinguished in name, branding, and even packaging from established South American brands. The mate sold in Arab and Latin American grocery stores comes in the same 500-gram and 1-kilogram Spanish- or Portuguese-language bags available in South America or the Middle East, but the new products for U.S. consumers are in helpfully labeled ounces. Perhaps more importantly, unlike the brands in South America, most of the new mate sold for North Atlantic consumers carries organic and fair-trade certifications, allowing us to explore the impacts of so-called ethical consumption. Beauty products aside, the new mate comes in two primary forms: as a tea (available in single-serving sachets or loose-leaf) where it is often the only or the chief ingredient; and as a blended energy drink, bottled or canned, ready-made for instant consumption.

A 2005 *Better Nutrition* article giddily declared mate "the newest coffeehouse 'it' drink," as if it were a trendy item of clothing debuted at Fashion Week.[3] For more than a century prior, the coveted North American market simply would not budge, immune to all commercial strategies and marketing inducements to take up the South American drink. What changed? One explanation might be that yerba mate products had never been available before the 2000s. But we know this is not the case from the history of trade fairs, holding companies, sales as coffee/tea replacements during the world wars, and more. Yerba mate was at the World's Columbian Exposition in Chicago (1893) after all. Or perhaps the door was opened for yerba mate because of a recent problem with

coffee or tea that created a vacuum in the market left by their decline. Perhaps increased prices or declining production made the
traditional beverages inaccessible. But coffee and tea remain as
popular as ever and, in fact, at record-high sales; and much of their
growth comes from premium, high-priced products. If deficien-
cies in the competition were not a factor, maybe the answer is that
something changed in mate production or preparation. Perhaps,
as with coffee and bananas, new plantations were installed in
U.S.-controlled territory under labor and pricing regimes newly
favorable for North Atlantic consortiums—a supply-side boon.
Indeed, no. *I. paraguariensis* is still only grown in traditional yerba
mate territory in South America's Atlantic Forest.

Or maybe the taste improved? Again, no. Much of the new mate
follows the bitter flavor profile of yerba consumed in South America. Or was mate finally introduced as part of a new recipe, presented
for the first time as a sweet, bottled drink? Cuban Americans know
the answer: Materva. Materva is a yerba mate soft drink first brewed
in Matanzas, Cuba, in 1920 with mate imported from South America
and copious sugar from Cuba's own cane fields.[4] The less sugary/
foams up nicely like a beer Club-Mate (formerly Sekt-Bronte) soft
drink got its start in Germany four years later in 1924. Materva was
so successful that manufacturer Cawy Bottling Company opened
factories throughout the island to produce the drink. When the
Cuban Revolution swept across the country in 1959, the company
and its factories were nationalized.[5] Production ground to a halt. But
like many Cuban exiles, Materva got a new start in Miami when
former employees resurrected Cawy Bottling Company in 1964. The
story goes that when Vincent Cossío (whose father had owned
Cawy) escaped from the island, he carried with him a copy of the
secret formula for Cawy's popular Limón soft drink. Cawy re-
launched Materva in the Sunshine State and it has enjoyed popularity in the United States ever since; it can be found on the menus of
Cuban restaurants and in Latin American grocers.

So, what changed? We are seeing the effects of new affects. The
turn of the millennium was accompanied by the development of new

needs in both the North Atlantic consumer and the North Atlantic market. A term with connotations from psychological analysis, "affect" may be thought of as how we wear our moods, the feeling of having feelings, or how we experience our bodies in the world.[6] New feelings, fears, and desires have arisen among postindustrial North Atlantic consumers that have made space for and have created a new kind of market demand for yerba mate. In previous chapters, we saw how changes in the production or in the commercialization of mate changed its trajectory, for example, the (re)discovery of cultivation or the incorporation of mate as tribute money in the Spanish Empire. But the North Atlantic case allows us to see how changes in the consumer opened a new chapter for mate. The distinction is worth emphasizing: something new about how North Atlantic consumers feel themselves and their bodies in the world, rather than changes in how yerba mate is produced, has made space for mate.

Untangling the new affects underlying new mate reveals how personal experiences of taste link to seemingly impersonal economic processes in the twenty-first century. As is true for any commodity analysis, to understand how mate finally made it in the North Atlantic, we need to know who the consumer is, what form of mate they are consuming, and where mate fits into the larger market of similar goods. That is, we need to distinguish new mate consumers from the core consumers of other psychoactive drinks. We need to attend to how mate is prepared—the recipes, the packaging—as well as the context in which it is drunk. And we need to map out brands, price points, vendors, and the commercial infrastructure of new mate. But the more interesting question is not how mate became popular but *why*.

Social theorist Max Weber (1864–1920) offers an explanation of what happened to create the desires and needs that the new mate satisfies. Weber argued that the political, economic, and social changes that characterized modernity led to the "disenchantment" of the West, brought on by government administered by bureaucracy, a rationally ordered economy, broad secularization following the Protestant Reformation, and the scientific revolution.[7] He went on to describe the modern political-economic order as an iron cage with a shell as hard as steel.[8] For Weber, the loss of wonder and mystery and the sense that life could be reduced to a formula or explained by a sufficiently powerful microscope left a psychological burden, leading many in the North Atlantic to seek out ways to reenchant reality. Fantasy, fiction, and theme parks provide a variety of ways to reenchant. But another common response has been to mine the cultural production of others who are seen as exotic.[9]

The quest for reenchantment may take different forms. One wonders if part of the appeal of New Age spirituality, crystals, sage-burning, yoga in contexts otherwise disconnected from Native American nations, the South Asian diaspora, and so forth might be explained by this search for reenchantment. Nature, romanticized and idealized as untouched, also serves as a resource for experiences and images that can combat disenchantment. While these pursuits might seem innocuous, the romanticization and alienation from community can carry with them harmful outcomes by masking and reproducing power structures and colonial violence. Rather than just analyzing the experience of consumption, the lessons of the past call us to put production in conversation with consumption.

There's a connection between what drugs do, the kind of economy in which they circulate, and the labor conditions in that society. But drugs also connect societies through the commodity chains running from their production to consumption. The new mate ostensibly reworks these connections through ethical consumption. But ethical consumption is not a simple category. Certification programs and corporate social responsibility initiatives, popular because they aim to address vicissitudes and injustices in the economy while affirming the power of capitalism to bring about human flourishing, have faced criticism because of how they actually function on the ground. They can conceal, rather than ameliorate, the problems on the production side of the commodity chain they purport to solve.[10]

To explore what changed for the new mate, this chapter unfolds three main points. First, the drugs of choice of a society reveal important dynamics about daily life in that society and so it matters that mate has gained traction as a postindustrial stimulant in the North Atlantic. Second, as mate delivers a desirable stimulant boost, it assuages anxieties around nature, the body, and ruptures between the two that beset Western worldviews. And, third, stories of how today's new mate is produced disrupt simplistic narratives about ethical consumption, either good or bad, which is why it's important to go deeper into the story of the mate produced in Paraguay's Mbaracayú Nature Reserve. The remedy for the shortfalls of ethical consumption begins with lessening the distance by learning more about the context that produces mate and the context that produces consumers who would pay premium prices for organic and fair-trade products.

Mate Energy Drinks

With names and taglines like "Guru: Organic Energy," "Virtue: Clean Energy," "Vida Maté," and "Soul Maté" (from Canada, the United Kingdom, the United States, and Finland, respectively), the cultural analysis almost writes itself. Unlike the adjacent sports drink category (of which electrolyte-replacing Gatorade is an example), energy drinks feature a stimulant, most often caffeine, as well as vitamins, amino acids, and/or a sweetener, to boost alertness. Ostensibly, energy drinks are meant to be consumed before or during exercise and other physically strenuous activities, but they have become lifestyle drinks linked, especially, to digital economy professions. In a market already brimming with soft drinks, traditional stimulant beverages, and recreational adult beverages, energy drinks have taken off in the North Atlantic since 2000.[11] If coffee and tea powered the Industrial Revolution, yerba mate energy drinks are decidedly postindustrial, designed for an economy where service has replaced manufacture as the productive engine.

FIGURE 7.1. Blended yerba mate drinks available in the United States. Image credit: author.

As we have seen in other parts of the mate story, because food is social, beverages can have racialized, gendered, and age resonances.[12] Since consumption is performative, we signal our membership in a community through what we consume. Mate energy drink brands know this and use targeted messaging on their products and in their advertisements to reach their idealized publics. Images from websites, visual media, and advertising promote mate energy drink users as a community that is youthful, physically fit, cosmopolitan, and postracial. On Guru's website, a racially mixed trio of surfers in wetsuits walk the California coastline, carrying their boards. One of them raises a can of Guru energy drink to her mouth.[13] Vida Maté's homepage features a solitary bearded hipster attired in hiking boots and a snow cap, with a beverage can and a mountain-climbing pick at his side as he gazes out at the sea.[14] Virtue's Instagram feed is populated by attractive twenty-somethings lifting weights, carrying beverage cans on a hike, reading on a picnic blanket, and practicing yoga.[15] Their feed includes images of African schoolchildren (country unspecified) and Tamil Nadu (India) villagers celebrating the arrival of clean drinking water as a result of Virtue's partnership with Drop4Drop, a water-access charity. Postracial images emphasize harmony, mixed-race social circles where peers engage in a shared activity, or joyful cooperation across ethnic difference as in charitable work. At the same time, they can unintentionally underscore a racial hierarchy that positions whiteness as the unmarked norm.

Mate energy drinks also have gendered valences. The activities in the ads—hiking, surfing, mountain biking, camping—skew masculine, though many of the participants are women. This disparity is backed by sales numbers: men are the main consumers of energy drinks.[16] The American Psychological Association has even published troubling connections between masculinity, energy drinks, and sleep problems.[17] By contrast, hot tea has historically been associated with feminized domesticity in North America; beer and wine also hold gendered resonances in North America.[18]

Consumption intended for exercise puts energy drinks in a different social space than other caffeinated beverages: neither leisurely like tea nor work-bound like coffee, and not a junk food meal accompaniment like caffeinated soda. So, what does it mean that the new mate is "postindustrial"? Analysts use the term to describe changes that began in the middle of the twentieth century and that matured in the twenty-first.[19] Postindustrial capitalist growth is driven by research and knowledge sectors, medical services and pharmaceuticals, financial services, and information technology. The shift from the factory and assembly line to the laboratory and computer terminal accompanied changes in the kind of labor (and laborer) at the core of productivity. And it cemented the two-wage household as the baseline. At the same time, the services economy reshuffled and solidified hierarchies as some of the jobs and sectors began to enjoy more prestige and better remuneration.

But energy drinks were not the first caffeinated brew that arose to slake postindustrial thirsts. Anthropologist William Roseberry, writing in the 1990s, argued that the rise of "yuppie coffees" was connected to new class identities and a strategy from the coffee industry to capture a premium market to make up for shrinking coffee sales.[20] The emergence of yuppies (young, urban, upwardly mobile professionals whose parents' or grandparents' generation had worked in a manufacturing base) was emblematic of the social impacts of postindustrial labor changes. New social groups beckon new ways to consume and concurrent with the yuppie came a burst of gourmet, specialty coffees and the expensive accoutrements to brew them—what has been called "third-wave coffee."[21] As a commodity, coffee had morphed into a mass-produced cheap staple for industrial workers on both sides of the Atlantic. But the 1980s saw a new inflection point for coffee with a proliferation of gourmet varieties at high price points that did not replace but rather augmented the mass-market coffees. No longer satisfied with just drip coffee from mass brands like Folgers or Maxwell House, now consumers shell out extra money for cappuccinos or lattes brewed from 100 percent Arabica beans sourced in Kenya or in the Kona districts of the Hawaiian archipelago.

The new coffees were critical in salvaging the industry from a precipitous decline in consumption and sales. According to the *World Coffee and Tea Journal*, 74.7 percent of the U.S. population drank coffee in 1962. By 1988, only 50 percent did.[22] Replacing the cheaper robusto beans in homogenized blends for 100 percent Arabica from a single region or even a single farm allowed producers to emphasize the terroir of their coffees and charge a premium for quality. And it encouraged consumers to develop preferences for certain locales of the coffee world, which meant they could thus demonstrate a gourmet ability to discriminate flavor.[23] Specialty coffees were displayed in rustic sacks in high-end grocery stores or in high production value bags that emphasized geographic origin, allowing consumers to experience a connection to place. Today, coffee imports to the United States are almost double what they were when Roseberry wrote his article and 66 percent of Americans eighteen and older drink coffee regularly.[24]

For the postindustrial new mate users in the North Atlantic, the beverage never evolved from mass production to niche. There was no "first" or "second" wave of yerba mate to be replaced by a "third." Rather, the new mate landed in the middle of a Millennial consumer base preconditioned to believe that quality and authenticity are important markers in caffeine. Energy drinks are for generations born into a full-fledged postindustrial society—not people living through the transition—where the ecological crises of capitalism, including climate change and despeciation, are in full bloom. The new beverage sector tracks with a particular kind of postindustrial employment where professional/personal life distinctions have shifted through trends like remote work and meals provided at the office. As part of the reconfiguration of the office, in the most desirable positions, recreational activities like foosball tables and complimentary yoga classes for mental and physical breaks are a job perk. Notably, energy drinks accompany outdoor adventures that reconnect users to nature or a mentally taxing high-intensity work environment.

Postindustrial postures toward nature also reveal anxiety around the body. On their website, GoMate boasts of its special combination of "yerba mate energy and brain-hacking nootropics," alongside an image of a white male GenZer levitating while sitting in a lotus pose.[25] Nootropics, sometimes called "smart drugs," are natural or synthetic compounds that improve cognition, a category of supplements and medicines that has gained popularity in the last three decades.[26] And to be clear, caffeine is a nootropic. Soul Maté invites drinkers to "enjoy the juicylicious mate" and MateMate promises to connect consumers to the "vibrant lifestyle of Berlin."[27] Amid imagery of active, attractive young people outdoors or on a dance floor, the suggestive notion of "hacking" positions yerba mate energy drinks with both the IT job sector and a particular idea about the body and mind.[28] Brain hacking sees the mind as a machine with living code that can be improved and tweaked with the right chemical inputs. The very language and verbal register of computer programming reveal how the brained is viewed as something that can be (should be?) altered, increasing optimal performance as a form of self-expression.

Free-market capitalism can also be hacked, it appears. CLEAN Cause donates profits to addiction recovery; Virtue "contributes to the conservation of plants, animals, [and] natural communities in the rain forest"; MateMate supports Youth Against AIDS; Yachak Organic combats deforestation.[29] Corporate social responsibility (CSR) sits front and center in yerba mate energy drink marketing as many of the new companies prominently announce how they give back to social causes. The idea here is that consumption can and indeed ought to be a way of expressing values—this goes beyond the understanding that value creation can happen within the relationship between loyal consumers and a brand that underlies so much of marketing theory. The CSR initiatives emphasized in yerba mate energy drinks also differ in important ways from ethical capitalist initiatives around organic and fair-trade production in loose-leaf/tea mate companies (more on this later).[30] Many mate energy drinks carry organic seals on their labels, but their websites and advertising schemes highlight work done with the proceeds of sales rather than work done in the sourcing of ingredients. That is, the focus is on the consumption side of the commodity chain, redirecting revenue to projects whose missions appeal to hip, youthful, adventurous buyers.

Skeptical readers might question the effectiveness of social interventions that border on advertising, but perhaps one important qualification might be the degree to which CSR is connected to the fundamental mission of the company. CLEAN Cause, for example, was started by an individual in addiction recovery who wanted to rethink a personal experience with beverages. The company publishes specific numbers on donations already given on the landing page of their website and tells stories of journeys to sobriety.[31] On the other hand, Pepsi-owned Yachak Organic, with the tagline "Inspired by the Amazon," partners with One Tree Planted to reforest the Madre de Dios region of the Peruvian Amazon. Guru: Organic Energy also announces that it is "Inspired by Amazonia's powerful botanicals." Colorful photographs of mist-covered rainforest treetops, a farmer, and a red howler monkey grace the Yachak Organic "Our Purpose" page.[32] Readers who want to know more are invited to "join the pack."

Yerba mate, of course, does not come from the Amazon. But this association of mate with the Amazon reveals something about the geographic imaginary of North Atlantic consumers. Geographic imaginary refers to the mental maps we have of the world, for example, what parts of the world we deem "exotic" or how we understand the dominant voting patterns of different regions in the country. The *New Yorker* published a now famous map on its front cover in 1976 called "View of the World from 9th Avenue" (sometimes called "A New Yorker's View of the World"). It depicted a few meticulously sketched blocks in Manhattan, the Hudson River, and then simplified land masses titled "Jersey," "Kansas City," "China," and "Russia." The humor comes from a sympathetic and yet acerbic rendition of the geographic imaginary of Manhattanites who think of New York as the center of the world. From the perspective of a mate energy drink, South America may appear so distant that the Amazon functions as a stand-in for an entire continent.

But if the purpose of conscientious capitalism is to lessen the gap between producer and consumer, this is a curious way to go about it. Instead, the danger of the mate energy drinks is to reproduce a twenty-first-century version of the *New Yorker* map with detailed and idealized renditions of life in a northern city, photogenic wilderness recreation, and a generic tribal South America. If they're only relying on mate energy drink labels, North Atlantic consumers may miss out on much of the mate story. They won't know, for example, that the bloodiest war in Latin America was fought over (or at least fueled by) mate, or that tangos and great Catholic conspiracies were inspired by the leaf, or that famous scientists who partied with Napoleon were kidnapped in South America because they got too close to the plant.

And yet it seems that mate energy drink brands go out of their way to provide their consumers with a wealth of information. Seals on mate energy drink labels proclaim "gluten-friendly," "carbon-neutral," "plant-based," "non-GMO," "vegan."[33] But with the exception of the fair-trade and organic certifications from third-party organizations, most of the seals seem to be designations created by the companies themselves.[34] The editors of *Hidden Hands in the Market: Ethnographies of Fair Trade, Ethical Consumption, and Corporate Social Responsibility* posit that labeling accompanies new ways of thinking about quality and even connoisseurship.[35] Labels allow users to exercise the discretion between high and low quality that evidences a connoisseur's discerning taste. Consumers who might feel uneasy about their unfamiliarity with the new beverage or hesitate to shop in Latin American or Arab grocery stores can nevertheless express a kind of confidence and even critical distinction in their choices. Labels convey useful health information. But they also satisfy a monetizable foodie need to consume as gourmands.

Mate as Tea

Mate-as-tea companies like Nativa, Maté Factor, EcoTeas, Guayaki, and Balibetov, on the other hand, seek the sweet spot between the two poles of blended mate energy drinks and the traditional South American mate companies. Maté Factor and Nativa, for example, sell loose-leaf yerba in one-pound rectangular bags that look like they were packed on the same assembly line machines used to fill Spanish- or Portuguese-language brands. Though the words on the bags are in English, the product they sell is nearly identical to what is sold in Asunción, Buenos Aires, or Montevideo (with two important caveats). Most of the companies hail from Brazil (Nativa and Maté Factor) or Argentina (EcoTeas), and though Guayaki does source from Paraguay, no one has created an exclusively Paraguayan brand tailored for the North Atlantic. Unlike the mate energy drink brands, mate-as-tea companies prioritize botanical accuracy about yerba, where it is grown, and by whom. EcoTeas and Guayaki have images of real *I. paraguariensis* trees on their websites' landing pages.[36] The vegetal motif on Nativa's bags is recognizably mate leaves. And there are no references to "the Amazon."

One key difference from most traditional yerba is the flavor. Unlike mate for South American and Middle Eastern consumers, the new yerba isn't roasted and so it doesn't have the iconic smoky flavor.[37] The second prominent difference between these new mate entries to the North American market and most South American mate brands is that the mate is certified organic and much of it is fair-trade.[38] This is also a point of continuity with many mate energy drinks. Whereas energy drink CSR efforts use profits or employees' volunteer time to support projects, organic and fair-trade are interventions focused on the production end of the commodity chain. As such, they are more closely tied to the product itself than CSR efforts, admirable though those may be. Mate energy drinks allow us to explore body hacking, geographic imaginaries, and postindustrial recreation. On the other hand, mate-as-tea centers the aims and shortcomings of ethical consumption.

At its base, ethical consumption may be thought of as a discourse, a narrative about how the world works (and how it ought to), rather than just a series of actions.[39] Following this line of thinking, recent scholarship has provocatively emphasized that the strongest motivator for the "ethical consumer" is identity, rather than budget or justice beliefs.[40] Beliefs and actions *follow* identity. That assertion can feel a bit jarring because it challenges the eco-

FIGURE 7.2. Loose-leaf and bagged yerba mate available in the United States. Note the difference between English- and Spanish-language products. Image credit: author.

nomic commonsense idea that price is the limiting factor and therefore a sufficiently large monthly budget would lead to behavioral changes. And it upends how we often like to think that our convictions are the result of a neutral decision-making process based on evaluating evidence.

Although the two get paired together, organic and fair-trade certification schemes arose separately. Organic certification emphasizes questions of agriculture, farming, the welfare of plants, animals, soils; fair-trade, instead, prioritizes the welfare of the communities who produce goods. Both use the power of price as a mechanism for justice to embed these values, expressed in a financial transaction. For most of human history, agriculture was de facto "organic"—cultivated or raised free of synthetic chemicals and laboratory-based genetic modification. The modern movement in the United Kingdom grew out of a self-conscious rejection of industrialized agriculture and the transposition of Indian soil management techniques to the United Kingdom and the rest of Europe.[41] What commenced as a philosophical-botanical movement became standardized through official protocols adopted by France in 1985, the United States in 1990, and the European Union in 1991.[42] To obtain USDA certification, for example, producers have to go through an evaluation and a three-year transition, and undergo annual inspections, even for farms located outside the United States. Organic standards were implemented for domestic production first. Fair-trade practices, on the other hand, began with an early attention to imports.

Fair-trade certifies the labor experience, seeking to keep more financial benefit in the producers' hands rather than the middleman through higher wages, infrastructural investments, and social benefits in education or health.[43] The pioneering fair-trade organization Ten Thousand Villages got its humble start in the trunk of a car. When Mennonite volunteer Edna Ruth Byler visited Puerto Rico just after the end of World War II, she met local women who struggled to provide for their families because they couldn't find a market for their fine lacework.[44] Byler herself paid the women a premium for their handcrafted needlework, which she sold out of the back of her car on the U.S. mainland. "I'm just a woman trying to help other women," Byler said.[45] Though handicrafts were the early fair-trade products, coffee was the first major food commodity.[46] Religious workers living among poor campesinos in Central America and Mexico during local political violence in the 1970s and 1980s used their personal and religious networks in Europe and North America to procure higher prices for smallholder coffee collectives. Pressure from university students, activists, and consumers in the early 2000s drove a massive expansion of fair-trade products with impressive gains. In 2008, Starbucks became the single largest buyer of fair-trade certified coffee in the world. Nestlé U.K. and Ireland's Kit Kat two-finger chocolate bar went fair-trade in 2010; with the addition of the four-finger Kit Kat in 2013, a full 2.5 percent of all the cocoa purchased by Nestlé worldwide was certified fair-trade.[47] The impressive gains, however, were short-lived.

The fact that so few South American (or Middle Eastern) mate brands are organic and that all the major loose-leaf mate brands sold in North America (and all the ones listed here) hold organic certification says a lot about North American market preferences. But what, exactly, does it say? For all the language about nature and environment in organic production, surveys in Europe and North America repeatedly show a puzzling finding.[48] When asked why they purchased organic products, European and North American consumers consistently respond that the number-one reason they purchase and consume organic goods is personal health.[49] Studies show that consumers who choose organic (and many who would but are put off by price) perceive that organic products are better for them and, especially, that they are free of pesticides consumers wish to avoid.[50] In a 2016 study, Pew found that 76 percent of Americans who purchased organic food said that getting healthier foods was a reason for their decision.[51] Less than half that number (33 percent) said helping the environment was a factor.

But if the surveys show that concern for the general environment ranks a distant second, the health and bodies of the agricultural workers who produce the food do not register at all. In fact, it appears that Pew didn't even bother to ask whether concern for agricultural workers might be a factor in purchasing organic food. Neither did a more recent survey of U.S. midwesterners, though they were given the options of "trying something new" and "trendy" as two separate reasons for choosing organic.[52] The organic designation is purportedly a concept about farming practices and protecting the quality of the natural environment. But the reasons that North Atlantic consumers choose organic food are Upton Sinclair–style fears about the contents of industrialized food.[53] In fact, one of the complaints I heard from yerba mate producers in Argentina was that organic standards were an imposition of preferences from the Global North without a real sense of the production process.

Like the branding strategies of new mate and the term "organic" itself show, the twentieth century saw the rise of "nature" and "ecology" as prominent frameworks in politics and culture. Yet when anxieties or problems of the social, political, and economic get transposed to language about nature or ecology rather than embedded within human relationships, the language of nature conceals and exacerbates problems. The trouble arises when nature is framed as separate from human community, as ideally pristine. This ideological distinction between humans and nature is actually an inheritance from ancient Greek and Enlightenment thought where culture and nature were opposing binaries.[54] But humans are part of nature. Cherokee Nation citizen and environmental scientist Clint Carroll and other Indigenous political ecologists have pointed out that all social, political, and economic dilemmas are also environmental issues.[55] Nature and land are implicated in every dimension of human community and human activity. And so to romanticize an untouched-by-humans nature or to ignore the ways environment and economics are always entangled results in worrisome blind spots.

The division between nature and human society mirrors the distance between the production and consumption sides of the commodity chain that Marx called the commodity fetish, and it leaves well-intentioned organic and fair-trade certification programs vulnerable. Without ongoing vigilance and pressure, scholars argue, organic and fair-trade certification programs can be co-opted or rewritten according to the objectives of the corporations they are meant to hold accountable.[56] Indeed, fair-trade gains in the early 2000s have been rolled back. Kit Kat ended their agreement with the Fairtrade Foundation in 2020, instead affiliating with the Rainforest Alliance, which focuses more on environmental conservation than on labor practices and does not have a guaranteed minimum price for producers. Two years later, in 2022, even in the face of public criticism, Starbucks withdrew from third-party fair-trade certification in favor of its own internal Coffee and Farmer Equity (CAFÉ) standard for all coffee sold in Europe, the Middle East, and Africa.

Critics also point out that certifications deepen the neoliberalization of the state.[57] For the sake of contrast, Keynesian capitalism in the early twentieth century saw the need for the state to build safety nets for society in order to soften the blow of economic downturns and maintain enough aggregate demand to keep the economy from full-on crisis. But advocates of neoliberalism have encouraged the rollback of state regulation to allow the market to more efficiently organize social goods.[58] When nongovernmental organizations have to certify labor and production conditions, ensure reasonable payments, and deliver community benefits to producers, private organizations take on the roles and responsibilities of the state that should be answerable to its citizens.[59] This lack of accountability leads to weakened governance. In this case, the critique goes, organic and fair-trade certification are indeed more than a marketing trick and may actually be detrimental to the long-term sustainability and quality of life of producers.

Yet the new yerba mate promises to reconnect North Atlantic consumers with nature and with themselves. And through trusted certification programs, it promises to reconnect consumers to the production of what they consume. Postindustrial crises are, after all, crises of disconnection.[60] By now, readers may be feeling apprehensive about whether the messaging and labels around new mate are anything more than mere advertising or unsure of what to make of the ways new mate beverages can reproduce a geography of distance while performing a reenchanting connection to the Amazon. It may be easier to sell the rainforest to consumers than to really interest them in the quality of life of the farm workers who pick the food. But even in the face of these challenges, we shouldn't underestimate the power of mate to surprise.

Fair-Trade, Organic Mate in Paraguay

The Mbaracayú Nature Reserve contains one of the largest remaining expanses of the once vast subtropical Atlantic Forest in Paraguay. Thousands of plant and animal species, many of them endangered, find shelter in the nineteen distinct ecosystems within the borders of the biodiversity hotspot. The locally run Moises Bertoni Foundation, named after a nineteenth-century Swiss naturalist who made his home on the Paraguayan banks of the Paraná River, was formed in 1991 with a laser-focused purpose to create and conserve the reserve, protecting the native forest from the rapidly encroaching soy and cattle (and marijuana) frontier all around.[61] The work is risky: an Aché Indigenous park ranger in the Mbaracayú Nature Reserve was killed in 2013 by unknown assailants while on patrol. And park rangers at other reserves administered by the foundation have also been murdered.

As part of its mission, the Moises Bertoni Foundation launched the shade-grown yerba mate project without even having a market secured. The twofold aim of the program was to conserve forests on the land held by farmers by giving them a financial incentive— meeting a material need for rural Paraguayans and protecting the environment. Since the success of the first harvest, enthusiasm has only grown. The foundation has started planting shade-grown yerba inside the Mbaracayú Nature Reserve, in those areas that were illegally deforested within the protected space (the areas of virgin forest inside the reserve remain untouched). The new trees are tended by students in the Mbaracayú Nature Reserve School, which exclusively educates local Indigenous and campesino girls in environmental management techniques, eco-tourism, and agroecology as a way to close the gender gap in education and to protect the environment.

The Guayaki Yerba Mate Company was started by friends at California Polytechnic State University in 1996 to bring the mate tradition to the United States as a for-profit firm that has always highlighted social mission as part of its aim. They source their organic, fair-trade mate from Argentina, Brazil, and Paraguay; the small flag on the shield on their product labels indicates which country yielded the yerba for that product. With iconic bright green and yellow packaging, today they are market leaders in both the loose-leaf and mate energy drink spaces in North America. Their collaboration with the Moises Bertoni Foundation is but one of several partnerships the company has in Paraguay.

Guayaki is actually a name for the Aché (with whom the yerba mate company has partnered for years, even before its association with the Mbaracayú Nature Reserve), an Indigenous nation that has suffered violence at the hands of Paraguayan political and economic elites for decades. During the military regime of Alfredo Stroessner (1954–89), the Paraguayan government embarked on several projects to open up the eastern region of the country in the ancestral territory of the Aché, including the construction of Itaipu Hydroelectric Dam with neighboring Brazil and clearing forest land for ranching and agriculture.[62] The development policy was accompanied by targeted violence as Aché villages were raided, men were slaughtered and reportedly hunted for sport, and women and children were raped before being killed or taken as trophies or enslaved in concentration camps in Paraguay.[63] An estimated 50 percent of the Aché disappeared between the 1960s and early 1970s.[64]

The systemic violence was denounced by human rights advocates, lawyers, and clergy to international courts. In an edited volume titled *Genocide in Paraguay* (1976), Auschwitz survivor and Nobel laureate Elie Wiesel wrote:

Until now, I always forbade myself to compare the Holocaust of European Judaism to events which are foreign to it. . . . And yet I read the stories of the suffering and death of the Aché tribe in Paraguay and recognize familiar signs. These men, hunted, humiliated, murdered for the sake of pleasure, these young girls, raped and sold; these children, killed in front of their parents reduced to silence by pain. Yes, the world impregnated with deliberate violence, raw brutality, seems to belong to my own memory.[65]

But no one in Paraguay was held to account. Instead, the anthropologists and clergy working with the Aché were arrested and terrorized by the Paraguayan government. The Aché who remained retreated further into the woods as soy and cattle ranching continued to spread even after the 1989 fall of Stroessner's dictatorship and the transition to democracy. Aché survivors filed a criminal complaint of genocide and crimes against humanity in Argentina in 2014 because Paraguayan officials refused to hear the case.[66] Histories like this help explain why local farmers step into fair-trade programs.

Fair-trade and organic certification do much more than grant a higher price for yerba produced by the Indigenous and mestizo farmers who live around the Mbaracayú Nature Reserve. They help make some of the most vulnerable people in Paraguay visible, in spite of years of government neglect (at best) and overt violence. For all the founded criticisms of how fair-trade and organic certification might (not) work in other parts of the world, in the case of Paraguay, there was no regulatory state to roll back. Neither was there a co-optation of previously fulfilled state responsibilities by civil society. After the War of the Triple Alliance (1864–70), Paraguay's economy was restructured into a booty of privilege attained through membership in the ruling elite.

That inequality continues today where, depending on the metric used, 60 to 80 percent of the economy is informal, which means that the legal minimum wage of about USD$375 a month is an aspiration for the majority.[67] Housing advocates assert that there is a deficit of 800,000 homes in a country of six million inhabitants— if each house is meant to minimally lodge a family of three or four, then at least one-third of all Paraguayans are unhoused or inadequately housed.[68] Poverty rates are higher in the countryside and even worse for Indigenous communities. The average age of death for Indigenous individuals in 2015 was thirty-seven, compared to sixty-eight for non-Indigenous individuals in Paraguay, a difference of more than thirty years.[69] And the coronavirus pandemic has only made things worse.

The data gathered in regular impact assessments and the international attention drawn to populations sometimes seen as eradicable obstacles to progress serve as a necessary but not sufficient step toward basic human rights. Because the Paraguayan government had not successfully conducted a national census since 2002, Moises Bertoni Foundation researchers themselves had to gather the most basic population data. Poor government data accompanies poor government services. It also makes it easier to say that there were no inhabitants on land converted to export-oriented agribusiness. If certification makes vulnerable people (who are normally very easy to erase) legible, more may have been lost besides income when Nestlé's Kit Kat and Starbucks terminated their third-party fair-trade agreements. Fair-trade advocates worried that it signaled a loss of influence, possibly because fickle consumer attention had shifted.

Ethical consumption has a scalar problem: consumer actions are individual, personal, but the social problems are structural, systemic, many of them built over multiple human lifetimes.[70] The purchase of one bottle simply cannot resolve chronic social problems. Similarly, a higher price for one or even ten harvests does not definitively counterbalance the histories of violence that lead to a community's present-day poverty. But leaving the analysis here leads to paralysis and to the status quo (or worse). Moreover, it discounts the efforts and experiences of communities on the ground who have done the hard work of getting certified and the real gains that have been made. Sustainable food has outcomes that are not measured in price but in the day-to-day experiences of social engagement and local politics. Food producers in Australia, for example, saw their participation in local farmer's markets as a way to simultaneously strengthen their relationships with consumers and their autonomy over what they produce.[71]

Paraguayans of all stripes were supportive of the certification scheme for the shade-grown mate in northern Paraguay because

of what they already knew about the downsides of other local economic options and because they are exceedingly proud of their
national drink. But they also had at hand a concrete positive example in organic, fair-trade sugar. Paraguay's sugar industry is old
(it dates to the beginning of Spanish colonialism), but in the 1990s
it was unclear whether it would survive into the new millennium.[72]
With antiquated technology and a changing international environment for the product coupled with the disappearance of government protection of national producers, Paraguayan producers
found themselves unable to compete with Brazil's or Argentina's
capacities to produce cheaper sugar at larger scales. Paraguay simply could not go lower than their neighbors' low prices.

But instead of folding, sugar producers in Paraguay decided to
go premium. With the collaboration of international partners,
nearly all of Paraguay's sugar industry was certified fair-trade and
organic for sale in the North Atlantic, revolutionizing the industry.
Today, there's a good chance that the organic, fair-trade sugar the
readers of this book can buy in their local grocery stores comes
from Paraguay. And a new distillery producing award-winning organic rums, gins, and brandies for export has just opened up next
to Paraguay's oldest organic sugar mill.

Conclusion

The drugs of choice elucidate key points about the values and structures of societies, especially in light of power asymmetries. And so,
the recent uptake of yerba mate in the coveted North American
market is a window into twenty-first-century anxieties about nature
as well as a testament to the creativity of capitalism to find new market niches. On the one hand, the new mate drinks are part of a new
commodity chain circuit, with new brands and processing techniques. On the other hand, new meanings around the body, caring
for the environment, and an ostensibly better way to do capitalism
have become attached to the psychoactive experiences of mate.
When people decide to consume yerba because it is organic, this too

is a sign of acquiescence to a narrative about the right embodied relationship to nature mediated through the market.

We can read political economic systems through the popularity of drugs, an argument that speaks to new psychoactive use today. On college campuses across the United States, the street price of off-script Adderall and other amphetamines follows the academic calendar, rising as midterms and finals approach.[73] The new mate use in North America sits at a time-sensitive health and environment nexus, with anxieties about the personal effects of industrialized food and about the planetary impacts of North Atlantic lifestyles. The hope placed in organic, fair-trade yerba mate is that it will be able to be many things to many: a better source of daily stimulants—better for the body and for the planet.

Epilogue

MERCADO 4 is a warren of open-air and indoor shops in the heart of Asunción, Paraguay, where nearly anything can be found for sale on rickety shelves or tacked to the walls. Shoppers can buy household goods, unlocked cell phones, off-brand clothes— almost all of it made in China, an irony because Paraguay does not have diplomatic relations with the People's Republic of China as it is one of the last countries in the world to formally recognize Taiwan. Along the labyrinthine corridors, peddlers carefully arrange piles of dried flowers, bundles of leaves, and stacks of newly harvested stems and roots, often lashed together with long blades of freshly cut grass (figures E.1 and E.2). One entire section of the market is dedicated entirely to *yuyos*, fragrant herbs that are used in combination with mate to make traditional remedies.

Amid the many shops, Tereré Literario stands out. A mass of thick vines growing from the edge of the street creates an impenetrable canopy over the sidewalk in front of the store, providing welcome shade and relief from the blistering Asunción sun. Mounds of herbs lie arranged on the sidewalk, overflowing from the store and the warehouse behind. On the wall near the entrance is a graffitied rendition of a cattle horn–shaped guampa, the traditional form of a vessel for drinking tereré, set against a jug of ice-cold water. The owners often sit outside their shop in the shade, drinking tereré with clients, surrounded by yuyos for sale. They chose the name of the store to convey their serious pursuit of plant

FIGURE E.1. Table with *yuyo* traditional herbal remedies in Asunción, Paraguay. From the Quechua ("yuyu") for weed, a loanword dating to the early Spanish Empire, as none of the Indigenous languages in Paraguay belong to the Quechua language family. Image credit: author.

knowledges applied to all kinds of ailments. For those who cannot visit the store, Tereré Literario boasts a very active Facebook page with daily posts and mini lessons on the properties and proper use of plants (local and exotic), not all of which are meant to be blended with yerba mate.

But many of the most popular yuyos are. And throughout the day, the rhythmic drumming of merchants pounding herbs in their wooden mortars fills the streets of the city: burrito (whitebrush) leaves for the stomach; boldo leaves for kidney health.[1] Ever in search of ways to distinguish their products from those of their competitors, yerba mate companies in Paraguay produce prepackaged

FIGURE E.2. Preparing *yuyos* for *tereré* in Asunción, Paraguay. Image credit: author.

blends of favorite combinations and experiment with new concoctions. Weight-loss yerba, a mix that includes the laxative senna, is a popular innovation and there are rumors of a yerba + cannabis brand about to launch. But in spite of corporate competition, yuyo merchants in Mercado 4 show no sign of slowing down.

Yerba mate is more than a drink; as a *recipe*, it is a window into questions of identity, community belonging, and how South America is inserted into the global economy. Social, economic, and political priorities get grafted onto plants via the recipe. Recipes showcase human knowledge about the material, non-human world and simultaneously represent human preferences. As the distinct mate-preparation styles between the South American markets that consume the drink demonstrate, recipes crystallize intense rivalries between neighbors and nations.[2] New recipes also point to new economic opportunities, new ways to consume. Though they have different social valences beyond the culinary, pharmaceutical patents and medical prescriptions are recipes, too.

The Book of Yerba Mate is a story of culture, consumption, cuisine, and commodities. By asking the deceptively innocuous question of why we in the North Atlantic don't drink mate, we have taken a journey across centuries and continents to explore how the modern world's political and economic order is put together. Our consumption practices are simultaneously intensely personal (what could be more personal than our individual taste?) and reveal the complicated social structures in which we live by exposing cultural priorities and supply-chain networks. Mate connects seemingly disparate people and places: cosmopolitan Latin American metropoles, mountain-top towns in the Levant, the ecologically sensitive energy drink sector, and more.

Time will tell whether the new mate in North Atlantic markets is just an "it" drink, destined to fade away once a new caffeinated trend arises. But a hint of the answer may come from the performance of the other *Ilex* beverages, yaupon and guayusa, in the North American market. Now that RUNA, the first major guayusa company in the North American market, has split its original hybrid social enterprise into a foundation and a separate for-profit company, the maintained involvement of RUNA's socially committed founders seems all the more crucial for the viability of its eco-social mission. Yaupon, on a rapid ascent as an *Ilex* drink that is local to North America, on the other hand, has a buffer from founder-dependencies because there are multiple companies in the new space—and because the shrub populates lawns and backyards in nearly one-third of the United States. The durability of mate's consumer base and the ability of companies to maintain independence from larger beverage conglomerates may determine whether the ecological values expressed in organic and fair-trade certification give way to bottom-line concerns about profitability. But even more is at stake.

The three *Ilex* drinks are more than just rivals in a zero-sum game in the North Atlantic. South American and Middle Eastern yerba mate coexists with other stimulating beverages in those regions. Having multiple companies offering different flavor profiles of yerba mate and even having different *Ilex* drinks available for consumers will, I suspect, cement the presence of mate, yaupon, and guayusa on the market. After centuries of taking a backseat to coffee and tea, the *Ilex* drinks of the Americas have carved out a resilient niche. As we have seen from the *Ilex* stories, the drinks we choose to give us an added boost in the morning link us to radically different regions in the world and to global histories. The cultural legacies of yerba mate wind through yaupon,

guayusa,
coca,
caapi,
datura,
coffee,
tea,
chocolate,
tobacco,
khat,
sugar,
kola,
marijuana,
and many other potent plants.

What we do when we take a sip of mate is connect to other mate drinkers across time and space and put ourselves in the ever-growing mate story in a drama with a plant as protagonist.

NOTES

Introduction

1. Blinn Reber 1985; Whigham 1991.
2. Matthee 1994.
3. Pepys 2003, 33; Varela Flor 2021.
4. Gonzalez 2019; Kurlansky 1998, 2003; Pendergrast 2010; Martin 2018; Shapiro 2015; Wilson 2007.
5. Kipple 2007.
6. Appadurai 1981.
7. Hopkins and Wallerstein 1986. In their pioneering essay on commodity chains, Hopkins and Wallerstein provide an important definition: "The concept 'commodity chain' refers to a network of labor and production processes whose end result is a finished commodity. In building this chain we start with the final production operation and move sequentially backward (rather than the other way around) until one reaches primarily raw material" (159). See also Bauer 2001; Bestor 2001; Roseberry, Gudmundson, and Kutschbach 1995; Topik, Marichal, and Zephyr 2006; Tsing 2015; Wolf 2010.
8. Carod-Artal 2013; Cañizares Esguerra 2006; Dauncey and Howes 2020; Dauncey and Larsson 2018; Manning and Rood 2016; Schiebinger 2017; Voeks and Greene 2018.
9. Marx 2011.
10. Coronil 1995.
11. Darwin and Darwin 1897, 573.
12. Chamovitz 2012.
13. Coccia 2018; Kohn 2013; Marder 2013; Myers 2015; Sheldrake 2020.
14. Courtwright 2001; Jankowiak and Bradburd 2003; Smith 1992.
15. Weinberg and Bealer 2002.
16. Buck 2001.
17. Jamieson 2001; Schivelbusch 1993.
18. Croegaert 2011, 473.
19. Bourdieu 2010.

20. Ever adept with on-point metaphors, Ortiz explains that "the result of every union of cultures is similar to that of the reproductive process: the offspring always has something of both parents but is always different from each of them" (1995, 103).

1: *Ilex* in the Americas and Indigenous Beginnings

1. Cabeza de Vaca 1542, 71–72.

2. Ren-You Gan et al. 2018.

3. Yao et al. 2021; Manen et al. 2010.

4. Schiebinger 2004, 3.

5. Camp Lee, S.C., March 2, 1862, Lenoir Family Papers, Personal Correspondence, 1861–1865, ca. 120 pp., Inventory #426, Manuscripts Dept., Southern Historical Collection, University of North Carolina at Chapel Hill. A note on terms: as will become clear from this chapter, there are various spellings of "yaupon" and "cassina" that are geographically marked and also the result of varied literacy. I have chosen to use the most common spelling of "yaupon" from Texas and North Carolina, where I live and teach and research. When I discuss a hot beverage made from yaupon, I sometimes refer to it as "yaupon tea" with "yaupon" as a crucial modifier. Any other use of the word "tea" (unmarked) is exclusively meant to refer to the beverage produced from *Camellia sinensis*, commonly called "tea" or "Chinese tea."

6. Wear 1999.

7. Food and Agriculture Organization of the United Nations (FAO), "Table 1: List of All Threatened Forest Occurring Single Country Endemics—Part 9," n.d., http://www.fao.org/3/ad655e/ad655e17.htm; J. Rzedowski and S. Zamudio, "Etapa final de la captura y catalogación del Herbario del Instituto de Ecología, AC, Centro Regional del Bajío," *Bases de datos SNIB-CONABIO proyectos* no. Q017, J097 and F014, Mexico City, 2001.

8. Gan et al. 2018.

9. Adair 1775, 46.

10. Crown et al. 2015.

11. Brickell 1737, 399.

12. Catesby 1763, 15.

13. Cattelino 2018.

14. Locke 1821 (1689), 216.

15. Hawkins 1806.

16. Stross 2011.

17. de Jesus and Hann 1993, n21. Recent feminist archaeological work has critiqued the discipline for its lack of attention to cookery techniques as a gender lacuna. See Sarah R. Graff, "Archaeology of Cuisine and Cooking," *Annual Review of Anthropology* 49 (2020): 337–54.

18. Galgano 2009.

19. Andry 1770, 425–26.

20. Arbesú 2017, fols. 568r–583v.

21. Coladonato 1992.

22. Palumbo, Talcott, and Putz 2009.

23. Hudson 1979.

24. Palumbo, Talcott, and Putz 2009; personal communication.

25. Capers 1822. See also Rollin 1837.

26. *Philadelphia Medical Times* 1872.

27. Earle 2012.

28. Mr. Drayton's Talk to the Cherokees 1775.

29. Alderman 1990 (1978); King 2007, 122.

30. Bartram 1791, 359.

31. Aiton 1789, 170.

32. Ibid.

33. Putz 2010; Wainwright and Putz 2014.

34. See Hale 1891; Venable 1885.

35. Hu 1979; Schultes 1950.

36. Charlevoix 1744.

37. *Daily Advertiser* 1775.

38. *Boston Gazette* 1769; *Medical Repository* 1806.

39. Eggleston 1888, 165.

40. *Medical Repository* 1806. See also *Southern Literary Messenger* 1838, 800.

41. Porcher 1863, 393.

42. M.S.B. 1861. Note the misapplication of *Ilex cassine* to yaupon, which would be rightly termed *Ilex vomitoria*.

43. Gallaway 1994, 185.

44. *Public Ledger* 1873.

45. Cobb 2007, 1.

46. See Catesby 1763; Harris 1891.

47. Brooks 2014.

48. Smith 2001.

49. Stick 1958.

50. Garrity-Blake and Amspacher 2017, 49.

51. Ibid.; Whisnant 2009 (1982), xxx.

52. American Institute of the City of New York 1864, 98.

53. Douglass 2008, 43; Northup 1855, 201.

54. Proctor 2002, 131.

55. Giltner 2008.

56. Dunbar 1956, 118.

57. Brimley 1955.

58. James Henry Rice, "The Story of a New Drink," *Nature Magazine* 62, no. 2 (1923): 53–54.

59. Brimley 1955, 10; *Medical Repository* 1806.

60. Brimley 1955, 10.

61. Fett 2002, 60.

62. See also Frank 2018, 57.

63. Carney 2013; Lovejoy 1980.

64. Fett 2002, 65.

65. Cheney 1925, 207.

66. Mitchell 1999.

67. Johnson 2016.

68. Opala 1987.

69. Johnson 2016, 61.

70. Mackintos et al. 2020; Um et al. 2020.

71. *Chambers Journal of Popular Literature, Science, and Arts* 1893.

72. Hale 1891, 7.

73. Mitchell and Sale 1922, 2.

74. Fairbanks 1922, 144.

75. American Yaupon Association, https://www.yauponamerica.org/; Lost Pines, "Post," Permaculture subreddit, Reddit, https://www.reddit.com/r/Permaculture/comments/3sks7b/wed_love_your_opinion_on_our_company_lost_pines/.

76. Whole Foods, "Top Food Trends 2023," www.wholefoodsmarket.com%2Ftrends%2Ftop-food-trends-2023&usg=AOvVaw0ZtnVGqp6TNxSrQwGQv0uV.

77. CatSpring, "People First," https://www.catspringtea.com/working-with-dignity.

78. Juan Lorenzo Lucero, S.J., to Melchor Navarra y Rocafull (Viceroy of Peru), August 23, 1683, p. 373, quoted in Victor Manuel Patiño, "Guayusa, a Neglected Stimulant from the Eastern Andean Foothills," *Economic Botany* 22, no. 4 (1968): 310–16, 311.

79. Wassén 1972.

80. Schultes 1972.

81. Shemluck 1979. On the domestication of plants in the Amazon, see Neves and Heckenberger 2019.

82. Loesener 1901, 311.

83. Spruce 1908, 453.

84. Ibid., 454.

85. Hudson 1979.

86. Lewis et al. 1991.

87. Villavicencio 1858, 373.

88. Lucero, p. 626, quoted in Patiño 1968, 311.

89. Hadwick Gayton 1928, 17.

90. Hugh-Jones 1995.

91. Shemluck 1979, 156.

92. Bennett 1992, 486.

93. Villavicencio 1858, 373.

94. Hugh-Jones 1979, 216: "yagé [e.g., ayahuasca] itself is compared to an umbilical cord that links human beings to the people's waking-up house and to the mythical past. Yagé is grown from cuttings and is thus thought to be one continuous vine which stretches back to the beginning of time."

95. Plowman 1984; Hugh-Jones 1995.

96. "How RUNA Built a Modern Brand on Ancient Shamanic Principles, with RUNA CEO Tyler Gage," episode 18, Snack Nation, January 29, 2018, https://snack nation.com/blog/tyler-gage-runa/.

97. Caballero 2018. The nonprofit Fundación Aliados (formerly Runa Foundation) supports Ally Guayusa, an Indigenous-owned small-batch guayusa tea export association. Fundación Aliados Ally Guayusa: Organic Guayusa Tea, https://www .losaliados.org/ally-guayusa.

2: Jesuit Conspiracies, Colonial Jealousies

1. "Solicitar al poder ejecutivo disponga la realizacion de campañas de promocion dirigidas a bares, confiterias, restorantes y afines, con el fin de incorporar en el menu a la yerba mate en sus diversas modalidades de infusion," Camara de Díputados de la Nación, Argentina, Expediente 5855-D-2008, Fecha: 16/10/2008, https://www .hcdn.gob.ar/proyectos/proyectoTP.jsp?exp=5855-D-2008. For more on culinary commodity nationalism, see Hirsch 2011; Monterescu and Handel 2019.

2. The ' is a glottal stop; the "c" and the "a" are pronounced as in Spanish. The report from the lower house of congress also cited criollo scribe Ruy Diaz de Guzman's first history of Paraguay in 1612, much of it eyewitness, wherein he described his contemporary Hernandarias's deeds. Ironically, Guzman was one of Hernandarias's strongest critics. And though he did author an important first history of Paraguay, the citation dutifully mentioned by Argentina's congress also appears to have been entirely fabricated.

3. The earliest reference I could locate was a handwritten French transcription of an article on yerba mate published in the Viennese newspaper *Wiener Zeitung*. Note that the file description in the archive describes the language as Spanish and that the newspaper in question is *Die Presse*. The transcription of the article, however, is in French and accompanied by a note on its (re)publication in *Wiener Zeitung* on January 24, 1865. "Traducción al castellano de un artículo sobre el Paraguay y la yerba mate publicado en el diario," *La Prensa* de Viena 345(16), fol. 281–85, Archivo Nacional de Asunción 1865.

4. del Techo 1897, 21; Cortes Ossorio 1677, n313.

5. Wolfe 2006.

6. "1567, instrucciones de Juan Ortega al capitan Ruiz (Ruy) Diaz Melgarejo, Asuncion Sept," in Garavaglia 1983. The letter can even be read in English as "Title granted in favor of Captain Rui Diaz de Melgarejo, appointing him Lieutenant Governor of the Province of Guayrá, and of Villa Rica del Espiritu Santo, in the Province of Coracivera, to be settled and apportioned" as part of Argentine evidence in a territorial dispute with Brazil over ownership of territory east of the Paraná River. Argentina lost its case. Estanislao S. Zeballos, *Argentine Republic Arbitration Upon a Part of the National Territory of Misiones Disputed by the United States of Brazil: Argentine Evidence Laid Before the President of the United States of America*, vol. 1 (New York: S. Figueroa, 1893), 187.

7. Lopez 1974.

8. Sarreal 2022.

9. Archivo Nacional, Asunción, Paraguay 1659, Libro de caja de la Real Hacienda, vol. 22, no. 1.

10. Whigham 1991, 14.

11. Garavaglia 1983, 68–83.

12. Ibid., 71; Lopez 1974, 498–500.

13. Ruiz de Montoya 1639, 8.

14. Ibid.

15. Archivo Nacional, Asunción, Paraguay, 1675, vol. 30, no. 7.

16. Ruiz de Montoya 1639, 9.

17. Garavaglia 1983, 46–47.

18. Lévi-Strauss 1997, 28–35.

19. Mauss 1967.

20. Vitoria 1975 (1532), 87.

21. Garavaglia 1983, 39; Lopez 1974, 498.

22. Fanelli 1962, 138, 139.

23. Allen 1981; Hafso 2019; Valdez, Taboada, and Valdez 2015.

24. Numhauser Bar-Magen 1998.

25. Cieza 2015.

26. Mintz 1979.

27. Antman 2023.

28. Gagliano 1963; Rodríguez-Alegría 2005.

29. du Biscay 1943 (1663), 41.

30. Ibid.

31. Burke and Burke 1757.

32. Vidal de Battini 1953; Villanueva 1985.

33. de León Pinelo 1636.

34. Other writers assert he was born in Portugal—a common trope among conversos that emigrated to the New World.

35. Hurtado Ruiz 2017, 183; Pisconte Quispe 2000, 1.

36. Silverblatt 2004.

37. Coro, or "wild tobacco" (*Nicotiana paa Mat Crow*), is native to South America; its root is still smoked by Indigenous groups in the region today.

38. de León Pinelo 1636, 65.

39. Dobrizhoffer 1822.

40. de Alcedo 1789, 119.

41. Campbell 1741, 240.

42. Betagh 1728, 328: "all East-Indian tea being there prohibited."

43. Byron 1768, 227.

44. Callcott 1824; Frézier 1902.

45. Raynal 1798, 168.

46. Molina et al. 1795.

47. Soler Lizarazo 2016.

48. "En Santa Fe el día 16 de Septiembre de 1793," Acta de Cabildo (digitized), vol. XVI A, fols. 208, 208v, 216–217v, https://actascabildo.santafe.gob.ar/actascabildo/default/ficha/5792-16_de_Septiembre_de_1793.

49. Eremites de Oliveria and Esselin 2015, 294.

50. Muello 1946, 47; *Le Maté ou Thé du Paraguay* 1914, 4.

51. Harris 1989, 31.

52. Furlong 1991, 114.

53. Dobrizhoffer 1822, 101; Charlevoix 1744, 221 (letter 33, dated April 5, 1722).

54. Furlong 1991, 118.

55. Albes 1916, 4; Daumas 1930, 7; Roger 1906, 11.

56. Furlong 1991, 117; per Furlong, this writing is originally found in *Paraguay Natural, II, cap: 14, 220–22*.

57. Nash 1993 (1979). For an account of the important expansion of coal mining in sixteenth-century Europe, extractivism, and its formative impacts on the Protestant Reformation (Martin Luther was the son of a coal-mining engineer), see Ryan Juskus, "The Ecopolitics of Truth and Sacrifice: An Ethnographic and Theological Study of Citizen Science, Environmental Justice, and Christian Witness in Coal's Sacrifice Zones"(PhD diss., Duke University, 2021); Gudynas 2011; Svampa 2011.

3: South American Cowboys and Nineteenth-Century Wars for Independence

1. From Uruguayan poet Bartolomé Hidalgo's "Diálogos satíricos," where Hidalgo, a gaucho and member of the armed guard, greets the Conde de Casa-Flores, who is on a mission on behalf of Ferdinand VII in the Americas. The "cielito" is a pre-independence folkloric musical style (both song and dance) from the Southern Cone region. In Peralto 1950.

2. Pérez Calvo 2013.

3. Borucki 2015; Edwards 2021, 18; Andrews 1980, 4; Frega et al. 2008, 5–102; Mallo and Telesca 2010.

4. Turner 1893.

5. Slatta 1997.

6. Sarmiento 2018 (1845), 261.

7. Alberdi 1852.

8. Hasbrouck 1935; Larson 2020.

9. Art. 25.: "El Gobierno federal fomentará la inmigración europea; y no podrá restringir, limitar ni gravar con impuesto alguno la entrada en el territorio argentino de los extranjeros que traigan por objeto labrar la tierra, mejorar las industrias, e introducir y enseñar las ciencias y las artes." Scobie 1964, 33.

10. Hernández 1872; Cymerman 1996.

11. Sarmiento 2018 (1845).

12. Gortázar 2006, 123–32.

13. Intendencia Montevideo ND Monumento Manuel Ledesma, https:// montevideo.gub.uy/areas-tematicas/personas-y-ciudadania/afrodescendientes /mapeo-afrodescendencia-resiliente/manuel-ledesma.

14. Comisión de Defensa Nacional 2020, "Joaquín Lenzina 'Ansina,' " folder no. 969 of 2020, document no. 299, Camara de Senadores, Uruguay.

15. Wilk 2006.

16. Moraes 2007.

17. Moraes and Thul 2018.

18. Goldman 2019.

19. Frega et al. 2008, 31; Thompson 2005.

20. Sociedad Académica de Amantes de Lima 1792.

21. Pereira Salas 1977, 74–75.

22. de Moesbach 1999, 90.

23. Couyoumdjian 2009; Munizaga 2017.

24. Ruschenberger and Waithman 1835 (1834), 161.

25. Orlove and Bauer 1997.

26. Ibid.

27. Cooney 1972.

28. White 1978.

29. Cooney 1972, 425.

30. Telesca 2010.

31. Agencia de Información Paraguaya 2018; Dos Santos 2019; Telesca 2013.

32. Bridges Abrams 1856.

33. Parish Robertson and Parish Robertson 1838, 140.

34. Ibid., 145.

35. Ibid., 146.

36. Reber 1985, 33.

37. See also Demersay 1867.

38. Deberle 1878, 290.

39. *Littell's Living Age* 1844.

40. Whigham 1994.

41. Pastore 1994, 299.

42. Huner 2011.

43. International Coffee Organization, table 1: Crop Year Production by Country, 2021, https://www.ico.org/prices/po-production.pdf; Vanali 2013.

44. Bondarik, Kovaleski, and Pilatti 2006.

45. Reichmann 1959, 139.

46. Font 2010.

47. Rodrigues Vegro 1994.

48. Campos Pessoa 2018.

49. Erickson, Corrêa, and Escobar 1984; Smith and Atroch 2010.

50. Lessa 1958[?].

51. The word *cimarrón* (from which we also get "maroon" in English) comes, per Price (1992), from the Taino and was originally used in Spanish to refer to the feral cattle that roamed the hills of Hispaniola, having escaped their enclosures in the early 1500s. It was then used to describe enslaved Natives who escaped from Spanish slavery and by the 1530s had come to commonly refer to enslaved Africans who had run away as "wild" or "untamed." The use of the term for yerba mate may come from its connotation of color (brown). For more on the history of maroon societies (of self-emancipated, formerly enslaved individuals) throughout the Americas, see Price 1979.

52. Martins 2018; Archivo do Estado de São Paulo, "Carta Regia ordenando a remessa de um caixao de congonha e a receita para o seu preparo (1721)," *Documentos interessantes para a historia e costumes de São Paulo* 18 (1896): 35–36.

53. Milan and dos Santos, n.d.

54. Da Silva Carneiro 1967; da Rosa and Santos de Souza 2019.

55. Fundação Instituto Brasileiro de Geografia e Estatística 1990, 351.

56. Linhares 1969.

57. Saint-Hilaire 1850, 50; Daniel 2009.

58. Linhares 1969.

59. Saint-Hilaire 1822, 351.

60. Ibid., 351n2.

61. Whigham 2017.

62. Whigham and Potthast 1999.

4: Botanical Imperialism and the Race for Plant Knowledge

1. Bell 2010, 78.

2. Archivo Nacional de Asuncíon, Colección Rio Branco, Catálogo 159, 10.V—1829, fol. 34: "apoderarse de territorio y yerbales pertencientes al Paraguay . . . como uno de [l]os espías observadores que viniero[n] a estos países con otros Franceses."

3. Von Humboldt and Bonpland 2009, 89–92.

4. Von Humboldt and Bonpland 1852, 439; Nedergaard 2003. Strychnine, typically sourced from the south/southeast Asian tree *Strychnos nux-vomica*, causes powerful involuntary muscle contractions. Both curare and strychnine cause death via asphyxiation.

5. Brockway 2002.

6. Ibid.

7. Amurrio 2001; Crawford 2016; Holland 1932.

8. Holland 1932.

9. Linnaeus 1753, 172. See https://www.biodiversitylibrary.org/page/26068141.

10. Sweet 1818, 157.

11. It was even identified after *Ilex vomitoria* (yaupon), but before *Ilex guayusa* (guayusa), which lacked great commercial circulation.

12. Osseo-Asare 2014.

13. Barrera 2006.

14. Gänger 2015.

15. Earle 2012.

16. Asúa 2014; Martin Martin and Valverde 1995. Titled copies of the manuscript can be found in Spain and Argentina; manuscripts with different (or no) titles can be found in Paraguay, Brazil, and the United Kingdom.

17. "Arbol de la yerva caāmini"—ca'a miri tree, note the orthography in the image indicating a distinct second "a" separated by a glottal stop and, possibly, an acute accent on the ultimate syllable of the word, unusual in Spanish and so marked.

18. De Montenegro 1711, 87.

19. Ibid.

20. Harris 1989, 31.

21. Mahmood 2005.

22. Ruiz de Montoya 1639, 9.

23. Anagnostou 2005.

24. Sayre 2007.

25. Boumedine 2020.

26. Mauss 1967.

27. Foster 1987. There is vigorous debate among anthropologists and ethnohistorians as to whether the humoral medicine common in popular medicine across Latin

America (among Indigenous as well as mestizo communities) is a remnant of classical humoral theory imported to the hemisphere as part of European colonialism or arises from precolonial, Amerindian medical knowledges that withstood colonialism. Foster makes the argument for the former based, in part, on the diffusion of medical knowledge through the work of Jesuit texts in the Americas and the hospital missionary work of the Catholic orders.

28. Scarpa and Anconatani 2019, 30.

29. Ibid., 41.

30. The Park at Malmaison: https://musees-nationaux-malmaison.fr/chateau-malmaison/en/park-malmaison.

31. "Death of Bonpland" 1858, 302.

32. Bell 2010.

33. Saint-Hilaire 1822, 351.

34. Ibid.

35. Ibid.

36. Saint-Hilaire 1824, xliii.

37. Miers 1826, 227.

38. Cribelli 2016, 81.

39. John Miers, *Viaje al Plata, 1819–1824*, trans. Cristina Correa Morales de Aparicio (Buenos Aires: Solar Hachette, 1968) only included chapters on the Argentine phase of the journey. Piwonka Figueroa (2009) translates chapters dedicated to Chile.

40. Piwonka Figueroa 2009.

41. Rippy and Pfeiffer 1948.

42. Miers 1826, 42.

43. Ibid., 42–43.

44. Ibid., 44.

45. Ibid.

46. Miers 1861.

47. Ibid., 389.

48. Pratt 2008, 8.

49. Said 1978.

50. Carta de Bolívar Para Gaspar Rodríguez de Francia, Fechada en Lima el 22 de Octubre de 1823, "En la cual le pide amistosamente la libertad del sabio Bonpland que el dictador Francia mantiene en prisión," Archivo del Libertador, Venezuela.

51. Miers 1861, 226.

52. Cribelli 2016.

53. Ibid., 26.

54. Ibid.; De Vos 2007.

55. Runge 1820.

56. Oudry 1827.

57. Jobst 1838; Mulder 1838.

58. Stenhouse 1843; Trommsdorff 1836.

5: New Ventures in Green Gold

1. Burton 1870. Even Friedrich Engels makes an offhand mention of the war in *The Origin of the Family, Private Property and the State*.

2. J.M.L. 1869. Although signed in 1865 in Buenos Aires, the secret treaty had been leaked to the British minister in Montevideo, who then sent a translation to the British foreign secretary. It was subsequently shared before Parliament and thus made inadvertently public.

3. Reber 1988; Whigham and Potthast 1990, 1999.

4. Linhares 1969.

5. Rodrigues Vacari de Arruda 2015; Webb 2020.

6. Eremites de Oliveria and Esselin. 2015, 280.

7. Eremites de Oliveria and Esselin 2015.

8. Epstein 1973, 41.

9. *Brazil Today* 1–2 (1940): 5.

10. Reginaldo Peralta 2012.

11. Warren 1985, 10.

12. Cimó Querioz 2010; Manoel Deodoro da Fonseca, Decreto N. 435 C. 4 de Julho de 1891, "Concede autorização a Thomaz Laranjeira para organizer uma sociedade anonyma sob a denominação de—Companhia Matte Laranjeira," Collecção das Leis da Republica dos Estados Unidos do Brazil, parte II (Rio de Janiero: Imprensa Nacional, 1891), 82.

13. Eremites de Oliveria and Esselin 2015, 301.

14. Warren 1978.

15. *Appletons' Annual Cyclopedia and Register of Important Events* 1878.

16. Ibid.

17. Decreto del 1 de enero de 1871: "El presidente de la República, teniendo conocimiento de que los beneficiadores de yerbas y otros ramos de la industria nacional, sufren constantemente perjuicios que les ocasionan los operarios, abandonando los establecimientos con cuentas atrasadas. . . . Art. 2—En todos los casos en que el peón precise separarse de sus trabajos temporalmente deberá obtener el dicho asentimiento por medio de una constancia firmada por el patrón o capataces del establecimiento. Art. 3—El peón que abandone su trabajo sin este requisito, será conducido preso al establecimiento, si así lo pidiere el patrón, cargándosele en cuenta los gastos de remisión y demás que por tal motive origine. . . .

Signed [President C. M.] Rivarola, [Vice President] Juan B. Gill. Rejistro oficial del gobierno provisorio de la República del Paraguay Año de 1871" (Asunción: Imprenta de la Nación Paraguaya).

18. Warren (1985, 205) asserts that La Industrial controlled 2 million hectares in eastern Paraguay alone. Parquet 1987, 9.

19. See *Don Pacífico de Vargas en pleito con la Industrial paraguaya* (Asuncíon: Imprenta de la Democracia, 1894).

20. Barrett 1910, 9.

21. Ibid., 18.

22. Reed 1995, 53.

23. *The Miscellaneous Documents of the House of Representatives for the Second Session of the Fiftieth Congress, 1888–'89* (Washington, DC: GPO, 1889), 652.

24. Documentos Diplomáticos y Consulares, boletin 28, vol. 6 (Ministerio de Relaciones Exteriories, Republica Argentina, 1904), 85.

25. Ruffin 1905, 268.

26. *Latin American Year Book for Investors and Merchants for 1920* 1920, 557.

27. Hanson 1937.

28. *South American* 1918. See also Rivarola 1993.

29. Linhares 1969, 163.

30. Centennial Notes 1876, 410.

31. Ibid.

32. Órgano Oficial, April–December 1888, https://files.core.ac.uk/pdf/1153/162451822.pdf.

33. Anuario Kraft 1913, 1416.

34. Brazilian Commission 1893, 14.

35. Ibid., 15.

36. Ibid.

37. Butler 1900; New Brunswick Daily Times Archives, January 16, 1904, p. 5, https://newspaperarchive.com/new-brunswick-daily-times-jan-16-1904-p-5/.

38. Caballero Campos 2017.

39. House of Commons Diplomatic and Consular Reports 1900, 7.

40. Eisenberg 1974.

41. Köhler 1998.

42. Friedrich Nietzsche to Elisabeth Förster, Niza, February 7, 1886, qtd. in Schneppen 2002, 83.

43. Elisabeth Förster-Nietzsche to Friedrich Nietzsche, Asunción, April 26, 1886, qtd. in Schneppen 2002, 82.

44. Schneppen 2002, 84.

45. Kurzwelly 2017, 29.

46. Kurzwelly 2017.

47. "Geographical Notes," *Scottish Geographical Magazine* 16 (1900): 719; *Bulletin of the Pan American Union* 40 (1915): 273.

48. Ruffin 1900a.

49. Ibid., 308.

50. Ruffin 1900b.

51. Ruffin 1900a, 307.

52. Embaixada dos E.U. do Brasil 1963.

6: Mate in the Middle East: Fatwas and Finger Puppets

1. ari ariel 2012; Avieli 2016; Hirsch 2011.

2. Bromberger 2020, 48.

3. Kanafani-Zahar 2020.

4. Ortiz 1995.

5. Ibid., 102.

6. Ibid., 98.

7. Balloffet 2020.

8. Civantos 2006.

9. Karpat 1985, 188.

10. *Bulletin of the Pan American Union* 1915, 825.

11. Karam 2004.

12. Civantos 2006.

13. Sutton, Vournelis, and Dickinson 2013, 351.

14. "Judgment Day," episode 17, season 2, *Top Goon* Day (2012).

15. "The Women of the Revolution," episode 7, season 2, *Top Goon* (2012).

16. Appadurai 1981.

17. Ibid., 495.

18. Ibid., 496. See also Cavanaugh and Riley 2017.

19. Sulaiman et al. 2021; see also Vered 2010.

20. Walid Jumblatt, senior leader of Lebanon's Progressive Socialist Party, frequently has his mate in hand during interviews and public speeches.

21. Fatwa number 106406: on mate, published Sunday, March 30, 2008, https://www.islamweb.net/ar/fatwa/106406/.

22. Agrama 2010.

23. Ibid.

24. Karababa and Ger 2011.

25. Dağlıoğlu 1940, quoted in Karababa and Ger 2011, 748.

26. Hattox 1985; Topik 2004.

27. El-Menyar et al. 2015; McGonigle 2013; Varisco 1986; Wagner 2005.

7: The New Postindustrial Hipster Mate

1. Spence 2000; West, Igoe, and Brockington 2006.

2. HOY 2020.

3. Brown 2005. The new "it" drink was accompanied by a burst of scholarly attention in English around its health effects. Riding the momentum from new attention to *I. paraguariensis*, the Yerba Mate Association of the Americas (YMAA) was formed in 2006 with a mission of advancing the scientific understanding of mate and expanding mate's public. The YMAA website even included full-text journal articles about *I. paraguariensis*. Although its U.S. counterparts the Tea Association of the USA (founded in 1899) and the National Coffee Association (founded in 1911) continue their course, YMAA members voted in 2009 to become part of the American Herbal Products Association, which advocates for a wider range of herbal and medicinal plants (including cannabis).

4. Coyula and Rigol 2005.

5. Cubanos Famosos, Vincent Cossío, https://www.cubanosfamosos.com/es/biografia/vincent-cossio.

6. Gregg and Seigworth 2010; Massumi 1995; Sedgwick and Kosofsky Frank 1995.

7. Weber 1958, 117.

8. Weber 1905 (1930), 98.

9. Di Leonardo 1998; Folch 2013.

10. Carrington, Zwick, and Neville 2016.

11. Nadeem et al. 2020; Tate 2009.

12. Harris and Munsell 2015.

13. Guru: https://www.guruenergy.com/en-ca/products/guru-organic-energy-yerba-mate/250-ml.

14. Vida Maté: https://www.drinkvidamate.com/our-maté.

15. Virtue Drinks: https://www.instagram.com/virtuedrinks/.

16. Heckman, Sherry, and Gonzalez de Mejia 2010.

17. American Psychological Association 2015; Levant et al. 2015.

18. Schlib 2017.

19. Castells 1976.

20. Roseberry 1996.

21. Castle and Lee 1999/2000.

22. Ibid., 764.

23. West 2012.

24. International Coffee Organization, Historical Data on the Global Coffee Trade: Imports, 1990–2019; National Coffee Association USA, Fall 2022 National Coffee Data Trends, https://www.ncausa.org/Research-Trends/Market-Research/NCDT.

25. GoMate: https://gomatedrinks.com.

26. Srivastava et al. 2019.

27. Soul Maté: https://soulmate.fi; MateMate: https://mate-mate.com/#mate-pate.

28. Kadlecová 2020.

29. Virtue: https://virtuedrinks.com/virtue-yerba-mate/.

30. Dolan and Rajak 2016.

31. CLEAN Cause: https://cleancause.com.

32. Yachak: Our Purpose, https://www.yachak.com/our-purpose/.

33. Gluten-free/friendly: Guru and Vida Maté; carbon-neutral: Virtue; non-GMO: Vida Maté; vegan: Virtue.

34. Though there are third-party certifications available for these designations.

35. Luetchford, Neve, and Pratt 2008.

36. EcoTeas: https://yerbamate.com; Guayaki: https://yerbamate.com.

37. This may be a matter of market and palate preferences; most of the black tea flavors sold in the North Atlantic, for example, are unsmoked. But there are also recent studies that suggest that smoked foods—charred, barbecued meats or processed meats like sausage or bacon—may be connected to an increased risk of cancer (Fritz and Soós 1980; Onopiuk et al. 2022). For a discussion on the health benefits of yerba mate, see Gawron-Gzella, Chanaj-Kaczmarek, and Cielecka-Piontek 2021.

38. Smith 2014.

39. Harrison, Newholm, and Shaw 2005, 1–8.

40. Andorfer and Liebe 2013. This is something science communication studies have also found regarding anthropogenic climate change. Belief that human activity is a principal contributor to global warming reflects political identity rather than educational level or familiarity with science.

41. Barton 2018.

42. Dankers 2003.

43. Barrientos 2016.

44. Ten Thousand Villages, History, https://www.tenthousandvillages.com/history; World Fairtrade Org and Our Movement, Our History, https://wfto.com/about-wfto/our-movement/#our-history.

45. Ten Thousand Villages, History, https://www.tenthousandvillages.com/history.

46. Jaffee 2014.

47. Starbucks Stories and News, "Starbucks, TransFair USA and Fairtrade Labelling Organizations International Announce Groundbreaking Initiative to Support Small-Scale Coffee Farmers," October 27, 2008; https://stories.starbucks.com/stories/2008/starbucks-transfair-usa-and-fairtrade-labelling-organizations-international/; Trading Visions, "Two Finger Kit Kat Goes Fairtrade," https://tradingvisions.org/content/two-finger-kit-kat-goes-fairtrade.

48. Schneider 2015; Campbell et al. 2014.

49. Torjusen et al. 2004.

50. Gundala and Sing 2021.

51. Pew Research Center 2016.

52. Gundala and Sing 2021.

53. Dürrschmidt 1999.

54. MacCormack and Strathern 1980; Klaus 1997.

55. Carroll 2015; Kimmerer 2013; Nadasdy 2017.

56. Jaffee and Howard 2010.

57. Jenkins 2004; Sharp 2006.

58. Peck and Tickell 2002; Harvey 2005.

59. Bacon 2010; Besky 2008.

60. Vaccaro, Harper, and Murray 2017.

61. Hetherington 2020; Reed 1990.

62. Comisión de Verdad y Justicia Sobre la Dictadura en Paraguay 2023; Folch 2019; Reed and Renshaw 2012.

63. Münzel 1974.

64. Arens 1976.

65. Wiesel 1976, 165.

66. Kearns 2014.

67. Pisani and Ovando 2019.

68. TECHO (Un techo para mi pais) presentation, June 2022, Asunción, Paraguay.

69. Sequera Buzarquis 2019.

70. Environmental activists will recognize the similarities between the scalar dilemma of ethical consumption and eco-anxiety/climate despair. Anthropogenic global warming and ecological crises such as despeciation are wicked problems that by definition cannot be resolved by switching to paper straws or recycling plastic bottles. Yet climate experts point out that while individual actions might not be enough, they do inspire others to take up similar actions, and those summed individual actions can pressure organizations to shift policy. Hayhoe 2018; McKinnon 2014; Stevenson and Peterson 2016.

71. O'Kane and Wijaya 2015.

72. Setrini 2011.

73. Bulthuis 2018.

Epilogue

1. *Aloysia polystachya, Peumus boldus*, respectively.

2. See Wilk and Barbosa 2012.

REFERENCES

Adair, James. 1775. *The History of the American Indians*. London: Edward and Charles Dilly.

Agencia de Información Paraguaya. 2018. "Casa de la Independencia recordará a afrodescendientes de la época colonial." https://www.ip.gov.py/ip/casa-de-la -independencia-recordara-a-afrodescendientes-de-la-epoca-colonial/.

Agrama, Hussein Ali. 2010. "Ethics, Tradition, Authority: Toward an Anthropology of the Fatwa." *American Ethnologist* 37(1): 2–18.

Aiton, William Townshend. 1789. *Hortus Kewensis; or, A Catalogue of the Plants Cultivated at the Royal Botanic Garden Kew*. Vol. 1. London: George Nicol.

Alberdi, Juan Bautista. 1852. *Bases y puntos de partida para la organización política de la República Argentina*. Buenos Aires: Imprenta Argentina.

Albes, Edward. 1916. *Yerba Mate: The Tea of South America*. Pan American Union. Washington, DC: Government Printing Office.

Alderman, Pat. 1990 (1978). *Nancy Ward, Cherokee Chieftainness: Her Cry Was All for Peace*. Johnson City, TN: Overmountain Press.

Allen, Catherine J. 1981. "To Be Quechua: The Symbolism of Coca Chewing in Highland Peru." *American Ethnologist* 8(1): 157–71.

American Institute of the City of New York. 1864. *Proceedings of the Farmers' Club, Together with the Rules and Regulations Adopted by the Committee of Agriculture*. Albany: Comstock & Cassidy.

American Psychological Association. 2015. "Connections Discovered between Masculinity, Energy Drink Use, and Sleep Problems." *ScienceDaily*, November 4. https://www.sciencedaily.com/releases/2015/11/151104150958.htm.

Amurrio, David. 2001. "La quinina: Historia y Síntesis." *Acta Nova* 1(3): 241–47.

Anagnostou, Sabine. 2005. "Jesuits in Spanish America: Contributions to the Exploration of the American Materia Medica." *Pharmacy in History* 47(1): 3–17.

Andorfer, Veronika A., and Ulf Liebe. 2013. "Consumer Behavior in Moral Markets: On the Relevance of Identity, Justice Beliefs, Social Norms, Status, and Trust in Ethical Consumption." *European Sociological Review* 29(6): 1251–65.

Andrews, George Reid. 1980. *The Afro-Argentines of Buenos Aires, 1800–1900*. Madison: University of Wisconsin Press.

Andry, Charles-Louis-François. 1770. *Matière médicale extraite des meilleurs auteurs, et principalement du Traité des médicamens de M. de Tournefort, et des leçons de M. Ferrein*. Vol. 1. Paris: Chez Debure fils jeune.

Antman, Francisca M. 2023. "For Want of a Cup: The Rise of Tea in England and the Impact of Water Quality on Mortality." *Review of Economics and Statistics* 105(6): 1352–65.

Anuario Kraft. 1913. *Gran Guía General de la República*. Vol. 1. Buenos Aires: Anuario Kraft.

Appadurai, Arjun. 1981. "Gastro-Politics in Hindu South Asia." *American Ethnologist* 8(3): 494–511.

Appletons' Annual Cyclopedia and Register of Important Events: Embracing Political, Military, and Ecclesiastical Affairs; Public Documents; Biography, Statistics, Commerce, Finance, Literature, Science, Agriculture, and Mechanical Industry (1876–1902). 1878. 18 (January 1): 677.

Arbesú, David. 2017. "La crónica de Juan de Paiva sobre el juego de pelota en Apalache/ Juan de Paiva's Chronicle on the Apalachee Ball Game." Transcription of la Crónica de Juan de Paiva. Archivo General de Indias, Escribanía de Cámara. *Anuario de Estudios Americanos* 74(2): 733–60. http://doi.org/10.3989/aeamer.2017.2.12.

Arens, Richard, ed. 1976. *Genocide in Paraguay*. Philadelphia: Temple University Press.

ari ariel. 2012. "The Hummus Wars." *Gastronomica* 12(1): 34–42.

Asúa, Miguel de. 2014. *Science in the Vanished Arcadia: Knowledge of Nature in the Jesuit Missions of Paraguay and Rio de la Plata*. Boston: Brill.

Avieli, Nir. 2016. "The Hummus Wars Revisited: Israeli-Arab Food Politics and Gastromediation." *Gastronomica* 16(3): 19–30.

Bacon, Christopher M. 2010. "Who Decides What Is Fair in Fairtrade? The Agri-environmental Governance of Standards, Access, and Price." *Journal of Peasant Studies* 37(1): 111–47.

Balloffet, Lily Pearl. 2020. *Argentina in the Global Middle East*. Stanford: Stanford University Press.

Barrera, Antonio. 2006. *Experiencing Nature: The Spanish American Empire and the Early Scientific Revolution*. Austin: University of Texas Press.

Barrett, Rafael. 1910. *Lo que son los yerbales*. Montevideo: Talleres Gráfico.

Barrientos, Stephanie. 2016. "Beyond Fairtrade: Why Are Mainstream Chocolate Companies Pursuing Social and Economic Sustainability in Cocoa Sourcing?" In *The Economics of Chocolate*, ed. Mara P. Squicciarini and Johan Swinnen. Oxford: Oxford Academic.

Barton, Gregory A. 2018. *The Global History of Organic Farming*. Oxford: Oxford Academic.

Bartram, William. 1791. *Travels through North & South Carolina, Georgia, East & West Florida, the Cherokee Country, etc.* Philadelphia: James & Johnson.

Bauer, Arnold J. 2001. *Goods, Power, History: Latin America's Material Culture.* Cambridge: Cambridge University Press.

Bell, Stephen. 2010. *A Life in Shadow: Aimé Bonpland in Southern South America, 1817–1858.* Stanford: Stanford University Press.

Bennett, Bradley C. 1992. "Hallucinogenic Plants of the Shuar and Related Indigenous Groups in Amazonian Ecuador and Peru." *Brittonia* 44(4): 483–93.

Besky, Sarah. 2008. "Can a Plantation Be Fair? Paradoxes and Possibilities in Fairtrade Darjeeling Tea Certification." *Anthropology of Work Review* 29(1): 1–9.

Bestor, Theodore C. 2001. "Supply-Side Sushi: Commodity, Market, and the Global City." *American Anthropologist* 103(1): 76–95.

Betagh, William. 1728. *A Voyage Round the World; Being an account of a remarkable enterprise, begun in the year 1719, chiefly to cruise on the Spaniards in the great South Ocean.* London: T. Combes et al.

Bondarik, Roberto, João Luiz Kovaleski, and Luiz Alberto Pilatti. 2006. "A Produção de Erva-Mate e a Iniciação Industrial do Paraná." Paper presented at ADM2006 190 Congresso Internacional de Administração, Ponta Grossa, Paraná, Brazil, September 19–22.

Borucki, Alex. 2015. *From Shipmates to Soldiers: Emerging Black Identities in the Río de la Plata.* Albuquerque: University of New Mexico Press.

Boston Gazette. 1769. "A Paragraph of a Letter from a Gentleman in Halifax, Nova-Scotia, to His Friend in Boston." May 8, p. 1.

Boumedine, Samir. 2020. "Jesuit Recipes, Jesuit Receipts: The Society of Jesus and the Introduction of Exotic Material Medica into Europe." In *Cultural Worlds of the Jesuits in Colonial Latin America.* London: University of London Press.

Bourdieu, Pierre. 2010. *Distinction: A Social Critique of the Judgement of Taste.* London: Taylor & Francis Group.

Brazilian Commission. 1893. *Catalogue of the Brazilian Section at the World's Columbian Exposition.* Chicago: E. J. Campbell.

Brickell, John. 1737. *The Natural History of North Carolina.* Dublin: James Carson.

Bridges Abrams, W. 1856. "A Chapter on the Yerva de Paraguay." *Journal of the Society of Arts* (March 21): 321.

Brimley, Herbert Huchinson. 1955. "Yaupon Factory." *State* 23(15): 9–11.

Brockway, Lucile. 2002. *Science and Colonial Expansion: The Role of the British Royal Botanic Garden.* New Haven: Yale University Press.

Bromberger, Christian. 2020. "Gilan (Northern Iran) Cuisine Specificity/La specificite de la cuisine du Gilan (Iran septentrional)." *Anthropology of the Middle East* 15(2): 47–54.

Brooks, Baylus C. 2014. "John Lawson's Indian Town on Hatteras Island, North Carolina." *North Carolina Historical Review* 91(2): 171–207.

Brown, Jordana. 2005. "The Newest Coffeehouse 'It' Drink May Beat Out Java for Health and Energy Benefits." *Better Nutrition* 8(67): 9.

Buck, Pem Davidson. 2001. *Worked to the Bone: A History of Race, Class, Power, and Privilege in Kentucky*. New York: Monthly Review Press.

Bulthuis, Noah. 2018. "As Finals Week Approaches, UCI Students Discuss Adderall Usage." *New University*, June 2. https://newuniversity.org/2018/06/02/as-finals -week-approaches-uci-students-discuss-adderall-usage/.

Burke, William, and Edmond Burke. 1757. *An Account of the European Settlements in America: In Six Parts*. London: Printed for R. and J. Dodsley in Pall-Mall.

Burton, Richard Francis. 1870. *Letters from the Battle-Fields of Paraguay*. London: Tinsley Brothers.

Butler, William Mill. 1900. *Yerba Maté Tea: The History of Its Early Discovery in Paraguay, Its Preparation in That Country and in Brazil, and Its Introduction into the United States*. Philadelphia: Yerba Maté Tea Company.

Byron, John. 1768. *The narrative of the Honourable John Byron (commodore in a late expedition round the world) containing an account of the great distresses*. London: Printed for S. Baker and G. Leigh, in York-Street; and T. Davies, in Russel-Street, Covent-Garden.

Caballero, Martín. 2018. "All Market Inc. Acquires Runa." BevNet, June 20. https:// www.bevnet.com/news/2018/market-inc-acquires-runa.

Caballero Campos, Herib. 2017. " 'Beba té de yerba mate y sea feliz!' La promoción de la yerba mate en lo estados unidos de América a fines del siglo XIX." *Revista Latino-Americana de História* 6(17): 80–95.

Cabeza de Vaca, Álvar Núñez. 1542. *La relación y comentarios*. The Wittliff Collections, Texas State University, San Marcos.

Callcott, Maria. 1824. *Journal of a residence in Chile, during the year 1822. And a voyage from Chile to Brazil in 1823*. London: Printed for Longman, Hurst, Rees, Orme, Brown, and Green, and John Murray.

Campbell, Benjamin L., Hayk Khachatryan, Bridget K. Behe, Jennifer Dennis, and Charles Hall. 2014. "U.S. and Canadian Consumer Perception of Local and Organic Terminology." *International Food and Agribusiness Management Review* 17(2): 21–40.

Campbell, John. 1741. *A concise history of the Spanish America; containing a succinct relation of the discovery and settlement of its several colonies*. London: Printed for John Stagg in Westminster-Hall, and Daniel Browne at the Black Swan without Temple-Bar.

Campos Pessoa, Thiago. 2018. "Underneath the Sign of Illegality: The Slave Trade in the Building of Coffee Complex in Rio de Janeiro (1831–1850)/Sob o signo da ilegalidade: O trafico de africanos na montagem do complexo cafeteiro (Rio de

Janeiro, c. 1831–1850)." *Tempo: Revista do Departamento de Historia da UFF* 24(3): 423–49.

Cañizares Esguerra, Jorge. 2006. *Nature, Empire, and Nation: Explorations of the History of Science in the Iberian World.* Stanford: Stanford University Press.

Capers, William. 1822. "Mission among the Creek Indians: Extract from the Journal of the Rev. William Capers to Tustunnuggee Opoi, Tustunnuggee Thlucco, General M'Intosh, and all the Chiefs of the Creek Nation." *Methodist Magazine* 5(1): 272.

Carney, Judith. 2013. "Seeds of Memory: Botanical Legacies of the African Diaspora." In *African Ethnobotany in the Americas,* ed. Robert Voeks and John Rashford, 13–33. New York: Springer.

Carod-Artal, F. J. 2013. "Psychoactive Plants in Ancient Greece." *Neurosciences and History* 1(1): 28–38.

Carrington, Michal Jemma, Detlev Zwick, and Benjamin Neville. 2016. "The Ideology of the Ethical Consumption Gap." *Marketing Theory* 16(1): 21–38.

Carroll, Clint. 2015. *Roots of Our Renewal: Ethnobotany and Cherokee Environmental Governance.* Minneapolis: University of Minnesota Press.

Castells, Manuel. 1976. "The Service Economy and Postindustrial Society: A Sociological Critique." *International Journal of Health Services* 6(4): 595–607.

Castle, Timothy J., and Christopher M. Lee. 1999/2000. "The Coming Third Wave of Coffee Shops." *Tea & Coffee Asia* 1(3): 14–18.

Catesby, Mark. 1763. *Hortus Britanno-Americanus.* London: W. Richardson and S. Clark for J. Ryall.

Cattelino, Jessica. 2018. "From Locke to Slots: Money and the Politics of Indigeneity." *Comparative Studies in Society and History* 60(2): 274–307.

Cavanaugh, J. R., and K. C. Riley, eds. 2017. "The Semiotics of Food and Language." *Semiotic Review,* issue 5.

Centennial Notes. 1876. "Glimpses in Agricultural Hall—Russia and the Argentine Confederation." *Friends' Intelligencer* 33(26): 409–11.

Chambers Journal of Popular Literature, Science, and Arts. 1893. "Holly Tea," April 29. 10(487): 262.

Chamovitz, Daniel. 2012. *What a Plant Knows: A Field Guide to the Senses.* New York: Scientific American/Farrar, Straus and Giroux.

Cheney, Ralph Holt. 1925. *Coffee: A Monograph of the Economic Species of the Genus Coffea L.* New York: New York University Press.

Cieza, Pedro. 2015. *The Travels of Pedro de Cieza de Léon, A.D. 1532–50, Contained in the First Part of His Chronicle of Peru.* Trans. Clements R. Markham. Project Gutenberg Ebook Chronicles of Peru.

Cimó Querioz, Paulo Roberto. 2010. "A grande empresa convencida como Mate Larangjeira e a economía ervateira na Bacia Platina (1882–1949)." Conference paper, Universidade Federal da Grande Dourados.

Civantos, Christina. 2006. *Between Argentines and Arabs: Argentine Orientalism, Arab Immigrants, and the Writing of Identity*. Albany: State University of New York Press.

Cobb, James. 2007. *Away Down South: A History of Southern Identity*. Oxford: Oxford University Press.

Coccia, Emanuele. 2018. *The Life of Plants: A Metaphysics of Mixture*. Trans. Dylan J. Montanari. Cambridge: Polity Press.

Coladonato, Milo. 1992. "Ilex vomitoria." In *Fire Effects Information System*. U.S. Department of Agriculture, Forest Service, Rocky Mountain Research Station, Fire Sciences Laboratory.

Comisión de Verdad y Justicia Sobre la Dictadura en Paraguay 1954–1989. 2023. *Informe Final: Ventanas Abiertas*. CODEHUPY: Asunción.

Cooney, Jerry W. 1972. "Paraguayan Independence and Doctor Francia." *The Americas* 28(4): 407–28.

Coronil, Fernando. 1995. "Transculturation and the Politics of Theory: Countering the Center/Cuban Counterpoint." In *Cuban Counterpoint: Tobacco and Sugar*, by Fernando Ortiz. Durham: Duke University Press.

Cortes Ossorio, Juan. 1677. *Reparos historiales apologéticos . . . propuestos de parte de los misioneros apostólicos del Imperio de la China representando los descuidos que se cometen en un libro que se ha publicado en Madrid en graue perjuizio de aquella misión*. Pamplona: Tomás Bazan.

Courtwright, David T. 2001. *Forces of Habit: Drugs and the Making of the Modern World*. Cambridge, MA: Harvard University Press.

Couyoumdjian, Juan Ricardo. 2009. "El mate, el té y el café en Chile desde la independencia hasta 1930." *Boletín de la Academia Chilena de la Historia* 75(118): 7–56.

Coyula, Mario, and Isabel Rigol. 2005. "La Calzada del Cerro Esplendor y Ocaso de la Habana Neoclásica." *Arquitectura y Urbanismo* 26(2): 28–41.

Crawford, Matthew James. 2016. "Between Bureaucrats and Bark Collectors: Spain's Royal Reserve of Quina and the Limits of European Botany in the Late Eighteenth-Century Spanish Atlantic World." In *Global Scientific Practice in an Age of Revolutions, 1750–1850: Discussing the Contingency/Inevitability Problem*, ed. Daniel Rood and Patrick Manning. Pittsburgh: University of Pittsburgh Press.

Cribelli, Teresa. 2016. *Industrial Forests and Mechanical Marvels: Modernization in Nineteenth-Century Brazil*. Cambridge: Cambridge University Press.

Croegaert, Ana. 2011. "Who Has Time for Ćejf? Postsocialist Migration and Slow Coffee in Neoliberal Chicago." *American Anthropologist* 113(3): 463–77.

Crown, Patricia, Thomas Emerson, Jiyan Gu, William Hurst, Timothy Pauketat, and Timothy Ward. 2012. "Ritual Black Drink Consumption at Cahokia." *PNAS* 109(35): 13944–49.

Crown, Patricia, Jiyan Gu, W. Jeffrey Hurst, Timothy J. Ward, Ardith D. Bravenec, Syed Alib, Laura Kebert, Marlaina Berch, Erin Redman, Patrick D. Lyons, Jamie

Merewether, David A. Phillips, Lori S. Reed, and Kyle Woodson. 2015. "Ritual Drinks in the Pre-Hispanic US Southwest and Mexican Northwest." *PNAS* 112(37): 11436–42.

Cymerman, Claude. 1996. "La ideología acarreada por el 'Martín Fierro' de José Hernández." *Anales de literatura hispanoamericana* 25:49–62.

Daily Advertiser (London). 1775. Friday, February 3. Issue 13767:1.

da Rosa, Lilian, and Taciana Santos de Souza. 2019. "Evolução do setor ervateiro durante o século XIX: Uma análise dos avanços tecnológicos na cadeia produtiva." *História Econômica & História de Empresas* 22:9–40.

Da Silva Carneiro, David Antonio. 1967. "O Mate e a Influencia Decisiva de Camargo Pinto." *Journal of Inter-American Studies* 9(4): 603–18.

Daniel, Omar. 2009. *Erva-mate: Sistema de produçao e processamento industrial.* Dourados: UFGD.

Dankers, Cora. 2003. *Environmental and Social Standards, Certification and Labelling for Cash Crops.* Rome: Food and Agriculture Organization of the United Nations.

Darwin, Charles, and Francis Darwin. 1897. *The Power of Movement in Plants.* New York: D. Appleton and Company.

Daumas, Ernesto. 1930. *El Problema de la Yerba Mate.* Buenos Aires: Campañía Impresora Argentina.

Dauncey, Elizabeth A., and Melanie-Jayne R. Howes. 2020. *Plants That Cure: Plants as a Source for Medicines, from Pharmaceuticals to Herbal Remedies.* Princeton: Princeton University Press.

Dauncey, Elizabeth A., and Sonny Larsson. 2018. *Plants That Kill: A Natural History of the World's Most Poisonous Plants.* Princeton: Princeton University Press.

de Alcedo, Antonio. 1789. *Diccionario geográfico-histórico de las Indias Occidentales.* Madrid: Benito Cano.

"Death of Bonpland." 1858. *American Journal of Science and Arts,* 2nd ser., 26(77): 301–4.

Deberle, Alfred Joseph. 1878. *Historia de la América del Sur desde su descubrimiento hasta nuestros días.* Barcelona: Jané Hermanos Editores.

de Charlevoix, Pierre Francois Xavier. 1744. *Journal d'un voyage fait par ordre du roi dans l'Amerique Septentrionnale.* Vol. 6. Paris: Chez Rollin Fils, Libraire, Quai des Augustins a S. Athanase & au Palmier.

de Jesus, Francisco Alonso, and John H. Hann. 1993. "1630 Memorial of Fray Francisco Alonso de Jesus on Spanish Florida's Missions and Natives." *The Americas* 50(1): 85–105.

de León Pinelo, Antonio. 1636. *Questión moral: Si el chocolate quebranta el ayuno eclesiástico.* Madrid: Por la Viuda de Juan Gonçalez.

del Techo, Nicolas. 1897. *Historia de la Provincia del Paraguay de la Compañía de Jesús.* Vol. 6. Versión del texto latino por Manuel Serrano y Sanz. Madrid: Librería y Casa Editorial A. de Uribe y Compañía.

Demersay, Alfred. 1867. *Étude économique sur le maté ou thé du Paraguay.* Paris: Ve Bouchard-Huzard.

de Moesbach, Ernesto Wilhelm. 1999. *Botánica indígena de Chile.* Santiago de Chile: Editorial Andres Bello.

De Montenegro, Pedro. 1711. *Libro primero de la propiedad y virtudes de los árboles y plantas de las misiones y provincia del Tucumán, con algunas del Brasil y del Oriente [Manuscrito]: Dividido en dos libros, en el primero se trata de la propiedad y virtudes de los árboles y de las plantas menores . . . en el segundo de las hierbas y raíces comestibles . . . / compuesto por el hermano Pedro de Montenegro, de la Compañía de Jesús, año de 1711, en las Misiones del Paraguay.* Biblioteca Nacional de España. Digitized by the Biblioteca Digital Hispánica.

De Vos, Paula S. 2007. "Natural History and the Pursuit of Empire in Eighteenth-Century Spain." *Eighteenth-Century Studies* 40(2): 209–39.

Di Leonardo, Micaela. 1998. *Exotics at Home.* Chicago: University of Chicago Press.

Dobrizhoffer, Martin. 1822. *An Account of the Abipones: An Equestrian People of Paraguay.* Vol. 1. London: John Murray.

Dolan, Catherine, and Dinah Rajak, eds. 2016. *The Anthropology of Corporate Social Responsibility.* New York: Berghahn Books.

Dos Santos, Augusto. 2019. "Asunción tuvo casi el 50% de población negra antes de la Independencia." *La Nación.* https://www.lanacion.com.py/gran-diario -domingo/2019/05/19/asuncion-tuvo-casi-el-50-de-poblacion-negra-antes-de -la-independencia/.

Douglass, Frederick. 2008. *Narrative of the Life of Frederick Douglass.* New York: Cosimo Classics.

du Biscay, Acarete. 1943 (1663). *Relación de un viaje al Río de la Plata y de allí por tierra al Perú con observaciones sobre los habitantes, sean indios o españoles, las ciudades, el comercio, la fertilidad y las riquezas de esta parte de América.* Trans. Francisco Fernández Wallace. Buenos Aires: Alfer y Vays, Editores.

Dunbar, Gary Seamans. 1956. "Historical Geography of the North Carolina Outer Banks." PhD diss., Louisiana State University.

Dürrschmidt, Jörg. 1999. "The 'Local' versus the 'Global'?: 'Individualised Milieux' in a Complex 'Risk Society': The Case of Organic Food Box Schemes in the South West." In *Consuming Cultures: Power and Resistance,* ed. Jeff Hearn and Sasha Roseneil, 131–52. New York: St. Martin's Press.

Earle, Rebecca. 2012. *The Body of the Conquistador: Food, Race and the Colonial Experience in Spanish America, 1492–1700.* Cambridge: Cambridge University Press.

Edwards, Erika Denise. 2021. *Hiding in Plain Sight: Black Women, the Law, and the Making of a White Argentine Republic.* Tuscaloosa: University of Alabama Press.

Eggleston, Edward. 1888. *A History of the United States and Its People: For the Use of Schools.* New York: D. Appleton & Company.

Eisenberg, Peter. 1974. *The Sugar Industry in Pernambuco: Modernization without Change, 1840–1910.* Berkeley: University of California Press.

El-Menyar, Ayman, Ahammed Mekkodathil, Hassan Al-Thani, and Ahmed Al-Motarreb. 2015. "Khat Use: History and Heart Failure." *Oman Medical Journal* 30(2): 77–82.

Embaixada dos E.U. do Brasil. 1963. *La Yerba Mate.* Montevideo: Serviço de Propaganda e Expansão Comercial (SEPRO).

Epstein, D. G. 1973. *Brasilia, Plan and Reality: A Study of Planned and Spontaneous Urban Development.* Berkeley: University of California Press.

Eremites de Oliveria, Jorge, and Paulo Marcos Esselin. 2015. "Uma breve história (indígena) da erva-mate na região platina: Da Província do Guairá ao antigo sul de Mato Grossos." *Espaço Ameríndio* 9(3): 278–318.

Erickson, H. T., Maria Pinheiro F. Corrêa, and José Ricardo Escobar. 1984. "Guaraná (Paullinia cupana) as a Commercial Crop in Brazilian Amazonia." *Economic Botany* 38(3): 273–86.

Fairbanks, Charles. 1979. "The Function of Black Drink among the Creeks." In *Black Drink: A Native American Tea*, ed. Charles Hudson, 120–49. Athens: University of Georgia Press.

Fanelli, Antonio María. 1962. "Relación de un viaje a Chile en 1698: Desde Cádiz, por mar y por tierra, escrita en italiano por el P . . . de la Compañía de Jesús." In José Toribio Medina, *Viajes relativos a Chile*, vol. 1. Santiago: Fondo Histórico y Bibliográfico José Toribio Medina.

Fett, Sharla M. 2002. *Working Cures: Healing, Health, and Power on Southern Slave Plantations.* Chapel Hill: University of North Carolina Press.

Folch, Christine. 2013. "Why the West Loves Sci-Fi and Fantasy: A Cultural Explanation." *The Atlantic*, June 13.

———. 2019. *Hydropolitics: The Itaipu Dam, Sovereignty, and the Making of Modern South America.* Princeton: Princeton University Press.

Font, Mauricio A. 2010. *Coffee and Transformation in Sao Paulo, Brazil.* Lanham, MD: Lexington Books.

Foster, George M. 1987. "On the Origin of Humoral Medicine in Latin America." *Medical Anthropology Quarterly* 1(4): 355–93.

Frank, Andrew K. 2018. "Red, Black, and Seminole: Community Convergence on the Florida Borderlands, 1780–1840." In *Borderland Narratives: Negotiation and Accommodation in North America's Contested Spaces, 1500–1850*, ed. Andrew K. Frank and A. Glenn Crothers, 46–61. Gainesville: University Press of Florida.

Frega, Ana, Karla Chagas, Óscar Montaño, and Natalia Stalla. 2008. "Breve historia de los afrodescendientes en el Uruguay." In *Población Afrodescendiente y Desigualdades Étnico-Raciales en Uruguay*, ed. Lucía Scuro Somma. Montevideo: PNUD.

Frézier, Amadeo. 1902. *Relación del viaje por el Mar del Sur*. Traducido por Nicolás Peña M. de la primera edición francesa de 1716. Santiago: Imprenta Mejía.

Fritz, W., and K. Soós. 1980. "Smoked Food and Cancer." *Bibliotecha Nutritio et Dieta* 29:57–64. https://pubmed.ncbi.nlm.nih.gov/7447916/.

Fundação Instituto Brasileiro de Geografia e Estatística. 1990. *Estadísticas Historicas do Brasil, 2a edição*. Rio de Janeiro: IBGE.

Furlong, Guillermo S. J. 1991. *Jose Sanchez Labrador, S. J. y su "Yerba Mate"* (1774). Buenos Aires: Distribuidora y Editora Teoría S.R.L., Abril.

Gagliano, Joseph. 1963. "The Coca Debate in Colonial Peru." *The Americas* 20(1): 43–63.

Galgano, Robert C. 2009. *Feast of Souls: Indians and Spaniards in the Seventeenth-Century Missions of Florida and New Mexico*. Albuquerque: University of New Mexico Press.

Gallaway, B. P., ed. 1994. *Texas, the Dark Corner of the Confederacy: Contemporary Accounts of the Lone Star State in the Civil War*. Lincoln: University of Nebraska Press.

Gan, R. Y., D. Zhang, M. Wang, and H. Corke. 2018. "Health Benefits of Bioactive Compounds from the Genus *Ilex*, a Source of Traditional Caffeinated Beverages." *Nutrients* 10(1682): 1–11.

Gänger, Stefanie. 2015. "World Trade in Medicinal Plants from Spanish America, 1717–1815." *Medical History* 59(1): 44–62. https://doi.org/10.1017/mdh.2014.70.

Garavaglia, Juan Carlos. 1983. *Mercado Interno y Economia Colonial*. Mexico City: Editorial Grijalbo.

Garrity-Blake, Barbara, and Karen Willis Amspacher. 2017. *Living at the Water's Edge: A Heritage Guide to the Outer Banks Byway*. Chapel Hill: University of North Carolina Press.

Gawron-Gzella, A., J. Chanaj-Kaczmarek, and J. Cielecka-Piontek. 2021. "Yerba Mate: A Long but Current History." *Nutrients* 13(3706): 1–19. http://doi.org/10.3390/nu13113706.

Giltner, Scott E. 2008. *Hunting and Fishing in the New South: Black Labor and White Leisure after the Civil War*. Baltimore: Johns Hopkins University Press.

Goldman, Gustavo. 2019. *Negros modernos: Asociacionismo politico, mutual y cultural en el Río de la Plata a finse del siglo XIX*. Montevideo: Perro Andaluz Ediciones.

Gonzalez, Sef. 2019. *All about the Burger: A History of America's Favorite Sandwich*. Coral Gables, FL: Mango Media.

Gortázar, Alejandro. 2006. "Ansina: ¿Un héroe en clave afro–uruguaya?" In *Los héroes fundadores: Perspectivas desde el siglo XXI*, ed. Carlos Demasi and Eduardo Piazza, 123–32. Montevideo: CEIU/Red académica "Héroes de papel."

Gregg, Melissa, and Gregory J. Seigworth. 2010. "An Inventory of Shimmers." In *The Affect Theory Reader*, ed. Melissa Gregg and Gregory J. Seigworth. Durham: Duke University Press.

Grondona, Eduardo M. 1954. "História de la yerba mate. II: Sinonimia, cariología y distribución geográfica." *Revista Argentina de Agrononomía* 21: 9–24.

Gudynas, Eduardo. 2011. "El nuevo extractivismo progresista en América del sur: Tesis sobre un viejo problema bajo nuevas expresiones." In *Colonialismos del Siglo XXI*, 75–92. Barcelona: Icaria Editorial.

Guedes da Silva, Walter. 2011. "Controle e domínio territorial no sul do estado de Mato Grosso: Uma análise da atuação da 'Cia Matte Larangeira' no período de 1883 a 1937." *Agrária*, São Paulo, no. 15: 102–25.

Gundala, Raghava R., and Anupam Sing. 2021. "What Motivates Consumers to Buy Organic Foods? Results of an Empirical Study in the United States." *PLoS ONE* 16(9): e0257288. https://doi.org/10.1371/journal.pone.0257288.

Hadwick Gayton, Anna. 1928. "The Narcotic Plant Datura in Aboriginal American Culture." PhD diss., University of California.

Hafso, Jasmine P. 2019. "Indigenous Identity and the Coca Leaf: Attitudes Towards the Coca Leaf in the Mid-sixteenth Century to the Late Seventeenth Century in Colonial Peru." *Constellations* 10(2): 1–22. https://doi.org/10.29173/cons29388.

Hale, Edwin M. 1891. "Bulletin No. 14." Washington, DC: Government Printing Office, Division of Botany.

Hanson, Simon. G. 1937. "The Farquhar Syndicate in South America." *Hispanic American Historical Review* 17(3): 314–26.

Harris, Jennifer L., and Christina R. Munsell. 2015. "Energy Drinks and Adolescents: What's the Harm?" *Nutrition Reviews* 73(4): 247–57.

Harris, Steven J. 1989. "Transposing the Merton Thesis: Apostolic Spirituality and the Establishment of the Jesuit Scientific Tradition." *Science in Context* 3(1): 29–65.

Harris, Thos C. 1891. "On the Carolina Banks." *Youth's Companion* 64(45): 571.

Harrison, R., T. Newholm, and D. Shaw. 2005. Introduction to *The Ethical Consumer*, 1–8. Thousand Oaks, CA: Sage.

Harvey, David. 2005. *A Brief History of Neoliberalism*. Oxford: Oxford University Press.

Hasbrouck, Alfred. 1935. "The Conquest of the Desert." *Hispanic American Historical Review* 15(2): 195–228.

Hattox, Ralph S. 1985. *Coffee and Coffeehouses: The Origins of a Social Beverage in the Medieval Near East*. Seattle: University of Washington Press.

Hawkins, Benjamin. 1806. "A Concise Description of the Creek Country." *Medical Repository of Original Essays and Intelligence, Relative to Physic, Surgery, Chemistry, and Natural History* (4):36.

Hayhoe, Katharine. 2018. "The Most Important Thing You Can Do to Fight Climate Change: Talk about It." TEDWomen. https://www.ted.com/talks/katharine _hayhoe_the_most_important_thing_you_can_do_to_fight_climate_change _talk_about_it?language=en.

Heckman, M. A., K. Sherry, and E. Gonzalez de Mejia. 2010. "Energy Drinks: An Assessment of Their Market Size, Consumer Demographics, Ingredient Profile, Functionality, and Regulations in the United States." *Comprehensive Reviews in Food Science and Food Safety* 9:303–17.

Hernández, José. 1872. *El Gaucho Martín Fierro*. Buenos Aires: Imprenta de La Pampa.

Hetherington, Kregg. 2020. *The Government of Beans: Regulating Life in the Age of Monocrops*. Durham: Duke University Press.

Hirsch, Dafna. 2011. " 'Hummus Is Best When It Is Fresh and Made by Arabs': Gourmetization of Hummus in Israel and the Return of the Repressed Arab." *American Ethnologist* 38(4): 617–30.

Holland, J. H. 1932. "Ledger Bark and Red Bark." *Bulletin of Miscellaneous Information* (Royal Botanic Gardens, Kew) (1):1–17.

Hopkins, Terence K., and Immanuel Wallerstein. 1986. "Commodity Chains in the World-Economy Prior to 1800." *Review (Fernand Braudel Center)* 10(1): 157–70.

House of Commons Diplomatic and Consular Reports. 1900. *Sessional Papers* 95(2426). London: Harrison and Sons.

HOY. 2020. "Productores de Villa Ygatimí elaboran yerba mate orgánica con precio premium." October 1. https://www.hoy.com.py/nacionales/productores-de-villa -ygatimi-elaboran-yerba-mate-organica-con-precio-premium.

Hu, Shiu Ying. 1979. "The Botany of Yaupon." In *Black Drink: A Native American Tea*, ed. Charles Hudson, 10–39. Athens: University of Georgia Press.

Hugh-Jones, Stephen. 1979. *The Palm and the Pleiades: Initiation and Cosmology in Northwest Amazon*. New York: Cambridge University Press.

———. 1995. "Coca, Beer, Cigars, and Yagé: Meals and Anti-Meals in an Amerindian Community." In *Consuming Habits: Drugs in History and Anthropology*, ed. I. Goodman, P. Lovejoy, and A. Sherratt, 47–66. London: Routledge.

Huner, Michael. 2011. "Sacred Cause, Divine Republic: A History of Nationhood, Religion, and War in Nineteenth-Century Paraguay, 1850–70." PhD diss., University of North Carolina.

Hurtado Ruiz, Pablo. 2017. "El Paraíso terrenal en la América del siglo XVII: Antonio de León Pinelo y Simão de Vasconcellos." *Catedral Tomada: Revista literaria latinoamericana/Journal of Latin American Literary Criticism* 5(8): 175–98.

International Coffee Organization. Historical Data on the Global Coffee Trade: Imports, 1990–2019. https://icocoffee.org/resources/historical-data-on-the-global -coffee-trade/.

Jaffee, Daniel. 2014. *Brewing Justice: Fair Trade Coffee, Sustainability, and Survival.* Berkeley: University of California Press.

Jaffee, D., and P. H. Howard. 2010. "Corporate Cooptation of Organic and Fairtrade Standards." *Agriculture and Human Values* 27(4): 387–99.

Jamieson, Ross W. 2001. "The Essence of Commodification: Caffeine Dependencies in the Early Modern World." *Journal of Social History* 32(2): 269–86.

Jankowiak, William, and Daniel Bradburd, eds. 2003. *Drugs, Labor, and Colonial Expansion.* Tucson: University of Arizona Press.

Jenkins, H. 2004. "Corporate Social Responsibility and the Mining Industry: Conflicts and Constructs." *Corporate Social Responsibility and Environmental Management* 11:23–34.

J.M.L. 1869. "The Extinction of a People." *The Spectator* 42(2160): 1356.

Jobst, Carl. 1838. "Thein identisch mit Caffein." *Annalen der Pharmacie* 25(1): 63–66.

Johnson, Roman. 2016. "Our Grandmothers' Ways: Complementary and Alternative Medicine Use by the Gullah-Geechee in McIntosh County, Georgia." Master's thesis, Georgia State University.

Kadlecová, Jana. 2020. "Body-hacking: On the Relationship between People and Material Entities in the Practice of Technological Body Modifications." *Historická Sociologie* 1:49–63.

Kanafani-Zahar, Aida. 2020. "The Lebanese 'Seven-Spice': A Propitious Substitute to Allspice?" *Anthropology of the Middle East* 15(2): 34–46.

Karababa, Emınegül, and Gülız Ger. 2011. "Early Modern Ottoman Coffeehouse Culture and the Formation of the Consumer Subject." *Journal of Consumer Research* 37(5): 737–60.

Karam, John Tofik. 2004. "A Cultural Politics of Entrepreneurship in Nation-Making: Phoenicians, Turks, and the Arab Commercial Essence in Brazil." *Journal of Latin American Anthropology* 9:319–51.

Karpat, Kamel H. 1985. "The Ottoman Emigration to America, 1860–1914." *International Journal of Middle East Studies* 17(2): 175–209.

Kearns, Richard. 2014. "Genocide of the Ache People of Paraguay Will Be Tried in Argentina." *Indian Country Today*, August 18. https://indiancountrytoday .com/archive/genocide-of-the-ache-people-of-paraguay-will-be-tried-in -argentina.

Kimmerer, Robin W. 2013. *Braiding Sweetgrass: Indigenous Wisdom, Scientific Knowledge, and the Teachings of Plants.* Minneapolis: Milkweed Ed.

King, Duane H., ed. 2007. *The Memoirs of Lt. Henry Timberlake: The Story of a Soldier, Adventurer, and Emissary to the Cherokees, 1756–1765.* Cherokee, NC: Museum of the Cherokee Indian Press.

Kipple, Kenneth. 2007. *A Movable Feast.* Cambridge: Cambridge University Press.

Klaus, Seeland, ed. 1997. *Nature Is Culture: Indigenous Knowledge and Socio-Cultural Aspects of Trees and Forests in Non-European Cultures*. London: Intermediate Technol.

Köhler, Joachim. 1998. *Nietzsche and Wagner: A Lesson in Subjugation*. Trans. Ronald Taylor. New Haven: Yale University Press.

Kohn, Eduardo. 2013. *How Forests Think: Toward an Anthropology beyond the Human*. Berkeley: University of California Press.

Kurlansky, Michael. 1998. *Cod: A Biography of the Fish That Changed the World*. New York: Penguin Books.

———. 2003. *Salt: A World History*. Toronto: Vintage Canada.

Kurzwelly, Jonatan. 2017. "Being German and Being Paraguayan in Nueva Germania: Arguing for 'Contextual Epistemic Permissibility' and 'Methodological Complementarity.'" PhD diss., University of Saint Andrews.

Larson, Carolyne R. 2020. *The Conquest of the Desert: Argentina's Indigenous Peoples and the Battle for History*. Albuquerque: University of New Mexico Press.

Latin American Year Book for Investors and Merchants for 1920. 1920. New York: Criterion Publishing Syndicate.

Le Maté ou Thé du Paraguay. 1914. "Ariel" Talleres Tipográficos y de Encuadernación. Asunción: Ministerio de Relaciones Exteriores. Sección Inmigración, Propaganda y Canje.

Lessa, Barbosa. 1958[?]. *História do chimarrão, 2a edição*. Pôrto Alegre: Livraria Sulina.

Levant, Ronald F., Mike C. Parent, Eric R. McCurdy, and Tyler C. Bradstreet. 2015. "Moderated Mediation of the Relationships between Masculinity Ideology, Outcome Expectations, and Energy Drink Use." *Health Psychology* 34(11): 1100.

Lévi-Strauss, Claude. 1997. "The Culinary Triangle." In *Food and Culture: A Reader*, ed. Carole Counihan and Penny Van Esterik. New York: Routledge.

Lewis, W. H., E. J. Kennelly, G. N. Bass, H. J. Wedner, M. P. Elvin-Lewis, and W. D. Fast. 1991. "Ritualistic Use of the Holly *Ilex guayusa* by Amazonian Jívaro Indians." *Journal of Ethnopharmacology* 33:25–30.

Linhares, Temistocles. 1969. *História Econômica Do Mate*. Rio de Janeiro: Libraria Jose Olympia.

Linnaeus, Carl. 1753. *Species Plantarum*. Vol. 1. Stockholm: Laurenti Salvi.

Littell's Living Age. 1844. "Opening of Commercial Intercourse with the Interior of South America." 3(32): 504.

Locke, John. 1821 (1689). *Two Treatises of Government*. London: Whitmore and Fenn.

Loesener, Theodor. 1901. *Monographia Aquifoliacearum*. Pt 1. Halle: Buchdruckerei von Ehrhardt Karras.

Lopez, Adalberto. 1974. "The Economics of Yerba Mate in Seventeenth-Century South America." *Agricultural History* 48(4): 493–509.

Lovejoy, Paul E. 1980. "Kola in the History of West Africa." *Cahiers d'Etudes Africaines* 20(77–78): 97–134.

Luetchford, Peter, Geert de Neve, and Jeffery Pratt, eds. 2008. *Hidden Hands in the Market: Ethnographies of Fair Trade, Ethical Consumption, and Corporate Social Responsibility.* B. Bingley: Emerald Publishing Limited.

M.S.B. 1861. "Letter 7—No Title." *Scientific American* 5(15): 230.

MacCormack, Carol P., and Marilyn Strathern. 1980. *Nature, Culture, and Gender.* Cambridge: Cambridge University Press.

Mackintos, Christopher, Chen Yuan, Fang-Shu Ou, et al. 2020. "Association of Coffee Intake with Survival in Patients with Advanced or Metastatic Colorectal Cancer." *JAMA Oncology* 6(11): 1713–21.

Mahmood, Saba. 2005. *Politics of Piety: The Islamic Revival and the Feminist Subject.* Princeton: Princeton University Press.

Mallo, Silvia C., and Ignacio Telesca, eds. 2010. *"Negros de la Patria": Los afrodescendientes en las luchas por la independencia en el antiguo Virreinato del Río de la Plata.* Buenos Aires: Editorial SB.

Manen, J. F., G. Barriera, P. A. Loizeau, and Y. Naciri. 2010. "The History of Extant *Ilex* Species (Aquifoliaceae): Evidence of Hybridization within a Miocene Radiation." *Molecular Phylogenetic Evolution* 57(3): 961–77.

Manning, Patrick, and Daniel Rood, eds. 2016. *Global Scientific Practice in an Age of Revolutions, 1750–1850.* Pittsburgh: University of Pittsburgh Press.

Marder, Michael. 2013. "What Is Plant Thinking?" *Klesis—revue philosophique* 25—*Philosophies de la nature.*

Martin, Laura. 2018. *A History of Tea: The Life and Times of the World's Favorite Beverage.* Clarendon, VT: Tuttle Publishing.

Martin Martin, Carmen, and Valverde, José Luis. 1995. *La farmacia en la América colonial: El arte de preparar medicamentos.* Granada: Servicio de Publicaciones de la Universidad de Granada.

Martins, Marcelo Thadeu Quintanilha. 2018. "Recovering Archives: The Custodial History of the Captaincy of São Paulo's Archival Holdings." *Revista Brasileira de História* 38(78). https://doi.org/10.1590/1806-93472018v38n78-03.

Marx, Karl. 2011. *Capital: A Critique of Political Economy.* Vol. 1. Mineola, NY: Dover Publications.

Massumi, Brian. 1995. "The Autonomy of Affect." *Cultural Critique* 31:83–109.

Matthee, Rudi. 1994. "Coffee in Safavid Iran: Commerce and Consumption." *Journal of the Economic and Social History of the Orient* 37(1): 1–32.

Mauss, Marcel. 1967. *The Gift: Forms and Functions of Exchange in Archaic Societies.* New York: Norton.

McGonigle, Ian V. 2013. "Khat: Chewing on a Bitter Controversy." *Anthropology Today* 29:4–7.

McKinnon, Catriona. 2014. "Climate Change: Against Despair." *Ethics and the Environment* 19(1): 31–48.

Medical Repository of Original Essays and Intelligence, Relative to Physic, Surgery, Chemistry, and Natural History. 1806. "Yapon-Tea, or Black Drink." 3:305.

Miers, John. 1826. *Travels in Chile and La Plata.* Vol. 1. London: Baldwin, Cradock, and Joy.

———. 1861. "On the History of the 'Maté' Plant, and the Different Species of *Ilex* Employed in the Preparation of the 'Yerba de Maté' or Paraguay Tea." *Annals and Magazine of Natural History* 3, 45(24): 220–28, 47(39): 389–401.

Milan, Pollianna, and Leandro dos Santos. N.d. "Erva-mate: O ouro verde do Paraná." *Gazeta do Povo.* https://especiais.gazetadopovo.com.br/erva-mate/producao/.

Mintz, Sidney W. 1979. "Time, Sugar and Sweetness." *Marxist Perspectives* 2(4): 56–73.

———. 1986. *Sweetness and Power: The Place of Sugar in Modern History.* New York: Penguin.

Mr. Drayton's Talk to the Cherokees. 1775. "A Talk from the Honourable Will H. Drayton Esq., One of the Beloved Men of South Carolina to the Beloved Men, Head Men & Warriors of the Cherokee Nation at the Congress," September 25. Reprinted in *The Historical Magazine, and Notes and Queries Concerning the Antiquities, History, and Biography of America (1857–1875); Boston* 1(5) (May 1867): 280.

Mitchell, Faith. 1999. *Hoodoo Medicine: Gullah Herbal Remedies.* Columbia, SC: Summerhouse Press.

Mitchell, George, and J. W. Sale. 1922. "Beverages Produced from Cassina. Reproduced from Type-written Copy." Washington, DC: USDA, Bureau of Chemistry.

Molina, J. Ignacio. 1795. *Compendio de la historia civil del reyno de Chile.* Trans. Nicolas de la Cruz y Bahamonde. Madrid: En la imprenta de Sancha.

Monterescu, Daniel, and Ariel Handel. 2019. "Liquid Indigeneity." *American Ethnologist* 46:313–27.

Moraes, María Inés. 2007. "Crecimiento del Litoral rioplatense colonial y decadencia de la economía misionera: Un análisis desde la ganadería December." *Investigaciones de Historia Economica* 9(9): 11–44.

Moraes, María Inés, and F. Thul. 2018. "Los salarios reales y el nivel de vida en una economía Latinoamericana colonial: Montevideo entre 1760–1810." *Revista de Historia Económica/Journal of Iberian and Latin American Economic History* 36(2): 185–213.

Muello, Alberto Carlos. 1946. *Yerba Mate: Su cultivo y explotación.* Enciclopedia Agropecuaria Argentina 31. Buenos Aires: Editorial Sudamericana.

Mulder, Gerrit Jan. 1838. "Ueber Theïn und Caffeïn." *Journal für Praktische Chemie* 15(1): 280–84.

Munizaga, José Gabriel Jeffs. 2017. "Chile en el macrocircuito de la yerba mate: Auge y caída de un producto típico del Cono Sur americano." *Revista Iberoamericana de Viticultura, Agroindustria y Ruralidad* 4(11): 148–70.

Münzel, Mark. 1974. *The Aché: Genocide Continues in Paraguay.* Copenhagen: International Work Group for Indigenous Affairs.

Myers, Natasha. 2015. "Conversations on Plant Sensing: Notes from the Field." *NatureCulture* 3:35–66.

Nadasdy, Paul. 2017. *Sovereignty's Entailments: First Nation State Formation in the Yukon.* Toronto: University of Toronto Press.

Nadeem, Ibrahim M., et al. 2020. "Energy Drinks and Their Adverse Health Effects: A Systematic Review and Meta-analysis." *Sports Health* 13(3): 265–77.

Nash, June. 1993 (1979). *We Eat the Mines and the Mines Eat Us: Dependency and Exploitation in Bolivian Tin Mines.* New York: Columbia University Press.

Nedergaard, Ove A. 2003. "Curare: The Flying Death." *Pharmacology & Toxicology* 92:154–55. https://doi.org/10.1034/j.1600-0773.2003.920402.x.

Neves, Eduardo G., and Michael J. Heckenberger. 2019. "The Call of the Wild: Rethinking Food Production in Ancient Amazonia." *Annual Review of Anthropology* 48:371–88.

Northup, Solomon. 1855. *Twelve Years a Slave.* New York: Miller, Orton and Mulligan.

Numhauser Bar-Magen, Paulina. 1998. "El comercio de la coca y las mujeres indias en Potosi del s. XVI." *Revista de História* 138:27–43.

O'Kane, G., and S. Y. Wijaya. 2015. "Contribution of Farmers' Markets to More Socially Sustainable Food Systems: A Pilot Study of a Farmers' Market in the Australian Capital Territory (ACT), Australia." *Agroecology and Sustainable Food Systems* 39(10): 1124–25.

Onopiuk, Anna, Klaudia Kołodziejczak, Monika Marcinkowska-Lesiak, and Andrzej Poltorak. 2022. "Determination of Polycyclic Aromatic Hydrocarbons Using Different Extraction Methods and HPLC-FLD Detection in Smoked and Grilled Meat Products." *Food Chemistry* 373(B): 131506. https://doi.org/10.1016/j.foodchem.2021.131506.

Opala, Joseph A. 1987. *The Gullah: Rice, Slavery and the Sierra Leone-American Connection.* Washington, DC: United States Information Service.

Orlove, Benjamin S., and Arnold J. Bauer. 1997. "Chile in the Belle Epoque: Primitive Producers, Civilized Consumers." In *The Allure of the Foreign: Imported Foods in Post-Colonial Latin America,* ed. Benjamin Orlove. Ann Arbor: University of Michigan Press.

Ortiz, Fernando. 1995. *Cuban Counterpoint: Tobacco and Sugar.* Durham: Duke University Press.

Orwell, George. 1946. "A Nice Cup of Tea." *London Evening Standard,* January 12.

Osseo-Asare, Abena Dove Agyepoma. 2014. *Bitter Roots: The Search for Healing Plants in Africa*. Chicago: University of Chicago Press.

Oudry M. 1827. "Note sur la Théine." *Nouvelle Bibliothèque Médicale* 1:477–79.

Palumbo, Matthew J., Stephen T. Talcott, and Francis E. Putz. 2009. "*Ilex Vomitoria* Ait. (Yaupon): A Native North American Source of a Caffeinated and Antioxidant-Rich Tea." *Economic Botany* 63(2): 130–37.

Pan American Union. 1915. *Bulletin* 40:825.

Parish Robertson, John, and William Parish Robertson. 1838. *Letters on Paraguay*. Vol. 2. London: John Murray.

Parquet, Reinerio. 1987. *Las empresas transnacionales en la economía del Paraguay*. Series Históricas 8976, Naciones Unidas Comisión Económica para América Latina y el Caribe (CEPAL).

Pastore, Mario. 1994. "State-Led Industrialisation: The Evidence on Paraguay, 1852–1870." *Journal of Latin American Studies* 26(2): 295–324.

Patiño, Victor Manuel. 1968. "Guayusa: A Neglected Stimulant from the Eastern Andean Foothills." *Economic Botany* 22(4): 310–16.

Peck, Jamie, and Adam Tickell. 2002. "Neoliberalizing Space." *Antipode* 34:380–404.

Pendergrast, Mark. 2010. *Uncommon Grounds: The History of Coffee and How It Transformed Our World*. New York: Basic Books.

Pepys, Samuel. 2003. *The Diary of Samuel Pepys*. New York: The Modern Library.

Peralto, A. Jover. 1950. *Cancionero del Mate*. Buenos Aires: Editorial Tupā.

Pereira Salas, Eugenio. 1977. *Apuntes para la historia de la cocina chilena: Santiago de Chile*. Santiago: Editorial Universitaria.

Pérez Calvo, Lucio E. 2013. "El condado de casa flórez y su progenie española y americana." *Hidalguía: La revista de genealogía, nobleza y armas* 361:819–40.

Pew Research Center. 2016. "Americans' Views about and Consumption of Organic Foods. The New Food Fights: U.S. Public Divides Over Food Science." https://www.pewresearch.org/internet/wp-content/uploads/sites/9/2016/11/PS_2016.12.01_Food-Science_FINAL.pdf.

Philadelphia Medical Times. 1872. "Editorial: The American Tea." September 26. 4(52):823.

Pisani, Michael J., and Fernando G. Ovando. 2019. "Brief Report: Measuring the Informal Sector in Paraguay." *Centro de Análisis y Difusión de la Economía Paraguaya (CADEP)*. https://www.cadep.org.py/uploads/2022/05/Measuring-the-informal-sector-in-Paraguay-CADEP-Eng.pdf.

Pisconte Quispe, Alan Martin. 2000. "Antonio de León Pinelo (1596–1660): ¿Perteneció a la segunda escolástica?" *Logos Latinoamericano* 5(5): 1–6.

Piwonka Figueroa, Gonzalo. 2009. "John Miers (1789–1879), viajero crítico de los chilenos en los comienzos de la República." *Cuadernos de Historia* 30:149–91.

Plowman, Timothy. 1984. "The Ethnobotany of Coca (Erythroxylum spp., Erythroxylaceae) Advances." *Economic Botany* 1:62–111.

Porcher, Francis Peyre. 1863. *Resources of the Southern Fields and Forests, Medical, Economical, and Agricultural. Being Also a Medical Botany of the Confederate States.* Charleston: Evans & Cogswell.

Pratt, Mary Louise. 2008 (1992). *Imperial Eyes: Travel Writing and Transculturation.* London: Routledge.

Price, Richard. 1979. *Maroon Societies: Rebel Slave Communities in the Americas.* Baltimore: Johns Hopkins University Press.

———. 1992. "Maroons: Rebel Slaves in the Americas." In *Creativity and Resistance: Maroon Culture in the Americas,* 62–64. Festival of American Folklife. Washington, DC: Smithsonian Institute. https://festival.si.edu/past-program/1992/creativity-and-resistance-maroon-culture-in-the-americas.

Proctor, Nicolas W. 2002. *Bathed in Blood: Hunting and Mastery in the Old South.* Charlottesville: University Press of Virginia.

Public Ledger (Philadelphia). 1873. "Spurious Substitutes." June 4, p. 1.

Putz, Francis E. 2010. "Yaupon Tea Has a Bad Name." *Gainesville.com,* April 8. https://www.gainesville.com/article/LK/20100408/News/604146341/GS/.

Raynal, Abbé. 1798. *A Philosophical and Political History of the Settlements and Trade of the Europeans in the East and West Indies.* Vol. 3. 2nd ed. Trans. J. O. Justamond, F.R.S. London: A. Strahan.

Reber, Vera Blinn. 1985. "Commerce and Industry in Nineteenth Century Paraguay: The Example of Yerba Mate." *The Americas* 42(1): 29–53.

———. 1988. "The Demographics of Paraguay: A Reinterpretation of the Great War, 1864–70." *Hispanic American Historical Review* 68(2): 289–319.

Reed, Richard. 1990. "Developing the Mbaracayú Biosphere Reserve, Paraguay: Chiripá Indians and Sustainable Economies." *Yearbook, Conference of Latin Americanist Geographers* 16:34–40.

———. 1995. *Prophets of Agroforestry: Guaraní Communities and Commercial Gathering.* Austin: University of Texas Press.

Reed, Richard, and John Renshaw. 2012. "The Aché and Guaraní: Thirty Years after Maybury-Lewis and Howe's Report on Genocide in Paraguay." *Tipití: Journal of the Society for the Anthropology of Lowland South America* 10(1): 1–18.

Reginaldo Peralta, Cleonice Alexandre le Bourlegat. 2012. "Trajetória da produção e da comercialização da Erva-Mate na fronteira sul de Mato Grosso Do Sul." *Revista Campo-Território* 7(13): 188–209.

Reichmann, Felix. 1959. *Sugar, Gold, and Coffee: Essays on the History of Brazil, Based on Francis Hull's Books.* Ithaca: Cornell University Library.

Ren-You Gan, Dan Zhang, Min Wang, and Harold Corke. 2018. "Health Benefits of Bioactive Compounds from the Genus *Ilex,* a Source of Traditional Caffeinated Beverages." *Nutrients* 10(1682): 1–17.

Rippy, J. Fred, and Jack Pfeiffer. 1948. "Notes on the Dawn of Manufacturing in Chile." *Hispanic American Historical Review* 28(2): 292–303.

Rivarola, Milda. 1993. *Obreros, utopías y revoluciones*. Asunción: Centro de Documentación y Estudios.

Rodrigues Vacari de Arruda, Larissa. 2015. "La Compañía Matte Larangeira: Las relaciones políticas de la primera multinacional lationamericana." *VIII Congreso Latinoamericano de Ciencia Política*, organized by the Asociación Latinoamericana de Ciencia Política (ALACIP). Presented at Pontificia Universidad Católica del Perú, Lima, July 22–24.

Rodrigues Vegro, Celso Luis. 1994. "Mercado da Erva Mate no Brasil: História, situação e perspectivas." *Informações Econômicas* (São Paulo) 24(12): 1–17.

Rodríguez-Alegría, Enrique. 2005. "Eating Like an Indian: Negotiating Social Relations in the Spanish Colonies." *Current Anthropology* 46(4): 551–73.

Roger, Leon. 1906. *Informe sobre el cultivo de la yerba mate*. Buenos Aires: Ministerio de Agricultura.

Rollin, David B. 1837. "Extracts from Mr. Rollin's Journal: Indian Harvest Feast; Creek Disturbances." *Baptist Missionary Magazine* 17(1): 22.

Roseberry, William. 1996. "The Rise of Yuppie Coffees and the Reimagination of Class in the United States." *American Anthropologist* 98(4): 762–75.

Roseberry, William, Lowell Gudmundson, and Mario Samper Kutschbach, eds. 1995. *Coffee, Society, and Power in Latin America*. Baltimore: Johns Hopkins University Press.

Ruffin, John N. 1900a. "Yerba-Maté Cultivation in Paraguay." June 7. Asunción, Paraguay. *United States Bureau of Foreign Commerce, Consular Reports: Commerce, Manufactures, Etc.* 64:307–8.

———. 1900b. "Paraguay." March 1. Asunción, Paraguay. *United States Bureau of Foreign Commerce, Consular Reports: Commerce, Manufactures, Etc.* 64:297.

———. 1905. "Yerba Maté in Paraguay." In *Monthly Consular Reports*, no. 296. Letter dated June 7, 1904, 267–68. U.S. Department of Commerce and Labor, Bureau of Statistics. Washington, DC: Government Printing Office.

Ruiz de Montoya, Antonio. 1639. *Conquista espiritual hecha por los Religiosos de la Compañia de Jesus en las Provincias del Paraguay, Parana, Uruguay, y Tape*. Madrid.

Runge, Friedlieb Ferdinand. 1820. "Neueste phytochemische Entdeckungen zur Begründung einer wissenschaftlichen." *Phytochemie* 144–59.

Ruschenberger, William, and Samuel Waithman. 1835 (1834). *Three Years in the Pacific; Including Notices of Brazil, Chile, Bolivia, and Peru*. Vol. 1. London: Richard Bentley.

Said, Edward. 1978. *Orientalism*. New York: Pantheon Books.

Saint-Hilaire, Auguste de. 1822. "Aperçu d'un voyage dans l'intérieur du Brésil, la province Cisplatine et les Missiones dites du Paraguay." *Mémoires du Muséum d'Histoire Naturelle* 9:337–80.

———. 1824. *Histoire des plantes les plus remarquables du Brésil et du Paraguay*. Paris: Chez A. Belin.

———. 1850. "Comparaison de la végétation d'un pays en parte extra-tropical." *Annales des sciences naturalles*. Vol. 14. Paris: Victor Masson.

Sarmiento, Domingo Faustino. 2018 (1845). *Facundo; o, Civilización y Barbarie*. Buenos Aires: Biblioteca del Congreso de la Nación.

Sarreal, Julia. 2022. *Yerba Mate: The Drink That Shaped a Nation*. Berkeley: University of California Press.

Sayre, Meredith Beck. 2007. "Cultivating Soils and Souls: The Jesuit Garden in the Americas." Master's thesis, Simon Fraser University.

Scarpa, Gustavo Fabián, and Leonardo Martín Anconatani. 2019. "La 'Materia Médica Misionera' atribuida al jesuita Pedro de Montenegro en 1710: Identificación, sistematización e interpretación de los usos medicinales de las plantas y sus implicancias para la etnobotánica actual." *Antiguos Jesuitas en Iberoamérica* 7(1):27–46.

Schiebinger, Londa. 2017. *Secret Cures of Slaves: People, Plants, and Medicine in the Eighteenth-Century Atlantic World*. Stanford: Stanford University Press.

Schivelbusch, Wolfgang. 1993. *Tastes of Paradise: A Social History of Spices, Stimulants, and Intoxicants*. New York: Vintage Books.

Schlib, Rene. 2017. "Beer Is for Boys; Wine Is for Women: How Women Perceive Portrayed Ideas of Masculinity in Alcohol Advertising." Master's thesis, University of Missouri.

Schneider, Regina. 2015. "Why Do People Buy Organic? An Analysis of the Attitudes and Intentions toward Organic Food Purchase." Master's thesis, Université Paris I Panthéon-Sorbonne.

Schneppen, Heinz. 2002. "Nietzsche y Paraguay: ¿El filósofo como campesino?" *Iberoamericana* 2(5):79–94.

Schultes, Richard Evans. 1950. "The Correct Name of Yaupon." *Botanical Museum Leaflets, Harvard University* 14(4): 97–105.

———. 1972. "Ilex Guayusa from 500 A.D. to the Present." In *Etnologiska Studier 32*, ed. Wassén. Göteborg.

Schuster, Adolf N. 1929. *Paraguay: Land, Volk, Geschichte, Wirtschaftsleben und Kolonisation*. Stuttgart: Strecker and Schröder.

Scobie, James R. 1964. *Argentina: A City and a Nation*. Oxford: Oxford University Press.

Sedgwick, Eve, and Adam Kosofsky Frank. 1995. "Shame in the Cybernetic Fold: Reading Silvan Tomkins." *Critical Inquiry* 21(2): 496–522.

Sequera Buzarquis, Víctor Guillermo. 2019. "Desigualdades que enferman y matan: Una aproximación a las desigualdades en salud en Paraguay." In *Salud, enfermedad y pobreza urbana. Estudio de los procesos de salud, enfermedad y atención de las familias en la periferia de Asunción*, 259–74. Asunción: Centro de Documentación y Estudios.

Setrini, Gustavo. 2011. "Clientelism and Fairtrade Farmer Organizations in Paraguay's Sugar Industry." PhD diss., Massachusetts Institute of Technology.

Shapiro, Howard-Yana. 2015. *Great Moments in Chocolate History: With 20 Classic Recipes from around the World*. Washington, DC: National Geographic.

Sharp, John. 2006. "Corporate Social Responsibility and Development: An Anthropological Perspective." *Development Southern Africa* 23(2): 213–22.

Sheldrake, Merlin. 2020. *Entangled Life: How Fungi Make Our Worlds, Change Our Minds and Shape Our Futures*. New York: Random House.

Shemluck, Melvin. 1979. "The Flowers of Ilex Guayusa." *Botanical Museum Leaflets, Harvard University* 27(5/6): 155–60.

Silverblatt, Irene. 2004. *Modern Inquisitions: Peru and the Colonial Origins of the Civilized World*. Durham: Duke University Press.

Slatta, Richard W. 1997. *Comparing Cowboys and Frontiers*. Norman: University of Oklahoma Press.

Smith, Franklin. 2014. "Exploring Fair Trade Yerba Mate Networks in Misiones, Argentina." PhD diss., University of Miami.

Smith, Nigel, and Andre Luiz Atroch. 2010. "Guaraná's Journey from Regional Tonic to Aphrodisiac and Global Energy Drink." *Evidence-Based Complementary and Alternative Medicine: eCAM* 7(3): 279–82. https://doi.org/10.1093/ecam/nem162.

Smith, Penne. 2001. "Appendix A: Transcription of Property Sale of Adam Dough Etheridge's Estate, July 13, 1869." In *Etheridge Homeplace: A History*. Outer Banks Conservationists. October. https://obcinc.org/wp-content/uploads/2022/05/etheridge_homeplace.pdf.

Smith, Woodruff D. 1992. "Complications of the Commonplace: Tea, Sugar, and Imperialism." *Journal of Interdisciplinary History* 23(2): 259–78.

Sociedad Académica de Amantes de Lima. 1792. *Mercurio Peruano*. Vol. 1. Lima: Imprenta Real de los Niños Huérfanos.

Soler Lizarazo, Luisa Consuelo. 2016. "Redes de comercialización de la yerba mate a partir de las operaciones mercantiles de Salvador Trucíos, Chile (1758–1798)." *RIVAR* 3(9): 26–49.

South American: A Journal for All Interested in Latin American Affairs. 1918. "The Paraguayan Tea Situation." 6(5): 12.

Southern Literary Messenger. 1838. "Botanical Notices of Interesting Plants." 12(4): 800.

Spence, Mark David. 2000. *Dispossessing the Wilderness: Indian Removal and the Making of the National Park*. Oxford: Oxford University Press.

Spruce, Richard. 1908. *Notes of a Botanist on the Amazon & Andes*. Vol. 2. London: Macmillan.

Srivastava, A., et al. 2019. "Phytomedicine: A Potential Alternative Medicine in Controlling Neurological Disorders." In *New Look to Phytomedicine Advancements in Herbal Products as Novel Drug Leads*, ed. Mohd Sajjad Ahmad Khan, Iqbal Ahmad, and Debprasad Chattopadhyay, 625–55. London: Academic Press.

Stenhouse, John. 1843. "On Theine and Its Preparation." *Memoirs and Proceedings of the Chemical Society* 2:215–21.

Stevenson, Kathryn, and Nils Peterson. 2016. "Motivating Action through Fostering Climate Change Hope and Concern and Avoiding Despair among Adolescents." *Sustainability* 8(1): 1–10.

Stick, David. 1958. *The Outer Banks of North Carolina, 1584–1958*. Chapel Hill: University of North Carolina Press.

Stross, Brian. 2011. "Food, Foam and Fermentation in Mesoamerica." *Food, Culture & Society* 14(4): 477–501.

Sulaiman, Naji, Andrea Pieroni, Renata Sõukand, Cory Whitney, and Zbynek Polesny. 2021. "Socio-Cultural Significance of Yerba Maté among Syrian Residents and Diaspora." *Economic Botany* 75(2): 97–111.

Sutton, David, Nefissa Naguib, Leonidas Vournelis, and Maggie Dickinson. 2013. "Food and Contemporary Protest Movements." *Food, Culture & Society* 16(3): 345–66.

Svampa, Maristella. 2011. "Extractivismo neodesarrollista y movimientos sociales: ¿Un giro ecoterritorial hacia nuevas alternativas?" In *Más Allá Del Desarrollo*, ed. Miriam Lang and Dunia Mokrani, 185–218. Grupo Permanente de Trabajo sobre Alternativas al Desarrollo. Quito: Editorial El Conejo.

Sweet, Robert. 1818. *Hortus suburbanus Londinensis; or, A Catalogue of Plants Cultivated in the Neighborhood of London*. London: James Ridgway.

Tate, Z. 2009. "The Eyes of the Forest." *Cultural Survival Quarterly* 33:12–13.

Telesca, Ignacio. 2010. "Sociedad y Afrodescendientes en el proceso de independencia del Paraguay." In *"Negros de la Patria": Los Afrodescendientes en las luchas por la independencia en el antiguo Virreinato del Río de la Plata*, ed. Silvia C. Mallo and Ignacio Telesca, 149–70. Buenos Aires: Editorial SB.

——— 2013. "Afrodescendientes en el Paraguay, de la colonia a nuestros días." *Todo es Historia*, no. 559 (February): 70–80.

Thompson, Robert Farris. 2005. *Tango: The Art History of Love*. New York: Pantheon.

Topik, Steven. 2004. "The World Coffee Market in the Eighteenth and Nineteenth Centuries, from Colonial to National Regimes." Working paper 04/04 presented at GEHN Conference, Bankside, London, September 17–20.

Topik, Steven, Carlos Marichal, and Zephyr Frank, eds. 2006. *From Silver to Cocaine: Latin American Commodity Chains and the Building of the World Economy, 1500–2000*. Durham: Duke University Press.

Torjusen, Hanne, Lotte Sangstad, Katherine O'Doherty Jensen, and Unni Kjærnes. 2004. "European Consumers' Conceptions of Organic Food: A Review of Available Research." Norway: National Institute for Consumer Research.

Trommsdorff, Johann Bartholomew. 1836. "Einige Bemerkungen uber den Paraguay-Thee." *Annalen der Pharmacie* 18(1): 89–96.

Tsing, Anna. 2015. *The Mushroom at the End of the World: On the Possibility of Life in Capitalist Ruins*. Princeton: Princeton University Press.

Turner, Frederick Jackson. 1893. "The Significance of the Frontier in American History." Paper presented at the American Historical Association, Chicago.

Um, Caroline Y., Marjorie L. McCullough, Mark A. Guinter, Peter T. Campbell, Eric J. Jacobs, and Susan M. Gapstur. 2020. "Coffee Consumption and Risk of Colorectal Cancer in the Cancer Prevention Study-II Nutrition Cohort." *Cancer Epidemiology* 67:101730.

Vaccaro, Ismael, Krista Harper, and Seth Murray, eds. 2017. *The Anthropology of Postindustrialism: Ethnographies of Disconnection*. New York: Routledge.

Valdez, Lidio M., Juan Taboada, and J. Ernesto Valdez. 2015. "Ancient Use of Coca Leaves in the Peruvian Central Highlands." *Journal of Anthropological Research* 71(2): 231–58.

Vanali, Ana Crhistina. 2013. *A erva mate e a politica paranense: Análise da legislaçao provincial para a economia ervateira (1854–1889)*. Curitiba: Instituto Memória Editora.

Varela Flor, Susana. 2021. " 'The Palace of the Soul Serene': Queen Catherine of Braganza and the Consumption of Tea in Stuart England (1662–1693)." e-*Journal of Portuguese History* 171–91. https://doi.org/10.26300/90dv-xn35.

Varisco, Daniel Martin. 1986. "On the Meaning of Chewing: The Significance of Qat (*Catha edulis*) in the Yemen Arab Republic." *International Journal of Middle East Studies* 18(1): 1–13.

Venable, F. P. 1885. "Analysis of the Leaves of Ilex Cassine." *American Journal of Pharmacy* (August): 389.

Vered, Ronit. 2010. "Pleasure Hunting/Just Their Cup of Tea." *Haaretz*, April 11. https://www.haaretz.com/2010-04-11/ty-article/pleasure-hunting-just-their-cup-of-tea/0000017f-e604-df5f-a17f-ffdef1ad0000.

Vidal de Battini, Berta Elena. 1953. "El léxico de los yerbateros." *Nueva Revista de Filología Hispánica* 7(1/2): 190–208.

Villanueva, Amaro. 1985. *El mate: Arte de cebar*. Rosario, Argentina: Ediciones del Peregrino.

Villavicencio, Manuel. 1858. *Geografía de la república del Ecuador*. New York: Robert Craighead.

Vitoria, Francisco de. 1975 (1532). *Relecciones sobre los indios y el derecho de guerra.* 3rd ed. Madrid: Espasa-Calpe.

Voeks, Robert, and Charlotte Greene. 2018. "God's Healing Leaves: The Colonial Quest for Medicinal Plants in the Torrid Zone." *Geographical Review* 108(4): 545–65.

Von Humboldt, Alexander, and Aimé Bonpland. 1852. *Personal Narrative of Travel to the Equatorial Regions of America during the Years 1799–1804.* Vol. 2. Trans. and ed. Thomasina Ross. London: Henry G. Bohn.

———. 2009. *Essay on the Geography of Plants.* Ed. Stephen T. Jackson. Trans. Sylvie Romanowski. Chicago: University of Chicago Press.

Wagner, Mark. 2005. "The Debate between Coffee and Qat in Yemeni Literature." *Middle Eastern Literatures* 8(2): 121–49.

Wainwright, Alisha E., and Francis E. Putz. 2014. "A Misleading Name Reduces Marketability of a Healthful and Stimulating Natural Product: A Comparative Taste Test of Infusions of a Native Florida Holly (*Ilex vomitoria*) and Yerba Mate (*I. paraguariensis*)." *Economic Botany* 68(3): 350–54.

Warren, Harris Gaylord. 1978. *Paraguay and the Triple Alliance: The Postwar Decade, 1869–1878.* Austin: Institute of Latin American Studies, University of Texas.

———. 1985. *Rebirth of the Paraguayan Republic: The First Colorado Era, 1878–1904.* University of Pittsburgh Press.

Wassén, S. Henry, ed. 1972. "A Medicine-Man's Implements and Plants in a Tiahuanacoid Tomb in Highland Bolivia." *Etnologiska Studier* 32. Göteborg.

Wear, Andrew. 1999. "The Early Modern Debate about Foreign Drugs: Localism versus Universalism in Medicine." *The Lancet* 354(9173): 149–51.

Webb, Philip Duncan. 2020. "Los Inmigrantes Españoles en Concepción (Paraguay): Entre la guerra guazú y la reconstrucción nacional (1869–1932)." *Naveg@mérica*; Murcia 24:1–31.

Weber, Max. 1905 (1930). *The Protestant Ethic and the Spirit of Capitalism.* Trans. Talcott Parsons. New York: Pantianos Classics.

———. 1958. "Science as a Vocation." *Daedalus* 87:111–34.

Weinberg, Bennett Alan, and Bonnie K. Bealer. 2002. *The World of Caffeine: The Science and Culture of the World's Most Popular Drug.* London: Routledge.

West, Paige. 2012. *From Modern Production to Imagined Primitive: The Social World of Coffee from Papua New Guinea.* Durham: Duke University Press.

West, Paige, James Igoe, and Dan Brockington. 2006. "Parks and Peoples: The Social Impact of Protected Areas." *Annual Review of Anthropology* 35(1): 251–77.

Whigham, Thomas. 1991. *La Yerba Mate del Paraguay (1780–1870).* Asunción: Centro Paraguay de Estudios Sociológicos.

———. 1994. "Paraguay and the World Cotton Market: The 'Crisis' of the 1860s." *Agricultural History* 68(3): 1–15.

———. 2017. *The Road to Armageddon: Paraguay versus the Triple Alliance, 1866–70.* Calgary: University of Calgary Press.

Whigham, Thomas L., and Barbara Potthast. 1990. "Some Strong Reservations: A Critique of Vera Blinn Reber's 'The Demographics of Paraguay: A Reinterpretation of the Great War, 1864–70.'" *Hispanic American Historical Review* 70(4): 667–75.

———. 1999. "The Paraguayan Rosetta Stone: New Insights into the Demographics of the Paraguayan War, 1864–1870." *Latin American Research Review* 34(1): 174.

Whisnant, David E. 2009 (1982). *All That Is Native and Fine: The Politics of Culture in an American Region.* Chapel Hill: University of North Carolina Press.

White, Richard Alan. 1978. *Paraguay's Autonomous Revolution, 1810–1840.* Albuquerque: University of New Mexico Press.

Wiesel, Elie. 1976. "Now We Know." In *Genocide in Paraguay*, ed. Richard Arens, 165–67. Philadelphia: Temple University Press.

Wilk, Richard. 2006. *Home Cooking in the Global Village: Caribbean Food from Buccaneers to Ecotourists.* London: Berg.

Wilk, Richard, and Livia Barbosa, eds. 2012. *Rice and Beans: A Unique Dish in a Hundred Places.* London: Berg.

Wilson, Bee. 2007. *The Hive: The Story of the Honeybee and Us.* New York: St. Martin's Griffin.

Wolf, Eric. 2010. *Europe and the People without History.* 2nd ed. Berkeley: University of California Press.

Wolfe, Patrick. 2006. "Settler Colonialism and the Elimination of the Native." *Journal of Genocide Research* 8(4): 387–409.

Yao, X., Y. Song, J.-B. Yang, Y.-H. Tan, and R. T. Corlett. 2021. "Phylogeny and Biogeography of the Hollies (*Ilex* L., Aquifoliaceae)." *Journal of Systemic Evolution* 59:73–82.

INDEX

Page numbers in *italics* indicate figures.

@ (arroba; at), 162–63

Abipón people, 66
acculturation, 14, 156. *See also* transculturation
Aché people, 168–69, 188–92
Adair, James, 26
Adderall, 8–9, 193
addiction, 9
affect, 171–73
agnotology, 21–23
Aiton, William, 31–32
Alawite community, 160–61
Alberdi, Juan, 83
Alcedo, Antonio de, 66
alcohol, 9
All Market, Inc., 46
allspice, 155
Alzagaray, Francisco de, 97–98
Amanda, 158
Amazon Rainforest, 180–81
American Psychological Association (APA), 176
amphetamines, 193
Anconatani, Leonardo, 115
anthropogenic global warming, 40, 178, 193, 215n70
anti-Arab sentiment, 157
antisemitism, 145–46
apalachine, 28, 32. *See also* yaupon holly (*Ilex vomitoria*)

Appadurai, Arjun, 160
Arab Spring protests (2011), 159
Argentina: Arab diaspora in, 157–58; coffee in, 48; consumption of yerba mate in, 11; cultivation of yerba mate in, 148, 150; Farquhar Syndicate in, 138–39; La Industrial Paraguaya in, 132–33, 138–40; Matte Larangeira in, 132–33, 135, 138, 139; nation-building and national identity in, 80–87, *81*; origin stories of yerba mate in, 48–49; scientific exploration in, 100, 116–17, 120–22; Spanish imperial political economy of mate in, 68; War of the Triple Alliance (1864–70) and, 81–82, 101–2, 127–28, 129–30, 135–37; yerba mate exports from, 150, 158–59, *158*, 181–82; yerba mate imports in, 139. *See also* Viceroyalty of La Plata
Aristotelian thought, 113
Artigas, José Gervasio, 77–79, 82, 84–86, 123
Artigas dictando órdenes a su secretario José Monterroso en Purificación (Blanes Viale), 77–78, *78*, 84, 86
Aryan supremacism, 127, 145–47
Assad, Bashar, 153–55, *154*, 159–61
Asunción (Barthe), 140, 143
O Auxiliadora (journal), 124–25
ayahuasca (yagé), 21, 44–45

243

A NOTE ON THE TYPE

This book has been composed in Arno, an Old-style serif typeface in the classic Venetian tradition, designed by Robert Slimbach at Adobe.